Journey into the Past

IVAN MAĬSKY

Soviet Ambassador to the United Kingdom, 1932–43.
Member of the Academy of Sciences of the U.S.S.R.

★

Journey into the Past

Translated from the Russian by
FREDERICK HOLT

HUTCHINSON OF LONDON

HUTCHINSON & CO. (*Publishers*) LTD
178–202 Great Portland Street, London, W.1

London Melbourne Sydney
Auckland Bombay Toronto
Johannesburg New York

★

First published 1962

*This book has been set in Bembo type face. It has
been printed in Great Britain by The Anchor Press,
Ltd., in Tiptree, Essex, on Antique Wove paper.*

To the memory of my old friend

M. M. LITVINOV

Contents

III AMONG THE ENGLISH

IV THE FALL OF TSARISM AND THE RETURN TO RUSSIA

Foreword

The hero of H. G. Wells's famous story *The Time Machine*, which the author calls a journey in Time, comes to the conclusion that time is a particular aspect of space, and by constructing a special machine which enables him to move with magic speed in this fourth dimension he travels for hundreds of thousands of years before and after the present day.

In the life of every man there are moments when he would very much like to imitate Wells's hero and have the wonderful 'time machine' at his disposal. Such a moment came for me in the autumn of 1932 when I arrived in London as the newly appointed ambassador of the Soviet Union. Two factors played a particularly important part.

The first was the circumstance that I was no stranger to London. In my youth I had lived there for five years as a political exile from tsarist Russia. It had been an important period for my spiritual development, in many ways determining my future course. With it were associated many weighty experiences, much joy and sorrow, many enthusiasms, many disappointments. The word 'London' always conjured up a whole gallery of scenes and images of long ago. So now when I was back in London it meant much more to me than a cold, dry, geographical expression. To me it was a living city. Its streets, squares, parks, even individual houses, brought back memories of the past and involuntarily carried my thoughts back to those half-forgotten days when, little more than a youth, I trod those very pavements and still had a fine head of bristling hair.

The second circumstance, which to a considerable extent reinforced the effect of the first, was that at the time of my arrival the King was not in London. He was to return to the capital in a few days. In accordance with diplomatic protocol, until the ambassador presents his letters of credence to the head of the State to which he is accredited he is not yet ambassador in the country to which he is appointed. He cannot represent his own government, has no official standing with the Foreign Office of that country, cannot pay or receive visits, give interviews or make speeches.

The result was that until the return of the King and the formalization of my status as ambassador I unexpectedly found myself a free man. I could and did avail myself of this little *entr'acte* to get a general idea of the political situation and familiarize myself with the Soviet institutions in London.

Yet my day was not occupied from morning to night. There was time to spare and when the hours for quiet reflection arrived and the autumn veil of London fog began to touch off elegiac music in my heart I found myself suddenly gripped by an irresistible desire to undertake a journey into the past and re-create, if only mentally, that world in which I had lived in my years of exile.

No 'time machine' was at my service: I had only ordinary human memory and imagination to help me. On the other hand my ambitions were much more modest than those of Wells's hero. I was dreaming of a journey of only twenty years back, not two hundred thousand. Everything is possible to a man who wants something badly enough and in fact I made the journey into the past. For a few days in succession, escaping from my secretaries and assistants, I wandered alone through familiar scenes and places in the giant city and the people and happenings of days long gone by came to life again before my mind's eye....

In 1944, during the Second World War, the House of Hutchinson published my memoirs of childhood and youth (1884–1901) under the title *Before the Storm*. These further reminiscences, published by the same House, are a continuation of the former, but it must be remembered that there was a gap of eleven years between the first period and the events of which I write in the present work.

J. Maisky

Moscow

PART ONE

★

London

1912

CHAPTER ONE

Three Arrivals

CHARING CROSS—one of London's most important
stations. It used to be England's link with the continent
of Europe. It is also considered the centre of the city,
from which distances north, south, east and west are measured.
Huge, gloomy and grimy, this station resembled some fantastic
monster clinging firmly to the ground with its claws and belching
forth columns of steam and smoke from its nostrils. Under the
dark vault of the station roof there was eternal bustle and din.
The blasts from the engines, the shouts of porters, the rumble of
cars, the clatter of luggage trolleys, the frantic rush of passengers,
the discordant buzz of the crowd—all this culminated in a sort of
feverish symphony of noise and movement. Nor is it surprising:
tens of thousands of passengers pass through Charing Cross every
day.

I stood outside this grimy, ponderous, ugly building, in the
autumn of 1932, gazing at the army of human ants swarming on
all sides and memory brought back scenes from days long past.

November, 1912. I was twenty-eight. Behind me I had a
history of the 1905 Revolution, prison, exile, misery and poverty.
I emigrated to England to learn about her politics and the working-class movement. I had very little money. In London I had
only one friend, who was a cashier in the Anglo-Russian Bank.
I had no idea what I would do or how I should make a living.
The future looked dark and problematical. But I was not dismayed. There was plenty of health and strength in my young
body and no lack of fire in my soul; I would win through.

The little steamer plying between Boulogne and Folkestone
was crammed with passengers. From the bar came the sound of
popping corks and the jingle of coins. Elderly Englishmen
sprawled in deck-chairs, their legs swathed in warm rugs. Young

girls, escorted by their smart swains, walked briskly round the deck, laughing happily at something or other. The rigging hummed and from time to time I got the spray full in the face.

Rolling slightly in the waves, the ship rumbled through the dark-blue depths. The French coast disappeared behind the horizon. The chalk cliffs of the southern shore of England quickly came to meet us. Every moment brought them closer and made them more distinct. What had looked like a smooth wall gradually turned out to be headlands, gullies, rugged cliffs. On a hill somewhat to the right the towers and walls of the old fortress of Dover glimmered in the dying light.

The steamer slowed down and, describing an elegant curve, carefully approached the quay. The passengers assembled on one side of the ship. The decks resounded with the clatter of the sailors' heavy boots as the baggage was collected at the appropriate exit.

So there I was on English ground. It was already nearly four o'clock. There was a slight haze, which played strange tricks with the appearance of both people and buildings. It was rapidly getting dark. I stood forlorn on the wet quayside with my two little bags, which contained all my earthly possessions. Following the crowd, I made my way to the customs shed. The formalities were short and simple; what sort of customs duties could they hope to get out of luggage like mine?

An official suddenly shot a question at me:

'Have you come third class'?

I did not yet know English and I asked the man to repeat his question in German. This annoyed him, but realizing that there was no other way of getting anything out of me he translated into that language.

'Yes, I've travelled third class,' I replied.

'In that case,' he continued, 'I'm afraid you'll have to show you have five pounds.'

'How do you mean, five pounds?' I asked in dismay.

The official quickly explained that in England there was a regulation that every third-class passenger must show he had five pounds on arrival. This was considered proof that he possessed means of existence and would not become a burden on the community.

I was extremely worried. In Paris no one had given me the

slightest warning about the existence of such a regulation. And
now this unexpected complication; for I was far from confident that I could produce this wretched five pounds then and
there.

I opened my purse, turned out my pockets and counted all the
money I could find. Alas! there was only three pounds, fifteen
shillings. Not a penny more. The officer's face assumed a grim
expression. He hesitated for a moment and then announced in an
official tone:

'You will have to return to France by the next boat, sir.'

'What! To France?' was my despairing cry.

'That's the law, sir,' the man coldly replied, and started to
walk away.

But I would not let him. I began to protest fiercely. I said I
had important business in London, and openly insinuated that I
had 'influential friends' who were expecting me and would
certainly be meeting me at the station. But none of this made
the slightest impression on the man. Then I tried to approach
him from another angle. I knew that in the nineteenth century
England had seemed the most hopeful asylum for emigrant
revolutionaries of all nations and descriptions. Here Marx and
Engels, Herzen and Bakunin, Hugo and Louis Blanc, Kossuth and
Mazzini, had lived and worked long years. Later on, in 1902–3,
Lenin had spent nearly twelve months here. It was here that in
1907 the fifth congress of the R.S.D.R.P.[1] was held after the
governments of the Scandinavian countries, in which it was
originally proposed to hold it, had refused permission. The
right of asylum had gradually become incorporated in the
tradition of English life. I appealed to that tradition and explained
to the officer that I presented myself as a political emigrant from
tsarist Russia and was seeking asylum in Great Britain.

'Look here!' my words tumbled out. 'It was here that Karl
Marx lived more than thirty years ago. . . . He was a refugee
from Germany . . . the well-known refugee!'

'I don't know anyone of the name of Marx, sir! I've never
heard of him, sir!' the officer calmly replied.

Thereupon he started to cross the room again, but stood
till for a moment and, after some hesitation, added:

'If you really are a political refugee, sir, it may be that . . .'

[1] Russian Social-Democratic Labour Party.

He did not finish his sentence and vaguely shrugged his shoulders. He made no promises and yet I felt there was a ray of hope. I burst out even more emphatically:

'*Of course* I'm a political refugee!'

The officer shook his head somewhat doubtfully, but explained that he would go and ask his superior. He disappeared through the doorway of some dark office and I waited, holding my breath; would they or wouldn't they admit me? Five minutes passed. My agitation mounted. At length my friend reappeared, accompanied by two others somewhat senior in age and rank. They looked at me with considerable curiosity and then the most senior asked me in German:

'You maintain that you are a Russian political refugee; how can you prove it?'

How could I prove it? At first I did not know what to say. I was completely flummoxed. Up to that moment it had never entered my head that I should ever have to prove that I was a Russian political exile. On the contrary, I had often had to conceal that fact, particularly in Germany. What could I do? What proof could I give?

An idea flashed through my head. I rummaged in my pockets and pulled out a piece of crumpled paper which my comrades in Paris had given me before I left. It was a certificate of the Central Bureau of Groups Abroad of the R.S.D.R.P. to the effect that I was a political exile and a member of the R.S.D.R.P. and it bore the seal and signature of Ornatsky,[1] secretary of the Central Bureau. The day before I had not wanted to have it; I thought it unnecessary. Comrade Ornatsky had almost had to stuff it in my pocket. But how handy it came in now!

The three Englishmen proceeded to study my certificate most carefully. Then they looked me up and down again and closely inspected the document once more. Ultimately the senior snapped out with a casual gesture:

'All right! Admit the passenger.'

I carefully replaced the precious document in my pocket and eagerly grasped my bags.

A long, noisy train, stubbornly cutting through the ever-thickening veil of yellowy-grey fog, quickly brought me in two

[1] At that time the party pseudonym of G. V. Chicherin, the future People's Commissar for Foreign Affairs.

hours from Folkestone to London. Towns, villages, stations, signals, bridges, flashed past.

London at last. Charing Cross station. The noise of the train drawing up at the platform. Bustle and commotion as the passengers poured out. The corrosive breath of the horrible fog.

I was met by the 'influential' friend about whom I had been so eloquent at Folkestone. He was wearing a battered hat and a faded overcoat. We debated quite a time whether it was worth taking a taxi. It would be cheaper by Underground. Finally we found ourselves seated in a taxi and travelling slowly to the modest lodgings of my friend in one of the northern suburbs of London. My mind was filled with a vague anxiety: what had England in store for me?

Such was my arrival in London in 1912.

Yet one more picture from those faraway days.

August, 1914. I was at Lausanne, in Switzerland. I had just arrived from Munich, to which I had returned three months earlier after a stay in England lasting nearly two years. At the very last moment, when the thunder of the guns of the First World War were already filling the air, I was lucky enough to get out of Germany and cross into Switzerland thanks to the help of my German Social-Democrat friends.

My mind was in a turmoil of confusion and dismay. The socialists of those days had long predicted the approach of war. At their international congresses they had debated that critical question and taken certain important decisions, the gist of which was that the proletariat, and more particularly its socialist vanguard, must engage in an implacable struggle against war and act resolutely against their governments if it broke out. And yet when it actually broke out it affected the socialists like a terrible earthquake. At once all was panic and disorder.

I well remember my thoughts in the first weeks after the war started. I was simply stunned and the very ground seemed to shake beneath my feet. My stock opinions and assumptions crumbled away. I had believed that the Socialist International was a solid rock; it collapsed before my very eyes like a house of cards. I had believed that German Social-Democracy was revolution-minded; it suddenly made common cause with that

B

satanic warmonger, the Kaiser. I believed that the traditions of
'the Commune' lived on in the French socialist movement; but
in August, 1914, the French socialists—even the old Marxist
Guesde—behaved no better than their German comrades. How
could all this happen, and why?

I searched feverishly for an answer to this monstrous question.
I spent long hours wandering by the peaceful shores of the ever-
blue Lake of Geneva and thinking, thinking, thinking. . . . I
discussed the question heatedly with some comrades who happened to be in Lausanne and Geneva at the time, but could get
little help from them. Like myself, they were all simple people
and just as stunned and perplexed as I was.[1]

The war disorganized my personal plans as well. In those
years I was making my living from literary work—I contributed
articles from abroad to Russian newspapers and journals. This
sort of work is possible when the correspondent lives in large and
important countries like Germany or England. But what sort of
articles could I send from small and petty-bourgeois Switzerland?

I gradually reached a decision to leave Lausanne and go back
to London. I should at least be able to make a living there. But
what mattered more was that London was a great watch-tower
from which it would be easier to get a comprehensive view of the
historic drama in progress and to grasp its inner significance.

But how could I get to England? The Germans were on the
Marne and communications between Switzerland and Paris
interrupted. No one could tell me anything definite about any
other route. In Lausanne and Geneva the most fantastic rumours
were in circulation as to what was actually happening in France
and everyone with whom I discussed my intention to make my
way to London looked at me as if I had gone off my head. But
I was absolutely determined to go and, as no one could tell me
anything sensible about the actual position inside France, I began
to pin my hopes on my own common sense and the elementary
logic of things.

I reasoned as follows: the closer to the front line, the greater
must be the disorganization of the normal life of the country,
including the normal functioning of transport. Contrariwise, the
greater the distance from the front line, the less must be the
interruption of normal life, including transport. Starting from

[1] See Appendix 1.

this assumption, I decided to choose for my journey across France the most westerly route possible, and after careful study of the map and the railway time-tables I established the nodal points of the sequence as Geneva–Lyons–Roanne–Moullens–Bourges–Tours–Le Mans–Rennes–St. Malo. Mobilizing all my cash and carrying a little portmanteau, I bade farewell to Lausanne one fine August morning and set forth on my journey, taking with me the good wishes of my friends and comrades.

All went comparatively smoothly as far as Lyons, but then the difficulties began. The roads were cluttered up with army transport, the stations crammed with people and rolling-stock. All existing time-tables were cancelled. There was no normal movement of trains. The direct routes were suspended. I had to change every hundred kilometres. We had to wait hours for engines to turn up. There was no food in the restaurants and nowhere to sleep when we stopped for the night, as all the rooms at the stations and all the hotels in the towns were full of soldiers. Sometimes our train stopped in the middle of open fields and had to wait a while for some mysterious signal before proceeding further. Everywhere there was an atmosphere of great calamity and superhuman tension.

Throughout a whole week I slowly progressed on my journey. But at least it was progress. Ultimately, early in the morning of the seventh day, a miserable provincial train deposited me in St. Malo. I had reached the Channel at any rate! Here I had to wait for a ship to take me to Southampton. I enquired about a time-table: it appeared that the boat had left the day before and the next crossing would be two days hence. There was nothing for it but to kill time in this little fishing town where there was nothing to do. I found quarters in a cheap little hotel, black with age, which was more like a tenth-rate boarding house. I anticipated forty-eight hours of boredom.

But fate was kind to me. The proprietor of the hotel, a picturesque old Breton with a shock of dirty grey hair, proved himself a remarkable conversationalist. In his earlier days he had been a fisherman, with a sideline in smuggling, and he had memorized hundreds of the most surprising stories about the sea, smugglers and pirates—in times past St. Malo had been a notorious pirates' lair. It was difficult to distinguish between truth, lies and feats of imagination in the old man's tales, but he

made them so interesting that I could listen to him for hours
without getting bored.

There was one other reason why I was not bored. Within
half an hour of my arrival my picturesque host suddenly asked me:

'Have you seen Chateaubriand's tomb?'

'Chateaubriand?' I replied in some surprise.

'Yes, Chateaubriand!' the old boy exclaimed. 'You must
certainly see his tomb!'

The name of Chateaubriand, one of the classics of French
literature, had been known to me since I was a boy.

And now it appeared that I was in the very town where he
was buried. But that is not quite right; he was buried not in the
town but in the sea.

A high gloomy rock rears its head far out in the sea. The
winds are always howling and the great breakers foaming around
it. Like wild beasts they leap up, lick its bare cliffs and, failing to
reach the top, fall back in impotent rage. A long, narrow stone
causeway links the island with the mainland. At high water this
causeway is submerged and then this lofty, gloomy rock becomes
a tiny island, guarding the entrance into the St. Malo bay like a
lonely sentinel.

Chateaubriand is buried at the very top of the rock. His
remains lie under a cairn on which is an iron frame, half eaten
away by time and weather, and a tall, black cross bearing the
inscription:

François René Chateaubriand
Born 4th September, 1768
Died 4th July, 1848

I sat by Chateaubriand's tomb for a long time, listening to
the breakers, watching the ships disappearing over the horizon
and thinking: What a romantic burial place! How mighty, how
magnificent, is the sea! One never tires of listening to it.

At the end of the second day the ship for which I was
impatiently waiting arrived from England. I boarded it with
some other passengers that night. But this time I was smarter
and bought myself a second-class ticket to avoid complications
in Southampton. Fortunately, visas were not yet required. Before
1914, speaking generally, they had not been heard of. In western

Europe at that time passengers crossing frontiers needed nothing in the way of documents. The visa system was born during the First World War and developed steadily afterwards.

So the worst was behind me. I was on board an English ship, and although some of the passengers hinted anxiously at mines, submarines and fast German cruisers preying on peaceful merchant ships, I just laughed and cheerfully resorted to the battle-cry of my schooldays: 'I'll take a chance!'

The ship sailed in the middle of the night. I went to bed and even undressed. Lulled by the gentle, rhythmic roll, I was soon lost to this world.

By midday next morning we were in Southampton. Nothing had gone wrong—no mines, submarines or cruisers. I ran quickly down the narrow gangway, passed through customs without a hold-up and took my seat in the train standing in the station.

Once again I was in England!

Such was my arrival in London in 1914.

How many years had passed since I first set foot on English soil? Only two decades. But what decades! They had witnessed world-shaking events and great historic changes, such as in another more 'organic' epoch would have been enough for two centuries. The gigantic four-year-war, the grandiose revolution in Russia, the birth of the Soviet State, far-reaching economic and political changes in Europe and other continents, bringing with them astounding transformations in the destinies of so many individuals. And need I go far to find an example?

Two days earlier I had again arrived in London, now not as a political exile hounded by tsarism, but as the ambassador of the Union of Soviet Socialist Republics!

At Dover the captain of the ship lowered a special gangway for me and my wife and took us ashore in person. There the harbour-master and local military and naval authorities were waiting for us. They welcomed the new Soviet ambassador on his arrival in the country to which he was accredited. There was no customs or passport control and we were led straight to the luxurious Pullman car of the London train, which was all ready to leave. A few minutes later porters brought our luggage, which, of course, had not been inspected. All the local high-ups accompanied us to the coach, bowing politely and wishing us a pleasant journey. The next moment the train, a blaze of lights, pulled out into the yellowish-grey gloom of a rapidly thickening fog (there had been no change as far as fogs were concerned!).

At the station I was welcomed by Mr. Monck, the head of the protocol department of the Foreign Office, and the Soviet colony in London turned out at full strength to meet me. There were lots of reporters and press cameras whirred tirelessly. The station-master led us to the Embassy car waiting by the platform. Policemen held back the crowd of sightseers thrusting forward on both sides. We took our places in the car and proceeded slowly in the direction of the Embassy accompanied by several other cars which were occupied by our Soviet comrades. The fog here was slight. The lights of the vast city were suffusing the dark and distant sky with a faint glow. I looked at this London which had so many memories of all kinds for me, and could not help thinking: Was it not different twenty years ago?

And my train of thought continued like this:

How has this fabulous change come about? How is it that I, whom in 1912 the English customs officers had wanted to keep out because I could not raise a miserable five pounds, am now being given such a splendid reception? Only because in that sixth of the earth's surface which was once the Tsar's empire the proletariat has conquered and built up the first socialist State in the world, a State as ambassador of which I am returning to England.

Such was my arrival in London in 1932.

CHAPTER TWO

In Highgate Cemetery

I HAD a long walk before I found what I was looking for. I thought that my memory had failed me. But no; at last I found the famous grave.

It was a little mound, framed by a rectangular surround of old white marble. Within the rectangle was a spread of green turf and a small flowering shrub. At the top end was a marble slab, set at a slight angle, and on it was the simple yet eloquent inscription:

> *Jenny von Westphalen*
> The beloved wife of
> Karl Marx
> Born 12th February, 1814
> Died 2nd December, 1881
>
> *And Karl Marx*
> Born May 5th, 1818 Died March 14th, 1883
>
> *And Harry Longuet*
> Their grandson
> Born July 4th, 1878 Died March 20th, 1883
>
> *And Helene Demuth*
> Born January 1st, 1823 Died November 4th, 1890

I do not like London cemeteries. They are as triste and prosaic as the streets of London suburbs. Here there is nothing romantic about death. The graves crowd together like the dark, grimy houses in a narrow street. At the far end of each grave is a headstone of coarse grey stone, semicircular at the top, on which the name of the deceased is inscribed. All the headstones look alike. They are all perpendicular, like sentries at a review by Death. Of

fine monuments there are very few; in such overcrowding there
is no room for them. Nor is there much in the way of turf and
flowers and what there is are skimpy and bedraggled. Wide alleys,
bordered by dreamy trees, are seldom found. One passes through
such a cemetery and gets impatient at the thought that this is no
realm of eternal rest but an overcrowded place of business for the
departed.

None the less, I always had a particularly warm feeling for
Highgate Cemetery. It was not merely a London cemetery no
different from dozens of others. It was the cemetery in which
Marx was buried. To me it bore a sort of bright halo and I was
often there during the years of my exile. I always took friends
and acquaintances arriving in London to visit it. I was always
present at the annual ceremony on the 1st May when wreaths
were laid on the famous grave. I also visited it alone whenever I
had a free moment. In those years I was studying Marx's works
and thinking a lot about him. Sitting at the graveside I liked to
review his life—his youth in Germany, his struggle in 1848, his
exile in London, his proud poverty and privation and his immortal
work for the ideological armament of the proletariat. In those
days I often saw his tomb as a flaming torch which burned with
a blinding light and scattered sparks to all corners of the earth.
The thought of that torch always gave me fresh inspiration.

Today, twenty years later, I stood by the same great tomb and
reflected sadly on the destructive work of time. The marble slab
had become dingy and begun to peel. The mound had settled and
was breaking up. The rectangular surround was all askew and
broken in one corner. The grass had faded and there were no
flowers at all. It was obvious that no one was looking after the
grave or waging a tireless, systematic war against the powers of
death and destruction.

One other thing struck me greatly. At the time of my exile
there was still plenty of room round Marx's tomb. It looked like
a little island in a bright-green sea. Now all available space was
occupied by later graves. All that was left was a little patch of
ground to the right of the marble surround. I looked at the
inscriptions on the headstones—all strange, meaningless, unknown
names.

Into a narrow crack between the marble surround and the
ground a number of visiting cards had been thrust by unknown

hands. I pulled them out and inspected them. Indian—Czech—Argentine—German—French—Chinese. And a faded Russian wreath, left by a party of Soviet sailors.

What an *International*! Could it be other than genuine, a real demonstration of the spirit of Marx's teaching? I sat down by the graveside and thought long and hard, recalling the events of these twenty years. What an amazing epoch! What vast changes in the political climate of the world! Among so much that was important and remarkable what could be more important and remarkable than the birth in an area comprising one-sixth of the world of the first socialist State in history? Yes, one of those sparks which had showered from all sides of this tomb had set fire to Russia! And here was I bowing my head before this famous grave, not as a homeless refugee hounded out of tsarist Russia but as the ambassador of my country which had become the beacon light of humanity.[1]

---

[1] After the Second World War Karl Marx's grave was removed to another part of Highgate Cemetery and a monument was erected to the great founder of scientific Communism.

CHAPTER THREE

The British Museum

IN GREAT RUSSELL STREET, almost in the centre of London, rises the huge, massive building which is famous as the British Museum. It is built in the classical style and embellished with forty-four antique columns. The architect obviously wanted to give the Museum beauty without too much weight, in accordance with the Hellenic genius, but time and the climate have prevailed. Today the smoke-blackened museum building confronts the world darkly from behind its iron railings.

If you make your way into it through the main entrance, to left and right you have long halls housing the greatest historical and artistic treasures. There are Greco-Roman sculptures, Egyptian mummies, Assyrian antiquities, collections of rare coins, sacred objects of various religious cults, weapons of Pacific races, women's ornaments thousands of years old and much else besides. To these halls a multitude of visitors anxious to know something about the past of the human race streams every day. Everything is open to everyone without payment.

Immediately ahead you see a glass door, guarded by an attendant, with a notice: 'Readers Only'. Here is the entrance to the far-famed Reading Room, of which not only the British Museum but the whole British nation has every right to be proud. From any guide-book you will learn that this circular, domed hall was opened in 1857 and that its creator was the Italian refugee Panizzi, who started as a reader and ended up as the director of the British Museum Library. You will hear further that it is 106 feet high and the diameter of the dome is 140 feet, that it will hold five hundred people, that the reference library in it runs to many thousand volumes and the total number of books reaches several millions and each is noted in the catalogue, comprising a thousand huge folios. But no words can convey the atmosphere which reigns in this remarkable laboratory of the human spirit.

When you have shown the attendant your reader's ticket, passed through the narrow corridor separating the Reading Room from the entrance and found yourself under its semicircular vault, you feel that you have entered a world of its own. Above your head is the high, beautiful dome, below which are twenty fine rectangular windows and underneath each the name of some great figure in English culture. The ventilation and lighting are perfect.

In the centre of the room are three concentric circles of yellow wooden counters; behind the inmost and smallest is the citadel of the administration, the second holds the catalogue of musical works, the third and largest the general catalogue with its thousand volumes. From these circles, like spokes in a wheel, radiate the tables for the readers which are distinguished by letters of the alphabet. Running down the middle of each table is a partition high enough to prevent a reader on one side from seeing his opposite number on the other. Each side is divided into numbered rectangular spaces, giving comfortable room for one reader to spread his books, manuscripts and so forth. To facilitate working, each rectangle is provided with a movable stand for books, an inkpot, blotting-paper, two pens—one with a steel nib, the other a goose quill. (I do not know whether there are goose quills now, but there certainly were in the days of my emigration.) The steel one is for use; the quill as a mark of respect to the spirit of the past. As a matter of fact, some present-day readers actually write with a quill. In front of each compartment is a comfortable, solid chair which positively invites you to sit down and lose no time over starting work. Everything about you—the vast, light room, the countless bookshelves round the wall, these black tables under the soft light of electric lamps, the great names you see under the windows—all incites you to give of your best in the search for truth and in the service of advancing human thought. But a quiet attendant, leading you to this temple of the spirit, is whispering in your ear:

'If there is any book you want, you get its title and number from the catalogue and write them on a special slip, together with the letter of the table and the number of your compartment at which you are sitting. Then you put the list in that urn over there. In twenty or twenty-five minutes the book will be brought to your place.'

Then, as if telling you a great secret, he lowers his voice even further and adds:

'If you haven't finished with your book today you can leave it for tomorrow, and even longer; before you go just put it on that counter. It will be kept for you in this room, so that next morning you'll get it without a fresh slip and unnecessary waste of time.'

Such was the famous Reading Room of the British Museum in which I began to work immediately after my arrival in London in 1912. I confess that my heart was beating fast the first time I took my place at the long black table and the first book I had asked for was brought to me. And why not! Had not this great room played an integral part in the intellectual history of our era? Here Karl Marx and V. I. Lenin had laboured. Louis Blanc and Mazzini had been here, and later on P. A. Kropotkin and S. M. Stepnyak-Kravchinsky. This room had inspired such leading lights in English literature as Tennyson, Dickens, Thackeray, Bernard Shaw and many more. Dozens of great leaders of popular movements in all quarters of the globe had gathered their materials and written their books here. Mighty shades from the past were all around me. I could hardly help asking myself whether I should ever prove in any way worthy of the great figures who had bent over those tables before me.

Then these first emotions passed. Man gets used to anything and I got used to the Reading Room and began to look about me and take in my new surroundings. By degrees I became a permanent visitor. I spent five years (1912–17) at these black tables and ultimately learned all the secrets of life and work within these walls.

As a rule I was at my place at ten o'clock every day. I worked without stopping until one o'clock and then knocked off for lunch and a breather until three o'clock. I always took my meal at the same place—the little popular restaurant run by Lyons. It was only a stone's throw from the Museum and for a shilling I could get some way towards assuaging my hunger. My means did not run to more. After lunch I went for a stroll in the vicinity of the Museum, having a look at the sights of central London or simply gazing into shop windows. Then I returned to the Reading

Room and stayed until seven o'clock, when it closed and all visitors went home. Such was my routine. I got used to regular hours at the British Museum and when some unpredictable occurrence broke the rhythm I always felt strange and ill at ease.

The object of my activities in the Reading Room was not invariable. It depended on time and circumstance and changed accordingly. Up to the beginning of the First World War I was mainly occupied in studying the English working-class movement —Chartism, trade unionism, the Labour movement and every-thing connected with them. I remember with what deep emotion I fingered the fading pages of old Chartist newspapers and gazed at the passionate appeals of the leaders—Stephens, O'Connor, Ernest Jones. When the 1914 war broke out, my attention was attracted to another aspect: I began a feverish examination of the sphere of international relations, of which humanity had been so sharply and painfully reminded. This close look at fundamen-tals could be regarded as my first training and preparation for my future work as a diplomat.

But whatever I was doing or thinking the Reading Room was the permanent centre of my activities. My room at Milton Road, Highgate, merely supplemented it. The Reading Room was my library, study and mental laboratory. Here I read, assembled my materials and wrote articles and contributions for the Russian press. It was here that I arrived at certain more profitable conclusions which were ultimately to inspire my way of life. That is why I never could, and never can, think of the Reading Room without a warm feeling of gratitude.

In this context I should like to offer a word of thanks to a man who kindly introduced me to the life and atmosphere of the Reading Room and gave me every help in my work. I refer to the old London exile, F. A. Rothstein, of whom I shall have a good deal to say later on. He himself worked for many years at the British Museum, and often gave me most interesting information about its history, traditions and visitors, past and present.

I subjected the visitors to the Reading Room to close inspec-tion, wondering which of them would be officially regarded as a reader in this unique institution. It certainly was a world of its own, with its own code, customs, values and traditions. At that

time I divided the readers into three main groups or 'curiae', each
with a special tag: (1) the casuals, (2) the nomads, (3) the settlers.

The casuals were the occasional 'extras' who turned up in the
Reading Room for a day or two for some special purpose and
then vanished for ever, or at any rate a long time. In this class came
journalists, visiting the British Museum to get material for
newspaper articles, secretaries of political and social figures
grubbing up information required for the next public appearance
of their employers, or senior clerks in commercial companies in
the City compiling historical facts and figures for their directors.
Numerically the casuals were the largest group, but their social
status in the Reading Room was very low. Most of the real
readers, and even the staff, treated them like pariahs, and indulged
in various unkind witticisms at their expense.

The nomads were the readers who worked systematically in
the Reading Room for weeks and months, disappeared for a
definite time, reappeared for weeks and months, disappeared
again, reappeared for a substantial period, and so on. They
included various professional workers—professors, university
lecturers and teachers who were writing treatises, preparing courses
of lectures or engaged in research. In this category also came the
more serious representatives of the literary world, collecting
material for some new work. It often had a substantial quota of
foreigners who had come from all corners of the earth to work for
a time in the Reading Room. This was a very valuable and
productive group of readers. When I think of it I can recall many
examples of the type, but here I will mention only A. M.
Kollontay, of whom I shall have more to say later on.

In the winter of 1913–14 she was preparing her great work
Society and Motherhood, which was published in Russia in 1915. She
had to collect material for her work and the British Museum
seemed the best place in which to find it. Alexandra Mihailovna
took her place at the long black table and in a few months became
one of the most assiduous readers. Here I met her and renewed
our previous, somewhat casual, acquaintance, which dated from
the International Socialist Congress at Copenhagen three years
before.

Without any doubt the 'first estate' among readers consisted
of the 'settlers', i.e. those who worked uninterruptedly in the
Reading Room for years on end. They made it their home, put

down roots, treated one another on a 'one of us' basis and to the staff became the fountain-head of opinion and the guardians of the code in this unique republic of readers. Usually they also occupied the same place at the table, which was carefully kept for them by the staff.

Who were the 'settlers'? Fundamentally, this category comprised two elements—the profound scholars and the 'down-at-heel' intellectuals.

I remember that at one time there was sitting close to me an old man with a shock of completely grey hair. At this moment I can see his noble head eternally bowed over in-folios of Chinese hieroglyphics. Who was he? One of the attendants told me that the old gentleman who interested me was a retired professor. He had spent all his life in some eastern British colony, was now living on his pension and writing a work in many volumes on the history of Chinese philosophy. I got to know this sinologue and we occasionally exchanged a few words. I found out that he had been working in the British Museum for three years and would need at least another three to finish the first draft of his book.

When the First World War broke out the professor was terribly shaken and worried. He immediately seemed ten years older, went to pieces and—what had never happened before—sometimes failed to turn up at the British Museum. I often noticed his vacant chair. One morning the attendant, bringing me the books I had left the day before, stopped for a moment and whispered:

'Our old professor is dead.'

'What of?' I said, greatly surprised.

'He died two days ago, from a heart attack. And he didn't finish his work either. After all, he'd had his day. . . . He must have been over eighty.'

All that day I was depressed by what I had heard. I went about in a dream, as if I had lost something intimate and familiar without which it was difficult to carry on.

Of these grey-haired scholars, fanatically devoted to their work, there were considerable numbers in the Reading Room and they gave it a flavour all its own.

But the 'down-at-heel' intellectuals formed the most numerous and active group. Among them were many interesting, energetic and talented people whose sole misfortune was that they

had little money, lived in gloomy attics and had no means of
buying the books and materials they needed. What could these
unfortunates do but spend whole days in the Reading Room,
which was light, warm and comfortable, and—most important
of all—a place where they had at their disposal sumptuous collections of any and every sort of book and periodical, all of which
they could use without paying a penny?

I considered myself in the category of such 'down-at-heel'
intellectuals. Many of my colleagues in the 'settlers'' group also
belonged to it. We all worked assiduously at the long black tables.
And not in vain. Several of the 'settlers' were one day to use the
knowledge gained here for the benefit of the toiling masses and
in the interest of human happiness.

It was a diversified sort of life, with its blend of the important
and the trivial, the serious and the comic. The British Museum
was no exception to this rule. At all times, side by side with the
great figures who were writing their names in History's golden
book, could be seen plenty of nonentities and victims of diseased
imaginations or just freaks. It was no different when I was there.
Let me give a characteristic example.

In one remote corner of the Reading Room I could always see
a tiny old lady, almost swamped by big orchestral and other
scores. She was very poorly dressed and her face clearly revealed
the ravages of privations. From a mere glance it was difficult to
tell exactly what she was doing. She was usually to be seen, her
chair tilted backwards, holding an open score, slowly turning the
pages and alternately opening and closing her eyes. She passed the
whole day that way. I met her once in the cloakroom and got
into conversation with her. She turned out to be French. With
the characteristic garrulity of her nation she revealed the secret of
her activities:

'I am very fond of music and used to play the piano quite
well, but now I am poor, horribly poor, and have had to get rid
of my instrument. I cannot even afford concerts. So I come here
every day, get out the works of my favourite composers and hear
them in my mind, note by note and beat by beat. It's just as good
as if I were at a concert. There's nothing like it! And it's so warm
and comfortable here, and so damp and cold in my garret!'

So *that* was what she was up to!

One fine morning I failed to see the old Frenchwoman in her

usual place. A few days later she was still absent. I questioned the
attendant and got the following answer:

'We don't know what to do. Of late this old Frenchwoman
has been going about like a tramp, her clothes in rags, her shoes
bursting, and worst of all she leaves a trail of dirt and mud behind
her. Finally the Director forbade her to come here. But it appears
that she has some influential friend. Some time or other she was
governess to an important lady, who at once took up her case and
has asked us to readmit her. Probably we'll have to let her in.'

Only two days after this conversation the old Frenchwoman
was back in her place and I again saw the familiar figure, blinking
hard as usual and holding an open score.

Nearly a year passed and then one day I arrived at the Reading
Room somewhat later than usual. One of the attendants I knew
caught sight of me, came straight to my table and whispered in a
tone of restrained agitation:

'You remember that old Frenchwoman?'

'Why, yes. We've talked about her occasionally. What about
her?'

'Something very odd has happened,' the man answered,
looking even more upset. 'She's dead!'

'Dear me!' I exclaimed, with a sympathetic gesture.

'That's not what's odd!' he continued, warming to his story.
'We've all got to die some time or other. But you can't have any
idea what's happened. You remember how she used to go about
like a tramp and we had to refuse her admission. Well, believe it
or not, a hundred thousand francs were found sewn up in the old
woman's mattress after her death! Fancy that!'

In those days a hundred thousand francs represented a very
considerable sum, about four thousand pounds. A woman living
by herself could have lived on the interest on that sum: yet the old
Frenchwoman pretended to be a pauper. The only parallel to a
psychosis like that is Molière's Harpagon or Gogol's Plyushkin!

Now, many years afterwards, I was standing on the pavement
in Great Russell Street, gazing intently at the huge, ponderous
block of the British Museum. Nothing, absolutely nothing, had
changed! The same dark stones, the same antique columns, the
same layer of London soot on the walls.

C

I strolled slowly through the adjacent streets: Bury Street, Museum Street, Montague Place, Bloomsbury Square. Everything was just the same—the second-hand booksellers with their faded volumes of old books set out on their shelves, the window displays of cheap reproductions of famous pictures, the motley shops with every kind of souvenir for foreigners. No change at all! How conservative is life in England!

I glanced at my watch. The sacred hour of lunch was at hand. Where should I go to renew my strength? An idea suddenly came into my head.

I turned a few corners in the maze of little streets adjoining the British Museum and stopped at a flight of steps. Above them the words 'Lyons and Co.' could be seen in gilded letters on a white ground. Here it was, that cheap restaurant which I knew so well in the days of my exile. It was in the very same place and looked no different.

I went in and glanced round. Nothing had changed. There was the cashier's desk, the same display of pastries on the same counter and, away in the corner, the little table at which I lunched for years. It was free at the moment and I sat down at it. Lots of London clerks, shop assistants and typists were eating and drinking all round me. There was a subdued hum of conversation.

A young woman in a plain black dress and a white cap came up and asked for my order. I examined the menu and chose Welsh Rarebit, one of my favourite dishes in the old days. After a few minutes the waitress brought my order and quietly walked away.

I picked up a fork and could not help thinking that I was back in the past.

CHAPTER FOUR

The Communist Club

ONE HUNDRED AND SEVEN, Charlotte Street—an address well known to us exiles. It played an important part in our sorry lives in those days. There, in one of the side streets of central London, a stone's throw from Soho—the French and Italian quarter—was to be found the Communist Working Men's Club and Institute (*Kommunistischer Arbeiter-Bildungs Verein*), usually abbreviated to Communist Club. It was traditionally said that Karl Marx was a member and that its name was associated with the celebrated *Communist Manifesto* published by Marx and Engels at the beginning of 1848.[1]

Tradition also records that during the next half-century the Communist Club became the meeting place of the revolutionaries of many races who took refuge in England from time to time during the political storms on the continent of Europe.

But when I lived in England as an exile, political emigration from Europe had ceased. Marx, Engels, Wilhelm Liebknecht,

---

[1] In those days we exiles had to be content with traditions and legends about the past history of the Communist Club. Today, thanks mainly to the efforts of Soviet scholars, we have more accurate, even if still inadequate, information about the story of this curious institution.

It was founded on the 7th February, 1840, by Carl Schapper and Joseph Moll, two exiled German revolutionaries, members of the secret society, the League of the Just. Its official name was the Educational Society of German Working Men, but its patent activities comprised peaceful propaganda in favour of socialism. It also seems to have been a legal cover for the secret designs of the League of the Just. At the start it made rather slow progress; in 1844 there were only thirty members. But subsequently it grew rapidly and even started its own press. In June, 1847, the first, and in November of that year the second, Congress of the League of the Just, now called the Communist League, were held in London. These congresses adopted a new constitution and organizational programme, the elaboration of which was entrusted to Marx and Engels. The result of this was the famous *Manifesto of the Communist Party*. The battle-cry of Marx and Engels, 'Proletarians of all countries, unite!', was also adopted. The Educational Society of German Working Men was very closely associated with both congresses and the *Manifesto of the Communist Party* was printed at its press. In December, 1847, Marx and Engels delivered addresses at the Society (see E. P. Kandel, *Marx and Engels—organizers of the Communist League*, Moscow, 1953). When Marx subsequently settled in England for good he kept up his association (though not continuously) with the Educational Society and more than once spoke within its walls.

35

Schapper and other German exiles had long been dead. Louis Blanc, Ledru-Rollin, Kossuth, Mazzini and other leaders of the bourgeois-revolutionary movement who had taken refuge in England had long vanished from the scene. All those Frenchmen, Germans, Italians, Hungarians and Austrians who had lived in England for a time awaiting constitutional changes in their own countries had gone home long before. The only exception was Russia. Political emigration from Russia to England had in fact been increasing numerically—and improving in quality—from the end of the nineteenth century. I shall have more to say about it later.

For the reasons already given, the make-up of the non-Russian membership and visitors of the Communist Club was gradually changing more and more. The great names and the eminent European figures had gone and their places had been taken by simple, ordinary folk. By the beginning of the twentieth century this levelling process could be considered at an end.

In my time most of the foreign habitués of the Communist Club were German Social-Democrats who had come to England for one reason or another. Among them could be found the London correspondents of German Social-Democrat newspapers, German clerks and workmen employed by English businesses, left-wing German intellectuals who had come to London to work at the British Museum, democratically minded German tourists seeing the sights of the British capital and so forth. There were no German political exiles in the usual sense of the word, i.e. persons persecuted by the German Government and for that reason unable to return to their own country.

The Communist Club occupied a fair-sized English-style house, having a main room for conferences which would hold two hundred people, some smaller rooms for meetings of groups and societies, a library, a billiard-room, card-rooms and a cheap restaurant where for a shilling or a few pence one could get a simple but adequate meal and even a tankard of genuine German beer. In our exile's life this restaurant played no small part.

The Communist Club was always full and noisy. Here conferences were held, evening discussions organized, amateur dramatics arranged, concerts given by instrumentalists and choirs, foreign languages taught and English learned. Friends and acquaintances could meet over a jug of beer and heatedly discuss the latest political news. Left-Socialist leaders arriving in London usually looked in.

I well remember a day in the middle of 1913 when Karl Liebknecht came on a visit to London. He was invited to the Communist Club and made a powerful, stirring and moving speech on a subject which was worrying us most at that time—the ever-growing threat of war. The main room of the Club was full to overflowing. You could not find a seat anywhere. People were packed together like sardines, standing on tables and crowding into the windows and fireplaces. The atmosphere was unbearably hot and close. The tension in the audience mounted moment by moment and the speech was frequently interrupted by frantic clapping. The speaker, a dark man with lively gestures, shot words at us like fiery darts, words which kindled anger and protest against governments which could drag their peoples into the bloody holocaust of war.

Karl Liebknecht was a very good speaker. There was not only the art of the orator in what he said but a ring of truth and sincerity which won us over completely. Nor was this feeling illusory. Little more than a year later he was the only one of 110 Social-Democrat members of the Reichstag who came out against the war, the outbreak of which was to a great extent imperial Germany's doing. During the course of that war he was ever a stout and open opponent of German imperialism and in January, 1919, the struggle brought him death at the hands of counter-revolutionary murderers.

After the meeting was over Liebknecht and some of the comrades had a meal at the Communist Club. He was accompanied by his wife, a young and lively brunette, Russian by birth. We sat at two adjoining tables and Liebknecht, in whom the oratorical fires had not yet died down, talked and jested uproariously. Someone asked him what the German proletariat would do if the Kaiser thought of declaring war.

'Oh, the German proletariat will certainly have something to say!' he emphatically exclaimed. And then, turning to me, he asked:

'And what will the Russian proletariat do?'

'It will be against the war,' I replied.

History was to prove our expectations unjustified, but the Russian proletariat got nearest to doing its duty: under the leadership of Lenin's party it staged the greatest of all great revolutions, a revolution which marked the beginning of a new epoch in the evolution of humanity.

It was midnight when we took Liebknecht home. It was a quiet, summer night, the great city was going to sleep and only here and there in the central area lingered the dwindling hubbub of the day's activities. I had Toni Hoffmann, a young German girl, with me. She was a Social-Democrat and a lively and intelligent person, quite untypical of Germans. I suggested seeing her home. On the way we talked of many things, including Liebknecht's speech, the danger of war and the role of the proletariat in averting it.

It was half past one when I left Toni at her door. I could not help a whistle of dismay: the Underground would be closed and the buses and trams have stopped running. There were taxis, of course, but they were beyond my means in those days. There was only one thing for it: walk all the way to Highgate where I was then living.

And so began my tour of London at night. I tramped the long, dreary streets, feebly lit by antiquated gas-lamps, and passed through empty squares with municipal employees busily washing them down. I crossed deserted bridges, catching glimpses of dark, shadowy canals beneath. I saw 'London's belly', the huge markets where the hours of darkness are consumed in preparation for the roar and racket of another day. I heard the calls of the prostitutes and the brazen laughter of their drunken escorts. I nearly fell over homeless creatures sleeping on the steps of closed churches. Sometimes I stopped at coffee-stalls and for a few pence fortified myself with a cup of strong tea and a sandwich of somewhat odorous fish. When I felt tired I had a rest on a seat in some park and gazed at the star-studded sky. All London's night life passed before my eyes as on a screen and its sickly grimaces almost became my own.

Time passed. The dark vault of the sky began to brighten a little in the east. There was a gentle morning breeze, which somewhat miraculously penetrated even the smallest fissures in this giant stone labyrinth. The first gleams of dawn caught the windows, setting them alight.

I walked on and on and only when the sun was above the horizon and a distant clock was striking seven did I reach the familiar pavement of my own street.

It had taken me all night to get back home to Highgate! Of course I had not taken the direct route, but had chosen a diversion through the north-eastern and north-western districts of the City.

It gives an idea of the size of London—and of what can happen if you walk a girl home!

PART TWO

*

Russian Political

Émigrés

CHAPTER FIVE

The Herzen Circle and its Members

U P TO the seventies of the last century the number of
Russian political émigrés in England did not reach
double figures, though they were usually eminent but
solitary personalities such as Herzen, Ogarev and Bakunin. The
eighties and nineties saw many changes. Their number increased.
Speaking generally, they came from the ranks of the *narodniki*[1]
and anarchists. P. A. Kropotkin and S. M. Stepnyak-Kravchinsky
were the most eminent amongst them. The twentieth century
brought further changes. With the extension and intensification
of the revolutionary movement in Russia the stream of Russian
emigration to England ran stronger. The number now reached
hundreds and thousands and sometimes included the real
'mountain tops', to use Herzen's expression. Everyone knows that
V. I. Lenin and N. K. Krupskaya lived in London in 1902–3.

When I settled in England at the end of 1912 the number
of political émigrés from Russia did not exceed four to five
thousand (exact figures were not available). The émigrés were
distributed all over the country but the bulk of them was to be
found in London. The intelligentzia predominated, but there was
a sizable contingent from the working classes. There were
practically no peasants.

In these pages I cannot give a detailed account of all sides of
the London political emigration of those days. This book is not
a specialist historical investigation into the subject and I must
confine myself to the most important and essential aspects.

As a rule the political émigrés of those days were people who
had escaped from prison or deportation and were being hunted
by the tsarist government. They were a very motley lot. As

---

[1] Sometimes called 'Populists'—a revolutionary Radical party.

43

regards nationality, they included Letts, Estonians, Poles, Ukrainians, Georgians, Armenians, Jews and Finns, though Russians largely preponderated.

There was always wide variation from the angle of political association. Representatives of all existing parties and groupings could be found in their ranks—Bolsheviks, Mensheviks, Socialist-Revolutionaries, Polish Social-Democrats, Latvian Social-Democrats, Jewish Bundists, anarchists of all brands and so on. I use the words 'and so on' advisedly. In 1914 when the International Socialist Bureau arranged a conference of the Russian Social-Democrats of various persuasions in Brussels and Kautsky tried to get them to unite (which incidentally was aimed at clipping the wings of the rapidly growing Bolshevik Party in Russia), it had to send out invitations to eleven organizations, all within one Social-Democratic fold.[1]

There was another category of émigrés—left-wingers not attached to any particular party. Among them predominated the *narodniki* of the end of the nineteenth century. They were not numerous, but on the strength of their revolutionary past they enjoyed great prestige and respect in the refugee colony. I shall come to some of them in the course of my story (see the sections on F. M. Stepnyak and A. I. Zundelevich). These people had no definite political programme but were all sworn foes of autocracy.

In the years of reaction following the suppression of the 1905–7 revolution many of the Social-Democrats, Socialist-Revolutionaries and others began to trim their sails and abandon—in fact, if not formally—their previous allegiance. Very few of them joined the Bolsheviks; most of them became left-wing Independents. I shall have more to say about one of them (see the section on P. V. Karpovich).

History was to show that of all the parties, groups and sects I have mentioned only the Bolsheviks held the key to the real meaning of revolution. All the rest were on wrong lines and when in the end the October Revolution triumphed too many of them passed over to the counter-revolutionary camp. But at the time, apart from the Leninist-Bolsheviks, only a few realized or foresaw what the future had in store.

Every party and ideology had local groups in London which

[1] See N. K. Krupskaya, *Reminiscences of Lenin* (English edn.) Moscow, 1959, p. 272.

held meetings of its members, carried on propaganda and agitation and tried to attract recruits. In numbers and activity the groups varied. The most powerful and best disciplined was the Bolshevik group under its leader and secretary, M. M. Litvinov, the future People's Commissar for Foreign Affairs in the U.S.S.R. It was much quicker in reacting to events occurring in Russia and more active in winning adherents to the Bolshevik cause among the émigrés in London. Other groups, in particular the Mensheviks and Socialist-Revolutionaries, fell far short of the Bolsheviks in influence and energy, and when collisions, which were not infrequent, occurred they usually gave way. Yet the number of members of the Bolshevik group was limited and increased rather slowly because every newcomer wishing to join its ranks was handled much more strictly than in other groups. M. M. Litvinov always refused to sacrifice quality for quantity.

The basic issues in the struggle of those days between the various groups, and primarily between the Bolsheviks on one side and all the rest on the other, naturally flowed from the general position of the parties and ideologies of which we know from the history of the C.P.S.U.[1] There is no need for me to go into the question here, but I think I should say that in the years of my exile there was no particular tension between the groups in London. This is partly explained by the fact that when I arrived in England at the end of 1912 the boundaries between the parties and ideologies had been clearly established long before and the number of doubters which each group tried to win over had greatly diminished. There was another reason, connected with the particular position of London as an émigré centre.

In the years between the two revolutions there is no doubt that Paris was the capital of the Russian political émigrés. Here was concentrated the main mass (in view of their numbers it is no exaggeration to speak of 'mass') of the exiles. The headquarters of the parties and groups were in this city, and a whole series of party and émigré organs were printed there. Everyone knows that Lenin and N. K. Krupskaya lived in Paris from 1909 to 1912, but it was also the home of other eminent Bolsheviks such as Semashko, Vladimirsky, Lunacharsky, Inessa, Armand, Stahl, S. Gopner and others. It was only in the middle of 1912 that Lenin, wanting to keep in closer touch with the rapidly growing

[1] Communist Party of the Soviet Union.

Labour movement in Russia, went to live in Cracow and then
Poronin, in Austrian Galicia. During the First World War he
had to take refuge in Switzerland.

The then leaders of the Mensheviks, Socialist-Revolutionaries,
Bundists, Poles, etc., also lived in Paris.

Under these circumstances it was quite natural that only in
Paris could the life and activities of the political émigrés be seen
in their full and racy vigour. There were frequent well-attended
conferences and meetings for the discussion of current affairs,
where there were sharp clashes of opinion between the champions of various points of view and concrete political formulae
and demands led to constant dissension, which slowly culminated
in a duel between the Leninist-Bolsheviks on one side and all the
rest on the other. Before the war the burning questions were the
character and destinies of the parties during a war, the nature of
war and how best to carry on the fight against it.

Looking back from the vantage point of a half-century later
it is easy to say that the fundamental duel was between the
Bolsheviks and the Mensheviks. The Bolsheviks stood for all that
was best and finest, most revolutionary and intelligent in the proletariat. They were its prophet and forerunner. The Mensheviks
on the other hand stood for all that was most retrograde, petty-
bourgeois and short-sighted in the proletariat and everything that
linked it with the old acquisitive and blood-sucking society.
They represented an era which was passing away and were the
Russian variation of European reformism—Bernsteinism in those
days—which after the October Revolution played, and still
plays, a counter-revolutionary role in the proletariat's fight for
freedom.

But for the honour of regarding Paris as their capital the
Russian émigrés (or, to be more accurate, the Paris colony) had
to pay a heavy price. Unemployment was rampant among the
exiles and thousands of them suffered terrible hardships and even
starved and got themselves involved in unnecessary worries and
troubles. There was much dissension with lots of feuds and
private quarrels, and though these were often only a kind of
reflection of the class struggle going on in Russia at the time they
none the less poisoned the atmosphere in the émigré colony in
Paris. The French environment—the hot-headed French character, the life in cafés and the streets, the confused state of politics—

also had a bad effect. All this complicated the serious and really important differences of opinion then being thrashed out between the various parties and groups.

N. K. Krupskaya, in her *Reminiscences of Lenin*, makes several references to this subject. Here are a few of her characteristic remarks:

'We had more than enough of squabbling and bickering . . . Life in Paris was a hectic affair.[1]. . . The conference[2] had told on Ilych, and he too was in need of a holiday somewhere out in the country, away from all the petty strife and squabbles of emigrant life. . . . The squabbling roused in one a desire to get away from it all. Lozovsky, for example, gave himself up entirely to the French trade union movement. . . . Another year or two of life in this atmosphere of squabbling and emigrant tragedy would have meant heading for a breakdown.'[3]

Speaking of this Paris period in Vladimir Ilyich's life, she also writes:

'In Paris we spent the most trying years of our emigrant life abroad. Ilyich always looked back upon them with a heavy feeling. He would often remark later, "What the devil made us go to Paris." It was not the devil who drove us there but the need to swing into the struggle for Marxism, Leninism and the Party in that centre of the Russian political emigrants which Paris was during those years of reaction.'[4]

Paris was undoubtedly the headquarters of the Russian émigrés in those days, but it began to lose that position in 1912 when Lenin went off to Galicia (then part of Austria-Hungary) before settling in Switzerland on the outbreak of the First World War. Looking back, it is easy to see that during that war, thanks to Lenin's presence, it was Switzerland that became the remarkable intellectual laboratory from which came the ideas which were to have such enormous influence not only on the history of our party but on the ultimate destinies of all mankind. From that point of view, in the years 1914 to 1917 Bern and Zürich, where Vladimir Ilyich was living, became the capitals of socialist thought, and history will never forget it. But even so, in the numerical and practical sense, even during the war Paris remained the main

---

[1] N. K. Krupskaya, *Reminiscences of Lenin*, Moscow, 1959, pp. 168, 193.
[2] It was held in July, 1910. The reference is to the extended session of the editorial board of the journal *Proletarii.*—I.M.
[3] N. K. Krupskaya, op. cit., pp. 198, 209, 214.
[4] *Ibid.*, p. 191.

émigré centre, with all the consequences flowing from that
position.

It was otherwise with London, which as an émigré centre
always remained modestly provincial compared with Paris. This
was attributable not only to the smaller size of the colony but to
a large number of other factors. London was a leviathan, not
only by virtue of its vast population but for sheer size. When I
was living there the population was double that of Paris and the
area it occupied at least three or four times bigger than the area
of the French capital. Excluding the City and a few central
districts, the British capital then consisted of a gigantic mass of
one- and two-storey houses, which meant that they took up a
lot of room. London had a diameter of 50 kilometres, 25,000
streets and 1,500,000 houses. In the course of centuries it had grown
in some elemental, disorderly fashion by a process of fusion of
large numbers of villages and suburbs with the City proper.

Four to five thousand Russian exiles were just lost in this
giant human anthill. Distances alone stood in the way of too
frequent meetings of the émigrés in one place. In contrast to
Paris, moreover, there was little unemployment among them;
somehow or other they usually managed to find work, and this
was particularly true of workmen, for whom there were open-
ings in factories and engineering works. And then the phlegmatic
character of the English, their tolerant and homely way of life
and their traditional moderation in politics, produced an atmosphere very different from that which prevailed in France. All
this made things very much easier for the émigré colony. Of course
there were feuds and private quarrels here too, but they never
reached the heroic proportions which were common on the
other side of the Channel.

Another very important factor was that at this time none of
the leaders of the parties or groups were living in London, it was
not a political centre and no newspapers or journals were published there. Such leaders in fact showed marked reluctance
to include London in those rounds of visits which were cus-
tomary in those days. Lenin did not come once during my five-
year residence. He had last been here in 1908 when he attended
at the British Museum to collect material for his well-known
book *Materialism and Empiriocriticism*. Such a master and lover of
tours of visitation as A. V. Lunacharsky did not put in a single

appearance, nor did we see the leaders of other parties and groups.

Ordinary émigrés preferred to avoid England, perhaps because they feared their ignorance of the language (which was seldom heard in tsarist Russia) or because they were put off by the widespread stories in our country about the English climate, the fogs and the standoffishiness and 'insularity' of Englishmen. It could really be said that the London émigré colony regarded itself as isolated and had few links with other émigré colonies and still less with Russia.

Unlike Paris, London never saw members of the Social-Democrat group in the Duma or the accredited Russian organizations charged with the duty of collecting information for the leaders and carrying out their directives. The outstanding representatives of the Russian intelligentzia—writers, artists, social workers—seldom put in an appearance. In turn the London émigrés, apart from those working for the Russian press, did not give much help in the political struggle for the mother country. Of course, they were very interested in that struggle and reacted strongly to what was happening at home in those days—the tsarist repression, the shooting at the Lena Goldfields and so forth. But they seldom had a chance of really showing what they were thinking. Of one such occasion I shall speak later.[1]

From what I have said it will be seen that the London émigrés lived far less turbulent lives than their counterparts in Paris. The struggle between the various parties and groups, which was going on in London also, took different forms from those in the French capital. There were very few big conferences and meetings at which the champions of conflicting opinions could come face to face. The London parties obtained fresh recruits preferably by quiet, solid spadework among individuals and clubs.

The First World War was as much of a shock to the London colony as to all the others. After a few weeks of consternation and dispersal, here as elsewhere, the process of gradual differentiation and crystallization set in. It was characteristic of this process that in all parties and groups except the Bolsheviks deep rifts appeared. Under M. M. Litvinov's leadership the Bolshevik group in London immediately took the Leninist line, but in other groups the position was different. The Menshevik group,

[1] See the chapter on Petro Zarechny.

D

for instance, was split between those who were in favour of the war and those who opposed it. The same thing happened to the Socialist-Revolutionaries, the Bundists and other groups. At the beginning of 1915 the position with regard to the war was that at one pole there was the Bolshevik group, rapidly growing thanks to the firm line it had adopted on a matter of principle, and at the other the 'Oborontsy',[1] a heterogeneous, ill-defined and ill-disciplined combination of Menshevik-Oborontsy, S.R. Oborontsy, Anarchist-Oborontsy and Oborontsy of every other type and tendency. Between these two poles was the great mass of émigrés occupying a central position, or perhaps I should say central positions, as the 'Centrists' were in turn divided into various subdivisions, some nearer to the Bolsheviks and others to the Mensheviks.

The influence of the Bolsheviks was all the greater because, in the first place, the Oborontsy among the London émigrés were numerically very weak (though their ranks included the mighty figure of P. A. Kropotkin) and secondly because 'left-wing' tendencies predominated among the Centrists. Such, for instance, was the Menshevik group which had for its leader G. V. Chicherin, a future People's Commissar for Foreign Affairs, and which adopted the standpoint of the Menshevik-Internationalists and resolutely refused to support the Entente.

Later on, as the war went on, the majority of the Centre Party openly recognized that it was imperialistic and passed from non-participation to active opposition.

Of course all this did not come about without much fluctuation, see-sawing and mental reservation and the Centrists, with few exceptions, could not rise to the sole true revolutionary position, Lenin's position, which demanded a complete break with the opportunists of all breeds and emphasized the necessity of converting the imperialist war into a civil war to unleash the socialist revolution. So though there were many among them who were perfectly sincere in their detestation of the war, in fact they did a lot of harm.

A characteristic case in this connection was the internationalist paper *Nashe Slovo*,[2] published in Paris in 1915–16. In May, 1915, Lenin, referring to it in the pages of *The Social-Democrat*, said:

[1] Those who considered it their duty to defend the country.
[2] *Our Word.*

'It[1] rises against Social-Nationalism but only to its knees, fails to expose the most dangerous advocates (such as Kautsky) of this bourgeois line of thought and instead of denouncing the war as opportunist maintains a rigid silence about it and takes no real steps to free socialism from its shameful servitude to patriotism.'[2]

This attitude of *Nashe Slovo* and such of the émigrés as supported it brought water only to the mill of the jingo Oborontsy and, in consequence, the imperialistic bourgeoisie, and it was the attitude adopted by a very large number of the London 'internationalists'.

Not long before the First World War there had been a growing idea among the London émigrés that there should be a single all-party centre which would meet the needs of the Russian colony as a whole. Round about 1910 this idea actually took shape and London saw the creation of a large émigré organization which, named after the great Russian exile of the nineteenth century, was officially called the Russian Circle named after Herzen in London (abbreviated in our plain émigré language to Herzen Circle). M. M. Litvinov played an active part in the creation of this organization and took over as secretary from the start.

The Herzen Circle was accommodated at the Communist Club, where it had a separate room for its modest office and committee meetings.

When there were members' meetings, amateur dramatics, lectures or musical evenings the big club-room was used and the restaurant was available. The activities of the Circle, as contemplated by its constitution, were not and could not be political. It was the émigré cultural and artistic centre, the place where people of all parties and convictions, homesick folk eating the sorrowful bread of exile, could meet in a free and easy atmosphere, play chess or dominoes, have a cup of tea or a glass of beer together, find Russian books and papers and hear Russian singing and music. There was a fund from which assistance could be given to émigrés most in need of it. From time to time amateur theatricals were organized and these were always particularly well

---

[1] *Nashe Slovo.*
[2] V. I. Lenin, *Works* (4th Russian edn.), vol. 18, p. 157.

received by the colony. Russians have a passion for the theatre!
I remember how I once appeared as Captain Zhevakin in Gogol's
Marriage.

The Circle gave us émigrés much of the homely warmth we
so sorely missed in the vast, cold stone labyrinth of London, and so
it, or rather its quarters in the Communist Club, were always
filled with Russian exiles drinking, eating, smoking, discussing
the news, arguing, quarrelling and making it up again, planning
the future—all amidst a cloud of tobacco smoke and a babel of
tongues.

When, in a very different era, my mind goes back to those
distant days, the name of the Herzen Circle recalls a long line
of figures now somewhat shrouded in the mists of time. Nearly
all of them have gone to that bourne from which there is no
return. I cannot sketch them all, but I should like to bring back a
few and show them as they were in the days of my exile.

CHAPTER SIX

M. M. Litvinov

OAKLEY SQUARE—a cramped little square in North London. A few sickly trees, a patch of green grass with its layer of fine soot, two or three benches, two rows of closely packed, monotonously similar, grimy houses, a glimpse of dull grey sky from which a sort of mist is always falling—such is my vision of the place. In a dense London fog Oakley Square and its vicinity are always particularly gloomy and forbidding. They are inhabited by labourers, tramwaymen and railwaymen, the lowest-paid categories of workers. Here the prosperous capital shows you not the dazzling façade of banks and ministries but the drawn face of poverty and privation. No, indeed, there is certainly nothing remarkable about Oakley Square, and yet this decaying square means so much to me.

It was the end of 1912 when I first arrived in London.

The times were difficult and dangerous. Europe was rushing towards a terrible disaster. All the great powers had their share of responsibility for this state of things, but that did not make it easier for the ordinary man. The butchery had already started in the Balkans—an immediate prelude to the First World War. Already the streets of German cities resounded to the heavy tread of troops awaiting the first summons to strike east or west. France and Russia, united in a military alliance, were already preparing to mobilize their forces to realize their imperialistic designs in the Balkans and Africa. The tattered Austro-Hungarian monarchy, governed, in the picturesque current jibe, by 'a despotism tempered only by inefficiency', was starting that last risky throw in the Balkans which led straight to Sarajevo. England, with its Asquith-Lloyd-George Liberal cabinet, was losing hope of making political capital out of keeping out of the approaching European conflict; Lord Haldane, her War Minister, was rapidly

preparing an expeditionary force to send to the continent and
Sir Edward Grey, her Foreign Minister, was putting the finishing
touches to the Anglo-Franco-Russian Entente. Many people,
including statesmen and politicians, realized what was happening
in the world and vaguely felt that things were going wrong, that
storm-clouds were piling up on the horizon, international tension
was growing and the European atmosphere was charged with
electricity.

In the east, behind the Vistula and the Dniester, the tsarist
colossus was rolling on just as swiftly towards its miserable end.
The shots of its soldiery were still echoing through the Lena
Goldfields, there was a fresh and mighty wave of strikes, meetings,
demonstrations and risings throughout the country, we had the
first stirring of revolt among the peasant masses, ground down by
poverty and losing patience and their legendary docility. Already
stepping into the forefront of history was the iron phalanx of
Communists which, guided by the genius of Lenin, was soon to
take the lead in bringing about the greatest of all great revolutions. And all this time the stupid, cruel, execrable, corrupt,
blood-sucking tsarist régime continued to dissolve and rot away
in its decrepitude. In its death-throes it tried to strangle that
young giant, the revolutionary proletariat, and finding its efforts
in vain threw itself only too eagerly into the bloody adventure of
imperialist expansion.

Such was the broad historical background against which
individual lives followed their individual patterns.

At the outset I found that London swallowed and suffocated
me. Not knowing the language and without money and any sort
of work, I felt lonely and lost in this giant stone ocean. I happen
to have preserved a letter to my mother which deals with those
very days (it is dated 28th December, 1912). I will quote from it.

'It will soon be two months since I arrived in London and
although, of course, I am not in a position to say that I know it
well (no one can get to know a vast place like this quickly) I have
already got some idea of the city and its life and I must frankly
admit that my impressions are not too favourable. London
certainly interests me greatly from the political and social-
economic point of view and I do not in the least regret that I am

spending the winter here. But I should be sorry to have to be buried in these parts for long. The very thought of possibly having to live here permanently sends a chill up my spine. No, I don't like London at all! It is huge, gloomy, uncomfortable, with its grim rows of little houses swallowed up in black fog and looking all alike. Sometimes the sun is not seen for weeks and this depresses people terribly. I understand now why spleen is called the English disease and also why Heine had such an aversion to the country of the proud British. He once said that the ocean would have swallowed England up long ago if it had not been afraid of indigestion. But I doubt whether he was quite right; digesting such a nut as England is no simple matter.'

It so happened that despite my then frame of mind I was 'stuck' in London for quite a long time. In various ways and capacities I was to spend eighteen years in all there. And my feelings about this city changed with the years. Before I had finished I even realized that there was a special charm about London. But at the start, during those first months of my acquaintance with the British capital, I was horribly cold and uncomfortable. I went looking for a little friendship and warmth to thaw out my frozen heart. I found them in that squalid and soot-begrimed Oakley Square.

At 30, Harrington Street, a stone's throw away, another Russian exile, Maxim Maximovich Litvinov, was living at the time. He was thirty-six years old and already had behind him a rich and varied revolutionary experience which had won him a special position and authority in émigré circles. I was eight years younger and looked up to him as a sort of god. When I arrived in London he was already an 'old inhabitant'. He had been in England since 1908 and in the past four years had mastered the language, established many local connections and acquired a good knowledge of the commercial and political set-up in the capital.

He was 'one of us' in this seven million strong anthill.[1] And indeed, despite our differences of opinion (he was a Bolshevik-Leninist, whilst I was then a Menshevik), Maxim Maximovich became my guide and patron in the first and inevitably hardest months of my residence in England. He helped me in learning the language and something about the country, taught me about its institutions and introduced me to people, gave me much

[1] The population of London in 1912.

information and sound advice. My friendship with him continued all his life and I recall it with more than ordinary warmth when I think of the end of 1912: then it proved particularly valuable.

In those days we had hardly a penny to our names and lived a dreary, uncomfortable life in our lonely, stuffy rooms. Every Russian hankers after a home atmosphere with a samovar and a plate of hors-d'œuvre on the table. If no samovar, at least a steaming teapot. Both of us were looking for some such home from home in which we could find relaxation and relief from the chilly monotony of our bachelor lives. Such a home was opened to us at 72, Oakley Square.

Here lived a Bolshevik, Platon Mihailovich Kerzhentsev, who, like myself and Maxim Maximovich, was an émigré and had come to London comparatively recently from the continent. I am not quite sure that I ought to talk about a 'home', as he occupied not a house but a large, damp and rather gloomy furnished room on the second floor of a grimy London house. But he was married, and this meant a very different atmosphere in his apartment. True there was no samovar, but an ever-ready teapot, some bread and cheap sausage always awaited the visiting comrade. Maria Alexandrovna, Kerzhentsev's wife, was ever a hospitable hostess and knew how to make her guests welcome.

There was another attraction in his quarters, the 'balcony'. It was not a real balcony, but one could get through a window on to a little railed-off roof from which, to the accompaniment of clattering hoofs and hooting motor-cars, the simple life of this poor district could be studied.

To speak of fresh air here would be almost sacrilegious. But we were not fastidious or spoilt.

When night was falling and figures could be seen hurrying along to light the gas-lamps, Maxim Maximovich, Kerzhentsev and I often resorted to the 'balcony' and, making ourselves as comfortable as we could, got involved in long discussions.

What did we talk about?

First and foremost, and the subject most frequently and hotly debated, was Russia—the struggle against tsarism, the workers' movement rapidly raising its head and the prospect of a revolution. We did not always agree, but there was no lack of heat and fire in our arguments.

We also talked quite frequently about England, her way of

life and national characteristics, her establishments and institutions, the strife of parties and the course of economic development. Maxim Maximovich was even then versed in the home and foreign politics of Great Britain and had close ties with the leaders of the English Labour movement (which was very useful to him later on when he became People's Commissar for Foreign Affairs), so that he was in a position to serve new arrivals like Kerzhentsev and me as guide and interpreter of contemporary England.

Even then I was greatly struck by certain qualities which later on made him one of the greatest statesmen in the Soviet Union —his sober and powerful mind, his strong character, his gift for quickly and firmly grasping the essentials of a question without getting lost in details, his bent for sarcasm, his fundamental dislike of empty talk, his genius for organization. He seemed to be able to do anything, unlike many émigrés who suffered from a chronic disability to get down to anything. He earned his living, plunged into social activities, read books, followed politics, toured the City on a bicycle on Sundays and even took part in amateur theatricals. I well remember one day when he appeared as the Tartar in Gorky's *Lower Depths*, which was staged by the colony's dramatic society. Yet with all this he never complained that he had too much to do and too little leisure. One always felt that the man one was dealing with was a convinced and faithful Bolshevik, tenacious, industrious and bursting with energy.

There was one particular evening on the 'balcony' which I shall always remember. The news coming from the continent was getting ever more alarming, the political atmosphere ever more oppressive and the spectre of approaching war was visible on the horizon. Maxim Maximovich looked more worried than usual. He gave Kerzhentsev and me a clear picture of the contending forces in the international arena and ended up with these words:

'If there is a great war the world will become unrecognizable. Revolution will triumph in Russia. And then—who knows what prospects will unfold for Russia and the Russian proletariat?'

No one answered him, but, watching the last rays of the sun dying away in the London sky, I could not help echoing his words:

'Yes, who knows?'

The hand of history was already writing words predicting great changes. Subterranean rumblings, marking the beginning of the end of an outworn system, were already making Europe totter.

The years passed. Maxim Maximovich continued to keep in close touch with Lenin, corresponding with him and receiving his directives and orders. He worked hard in the London Bolshevik group and acted as secretary of the Herzen Circle. He kept a close eye on the political life of England and the course of affairs in Europe. As I have said, when the First World War broke out he adopted Lenin's position and campaigned stubbornly for the Bolshevik line in the émigré colony. On Lenin's behalf he represented the Bolsheviks at the International Socialist Conference (or, to be more accurate, the conference of socialists from the Entente countries) which was held in London in February, 1915. Here Litvinov tried to read the Bolshevik declaration, and when the chairman of the Conference refused to allow him to do so he walked out of the assembly. The declaration was thereupon published in the press.

About that time my relations with Maxim Maximovich cooled off to some extent, the reason being political. As I have already said, during my years in London I was a Menshevik. When the war broke out I shared the views of those middle-of-the-road internationalists who were so fiercely and justifiably attacked by Lenin. I did not sympathize with the Oborontsy, however, and in fact frequently opposed them, both verbally and in print. But I could not take the Lenin line and in fact adopted a sort of central position and so sometimes fell into the Socialist-Chauvinist trap. This came out very clearly in the above-mentioned Socialist Conference in London in February, 1915.

At this Conference Martov was to have come from Paris as representative of the Mensheviks, but at the last moment the British authorities refused him a visa. He sent me the declaration which he had intended to make public at the Conference and asked me to take his place. Although the Menshevik declaration was framed in the spirit of what Lenin called 'a rising, but only to one's knees', it aroused the wrath of the French delegates (Vaillant, Compère-Morel, Sembat, Longuet, Thomas), who were very chauvinistically minded, and was not read at the Conference but merely included in the minutes. I was irritated by the chairman's behaviour but did not retire from the proceedings—thereby displaying that same temporizing which was so characteristic of all Menshevik-Internationalists.

Of course my appearance at this Conference was a great political mistake, a mistake arising out of my erroneous views on the question of the war; but at the time I did not appreciate it. I realized the falseness of my 'internationalist' ideas during the First World War when in 1919–20 I broke with Menshevism, at first in practice and afterwards officially by a letter published in Pravda.

In February, 1921, I was admitted to the R.K.P.[1]

The explanation and circumstances of my break with Menshevism and adhesion to the Bolsheviks are given in detail in my little book *Demokraticheskaya Kontrrevolyutsia*,[2] which was published by the State Publishing Institution in Moscow in 1923.

Returning to my relations with Litvinov, political differences of opinion could hardly fail to affect them at such a critical time as the First World War. But there was no complete break and when there was a big change in his private life in 1916 we began to meet again. The change was that he got married. The Litvinovs set up house in Hampstead and I visited them several times.

My old friendship with him was completely restored in the Soviet Union in January, 1922, when I returned to Moscow from Siberia where I had been president of the Siberian *Gosplan* Committee. I was bringing with me the first economic plan for Siberia for 1922 for confirmation by the Central *Gosplan* and called on him at the Narkomindel[3] for old times' sake. I remember that I was dressed in the fashion of those days—leather jacket, high boots and a sheepskin coat with a high fur collar thrown over my shoulders. Maxim Maximovich gave me a very friendly reception but glanced somewhat ironically at my get-up. At the close of our conversation, which was mainly about memories of the past, he suddenly shot a question at me:

'You haven't forgotten your foreign languages, I suppose?'

[1] Russian Communist Party (Bolsheviks).
[2] *The Democratic Counter-revolution.*
[3] The People's Commissariat for Foreign Affairs.

'No, I haven't forgotten them,' I replied, somewhat taken aback.

'Wouldn't you like to come and work in Narkomindel?' he continued.

I hastened to assure him that I very much liked my work as head of the Siberian *Gosplan* and did not want to change it for any other. Litvinov said nothing, but laughed in a very odd way. A week later I received an intimation from the Central Committee of the party of my appointment as head of the press department of the Narkomindel. So here I was back with Litvinov.

Our friendship deepened with the passing of the years. It has always remained one of my finest memories.

In May, 1917, not long after the February Revolution, I returned to Russia. The émigrés had agreed among themselves on a rota for using the scanty and difficult means of transport available during the war (I shall have more to say about this later) and so Maxim Maximovich found himself detained in London longer than he wished. When his turn came there had been a swift change in the situation.

The international position at that moment was quite critical. The bourgeois world had only just realized that the Soviet Republic had been born. The Soviet Government's proposal that the war should be quickly ended by a general democratic peace without annexations and indemnities was rejected by both the warring coalitions, and in consequence negotiations were in progress at Brest-Litovsk for the conclusion of peace between the German bloc and Soviet Russia. Among the Entente countries, and, in particular, ruling circles in England, the mood was rapidly growing which subsequently led to intervention and support for the White Guard counter-revolution. At the same time a substantial proportion of the British proletariat had strong sympathies with the October Revolution and was looking only for some concrete way of showing this sympathy.

In these circumstances the Soviet Government badly needed someone who, knowing the country and the language and having links with proletarian circles, might be able to take advantage of the mood of the democratic masses in the struggle against the attempts forcibly to suppress the Soviet Republic. Litvinov seemed to have special qualifications for the task and that is why

Lenin secured his appointment by the Council of People's Commissars. As a result Litvinov had to unpack the trunks which he had already packed and immediately address himself to a very important and complicated task which was quite unfamiliar to him.

On the 5th January, 1918, the day after his appointment, he sent Arthur Balfour, the British Foreign Secretary, a note informing him of the fact and requesting a meeting—the first Soviet Note in London. A few days later he received a polite reply to the effect that since the Soviet Government was not officially recognized by England, Mr. Arthur Balfour could not receive Mr. Litvinov, but if the latter wished to keep in contact with him he would appoint one of his officials, Mr. Rex Leeper, through whom Mr. Litvinov could communicate anything he thought necessary to Mr. Balfour.

Why this comparative punctiliousness on the part of the English Foreign Secretary?

The explanation must be sought in the following piece of history.

As early as the end of 1917, Lloyd George, at that time Prime Minister, came to the conclusion that the then British ambassador in Russia, Sir George Buchanan, was quite unfitted to maintain relations with the new men at the top and to perform the other, more 'delicate', tasks which the British Government might require of him in Soviet Russia. He was recalled. In his place Lloyd George wanted to send a younger man, someone more supple and resourceful. His choice fell on R. H. Bruce Lockhart, previously British vice-consul in Moscow, who had returned to London from Russia on the eve of the October Revolution. The British Government was looking for a chance to send him to Russia and M. M. Litvinov's appointment as Soviet plenipotentiary seemed a propitious moment.

Lockhart lost no time in getting into touch with M. M. Litvinov and met him at one of Lyons' democratic little restaurants in the Strand. Although there were no official diplomatic relations between British and Soviet governments, it was agreed that Litvinov in London and Lockhart in Moscow should enjoy the established diplomatic privileges, including the right to use cypher and the diplomatic bag. Here, on a coarse tablecloth, M. M. Litvinov wrote a letter to the People's

Commissar for Foreign Affairs which he handed to Lockhart. It
was to serve as a visa for the latter. On the 14th January, 1918, he
left England for Soviet Russia.

Many years later I heard from Maxim Maximovich's own lips
the story of his work as plenipotentiary—the first Soviet
plenipotentiary to England—which was so closely linked with his
years of exile. It happened in the following way. In 1933, when
he was People's Commissar for Foreign Affairs, he came to
London for the World Economic Conference which was being
held there. I was then Soviet ambassador to Great Britain and
also taking part in the work of the Conference. In our spare time
(there *was* spare time, as the delegates did not like being over-
burdened with work) he and I often went walking in the London
parks. On one occasion he led me to an unoccupied bench under
ancient oaks in one of these parks and with a laugh suddenly
opened up.

'Would you like to hear how my diplomatic career began?'

'How?' I asked, with some surprise.

'Like this,' he replied as he sat down.

He went on to tell me such a vivid and remarkable story that
when I got home I wrote it out at once. Afterwards I gave him
what I had written and he read it and made a few minor correc-
tions. Later on two copies were typed. Maxim Maximovich had
one and with his permission I kept one for myself. I am taking
the liberty of reproducing the text.

'There I was as plenipotentiary,' he said, 'and I had nothing,
absolutely nothing—no instructions from Moscow, no money, no
staff. It is superfluous to add that I had no experience or training
for diplomatic work. I simply had to start from scratch.

'First of all it was absolutely essential to establish some sort of
contact with Moscow. I availed myself of the services of one of
the émigrés who was returning to Soviet Russia to take the newly
created People's Commissariat for Foreign Affairs a letter in
which I asked for instructions and money. By the same comrade
I sent Narkomindel a cypher which I got out with the help of one
of the members of the former tsarist Purchasing Commission in
London who sympathized with us. Hitherto we had lacked a
cypher and all communications between N.K.I.D. and myself

had been by telegram *en clair*. The cypher I sent was altered in some respects and afterwards distributed to all our plenipotentiaries abroad. Now that correspondence in cypher between N.K.I.D. and myself had become possible our relations became somewhat closer but only "somewhat", as one characteristic example will show.

'After sustained pressure on my side, in March, 1918, I was at length informed by Moscow that N.K.I.D. was sending me the first diplomatic courier. It is easy to imagine how impatiently I awaited his arrival! I followed the various stages of his long and complicated journey (he was coming via Finland, Sweden and Norway) with the closest attention and went in person to the station to meet him. The courier arrived with a large bag covered all over with diplomatic labels, and it was in a state of great excitement that I carried it from the station to my rooms. Even greater was my excitement as I started to open this precious receptacle which I expected to contain all the instructions and orders I needed. Imagine my dismay on finding a pile of the latest Moscow papers but not a single directive! True enough, G. V. Chicherin, who was then Deputy People's Commissar for Foreign Affairs, had included a little letter addressed to me in the bundle of newspapers. But this letter was in the most general terms and gave me no definite instructions whatever on the matters in which I was particularly interested. At the time I was very angry, but today I understand well enough that I could not have expected anything else. In March, 1918, thousands of pressing problems, including the question of the Brest-Litovsk Treaty, had the Soviet Government by the throat. Their solution was a matter of life and death to the Soviet State. Lenin had his hands too full for him to concern himself with instructions to the London Embassy, and the People's Commissariat for Foreign Affairs, which had only just been established and was taking its first timid steps in its own sphere, could hardly be expected to direct my activities by itself. As before, I was left to myself.

'The diplomatic bag did, indeed, solve one of my problems; it contained a draft for two hundred thousand roubles in tsarist banknotes, which were then still being accepted in London, and I managed to convert them into pounds, though at a very poor rate of exchange. Now I could at least get down to setting up the first Soviet Embassy in London officially. I took special premises

for it at 82, Victoria Street, S.W.—hitherto my own rooms had
had to serve—ordered seals and headed notepaper and invited a
few people to join me. My wife was the secretary and conducted
all the English correspondence. I also secured the services of three
or four more émigré comrades or former employees of the
tsarist War Purchasing Commission.

'On the doors of the Embassy a brass plate with the inscription
"Russian People's Embassy" was fixed. The consulate, entitled
"Russian People's Consulate", was also accommodated there. I
gave myself the title of "Russian People's Ambassador". All these
denominations were my own invention; as I have said before, I
had had no instructions at all, not even as to my official description, from Moscow.

'What about my relations with the British Government and
English society? Here it is necessary to make a sharp distinction
between the period preceding the treaty of Brest-Litovsk and
that which followed it. Up to that treaty the attitude of official
and unofficial England towards me was comparatively favourable,
allowing for the times and circumstances.'

Referring to the before-mentioned exchange of notes with the
British Foreign Office Maxim Maximovich continued:

'Later on my link with the British Foreign Office was actually
provided by a young official from that department, Rex Leeper.[1]
I had known him before. I met him for the first time at the house
of the Spanish émigré, Madariaga (who was subsequently Spanish
delegate at the League of Nations), and up to the revolution I had
been giving him Russian lessons. Now the Foreign Office decided
to use my old acquaintance with Leeper for diplomatic purposes.

'At the outset my business meetings with him were not
without a certain "romantic flavour", as we used to forgather in
cafés or restaurants, and even in London parks.'

Litvinov nodded at the seat on which we were sitting and
smilingly added:

'One of our talks was on this very seat. . . . Afterwards he used
to come to my rooms and towards the end I began to visit him at
the Ministry.'

But let me return to my story.

---

[1] In years to come Rex Leeper was to have a very successful diplomatic career. After
the Second World War he held the post of British minister to Greece and subsequently
became ambassador to the Argentine.

'It goes without saying,' continued Maxim Maximovich, 'that when I had received *de facto* recognition from Balfour I decided to try to liquidate the former tsarist Embassy which was still prolonging its existence in London. I wrote a letter to Constantine Nabokov, then considered the *chargé d'affaires*, and demanded that the comedy should cease and Chatham House, the Embassy, be handed over to me. I sent the letter to him by one of my colleagues. He accepted it and replied quite politely that if the British Government officially recognized the Soviet Government he would not hesitate to retire and relinquish the Embassy, but pending such recognition he considered my claims unfounded.

'I dispatched a letter in similar terms to the tsarist consul-general, Mr. Onou,[1] but he turned out to be a much tougher proposition and told my messenger to make himself scarce.

'I had more success in other directions. I sent the Bank of England a letter demanding that a stop should be placed on all monies deposited with it by the tsarist Government for the payment of its Embassy and the tsarist War Purchasing Commission in London. The Bank complied with my request and the Embassy and mission got no more money.

'As regards my relations with the press and public opinion, here again I had no particular cause for complaint, considering the situation and circumstances, in the first period. I was always being interviewed and photographed, my wife's relations were described in detail, but there was comparatively little defamation or abuse.

'Even better were my relations with the British working man and leading circles in the British Labour movement. In the middle of January, 1918, I sent the leaders of the Labour Party and the trade unions a letter in which I informed them of my appointment and expressed my confidence that I should get full support for my work from the British proletariat. I followed up my letter with personal visits to the Labour leaders. Speaking generally, I had a friendly reception, but there were exceptions. Bowerman, the leader of the printing union, for instance, was distinctly hostile. On the other hand, the Labour leader, Anderson, was particularly friendly and subsequently gave me steady support.

[1] The last tsarist ambassador in London, Count Benckendorff, had died in January, 1917, and the Provisional Government did not appoint a successor. C. Nabokov, a counsellor (brother of V. Nabokov, head of the secretariat of the Provisional Government), was in charge of the Embassy in the capacity of *chargé d'affaires*.

E

'At the very outset of my activities as plenipotentiary I worked hard at meetings and in the press to enlighten people about the October Revolution and raised my voice in no uncertain terms against the prolongation of the war. I published a number of articles in the Independent Labour Party's weekly, *The Labour Leader*, and several other papers and issued a large quantity of leaflets and pamphlets.[1] I appeared and spoke at the 17th Conference of the Labour Party at Nottingham. At many meetings I found myself involved in hot disputes with opponents of the October Revolution.

'I well remember a particular meeting held in the Caxton Hall. It came about in the following way.

'In the summer of 1918 Kerensky arrived in London and made a slashing attack on the Bolsheviks at the Labour Party Conference at which Arthur Henderson was in the chair. I was present at this Conference but was not allowed to reply to Kerensky, despite the clamours of the audience. A few days later some Labour left-wingers and several radical Members of Parliament, Joseph King and others, arranged a special meeting at Caxton Hall at which I was the principal speaker.[2] The hall was full to overflowing, the mood of the audience quite exhilarating and the resolutions passed were extremely sharp.'

When Britain changed over to open political intervention the position of the Soviet Embassy quickly deteriorated, a development which took the most various forms.

'Arriving at the Embassy one morning,' M. M. Litvinov continued, 'I found it locked. It appeared that the landlord of the premises at 82, Victoria Street had decided to liquidate permanently such a dangerous institution as the Soviet Embassy and, tearing up the contract between us, had arbitrarily taken away the key. I took the matter to court. The judge went into my complaint and held that the landlord had in fact repudiated the agreement he had signed. The defendant then justified his action, pleading that I was in England engaged in "dangerous propaganda against the Crown and society". The judge was obviously on his

---

[1] Of these the most important was the brochure, *The Bolshevik Revolution, its Rise and Meaning*, which appeared in English in the spring of 1918. In the drafting of this document M. M. Litvinov was greatly helped by several London Bolshevik émigrés, mainly F. A. Rothstein.

[2] In *The Labour Leader* of 4th July, 1918, M. M. Litvinov also published a crushing 'Reply to Kerensky'.

side and the judgment was that though the defendant had broken
the contract my claim must be rejected. I even had to pay the
costs. In view of the complicated situation I decided not to appeal
against this decision and put an end to the litigation. As a result,
the "Russian People's Embassy" ceased to exist at 82, Victoria
Street and I had to transfer it to my own rooms at 11, Bigwood
Avenue, Golders Green, N.W.

'My position as Soviet representative in England became more
difficult every day. The Conservative press raged and government
circles found it increasingly hard to reconcile themselves to the
presence of an agent of Soviet Russia, even if unofficial. The
general atmosphere of hostility also had its effect on the Labour
leaders. Some of them soon cooled off, while others wavered.
But there were a few, notably Anderson, whom I have already
mentioned, who continued to give me firm support despite the
changed atmosphere.

'In the summer of 1918 I became convinced that the centre
of the intervention movement was being shifted to Washington
and I accordingly wrote to Vladimir Ilyich pointing out that
under existing conditions I thought I could do more good to the
Soviet Government in the U.S.A. than in England. He agreed
with that point of view and I was appointed Soviet plenipotentiary in Washington. He also sent me a courier with all the
necessary documents, including a diplomatic passport with
signatures and seals, which in those days were for some reason
triangular. I informed the American Embassy in London of my
appointment and asked for a visa for Washington. The Embassy
was comparatively favourable but Washington definitely thought
otherwise. The visa was refused and so my journey to the U.S.A.
never materialized. I had to stay on in London and continue my
work as Soviet representative in England.

'When Bruce Lockhart was arrested in Moscow on the 3rd
September, 1918, for counter-revolutionary activities, the British
Government, by way of reprisal, searched my rooms and arrested
me on the 6th September. Almost all my employees had their
homes searched and were arrested at the same time. I was lodged
in Brixton gaol. I was treated perfectly decently in the prison and
the lower ranks of the staff (gaolers and so forth) showed me open
sympathy. They vied with one another in trying to do me little
services and so it was not difficult for me to keep in touch with

the outside world. I remember that when I was released one of the gaolers pressed me to take him with me to work in Soviet Russia.

'A few days after my arrest Leeper came to see me in prison. There was a purpose in his visit. Before I was incarcerated the Foreign Office could communicate with the Soviet Government through me and the moment Lockhart went to prison there was no other link. Yet negotiations with Moscow were essential if only for the purpose of procuring his release. Then the F.O. recalled my existence and sent Leeper to see me. Leeper asked me to send a note in cypher to Moscow proposing that Lockhart should be exchanged for me. I told him that I would not send cypher messages from prison. One thing or the other; either the British Government considered me the representative of the Soviet Government—in which case I must be released—or they regarded me as under arrest—in which case they had no business to be coming to me asking me to send a message in cypher. They must choose. Having failed in his mission, Leeper left.

'Ultimately my stand had its effect. Ten days after my arrest I was released and went home. On my categorical demand the members of my staff were released simultaneously. It is true that even after my return I was visited by representatives of Scotland Yard, who were always on my track, but I was now a free man and therefore agreed to transmit the F.O.'s proposal to the Soviet Government. Moscow agreed and so the question of my leaving England was decided in principle.

'Yet all sorts of obstacles had to be overcome before effect could be given to that decision. Lockhart was in Moscow, I was in London, and railway, telegraph, telephone and all other communications between the two capitals were at that time, if not completely interrupted, at least precarious and complicated. In these circumstances it was simply impossible to arrange that Lockhart should cross the Soviet frontier and I the English on one and the same day; it all boiled down to which of us should pass the frontier first. I suggested to the F.O. that I should leave England first but, instead of going straight on to Soviet Russia, should stop at Christiania [Oslo nowadays] and remain in Norway until Lockhart left Russia. Ultimately, with a heavy heart Balfour accepted my suggestion.

'The exchange took place in September, 1918. Communications between England and Soviet Russia at that time were through Scandinavia and being made extraordinarily difficult by the German submarine blockade of England and the vast quantity of mines in the North Sea. In practice I would have to travel from London to Aberdeen, there board a ship which, escorted by two destroyers, made more or less regular crossings between Aberdeen and Bergen, and make my way from Bergen to Soviet Russia via Christiania and Stockholm.

'When the time came for me to leave London there was a strike on the English railways. The F.O. offered to take me and my companions (I had with me about forty Bolsheviks who were still living in London) by motor-bus. I agreed. Leeper accompanied me to Aberdeen, and we also had with us the Norwegian vice-consul in London, who was also concerned in my evacuation from England.

'The passage from Aberdeen to Christiania was quite uneventful. On arriving in the Norwegian capital I presented myself at the Ministry for Foreign Affairs, told them the conditions on which I had left England and that I was entirely at their disposal. The Minister was extremely embarrassed. He said that my arrangement with the English Foreign Office was no concern of his at all and that I could act now as I thought fit. I left him and paid a visit to the British Embassy in Christiania, where I told them that I was carrying out my agreement with the F.O. and would remain in the Norwegian capital until the news came through that Bruce Lockhart had left Russia.

'There was some delay over his release and evacuation and it was not until early in October that he passed Russia's frontier with Finland. Then my agreement with the F.O. came to an end—and with it the story of the first Soviet Embassy in London.'

With it also ended the story of M. M. Litvinov's years of exile. Before him now opened the most important page of his life.[1]

---

[1] See Appendix 2.

CHAPTER SEVEN

G. V. Chicherin

OAKLEY SQUARE once more. . . .
The storm-clouds piling up on the political horizon of Europe had burst. The First World War broke out. The German battalions poured into Belgium and France. A wave of continental refugees swept up to the shores of England.

G. V. Chicherin arrived in London with that wave. At the time of the German onslaught he was on holiday at one of the little German spas. The onrush of the German armies cut him off from Paris, where he had been residing. He was determined not to live 'under the Germans' and he just managed to catch the last steamer leaving for the only country to which it was possible to go—England.

Hence his appearance in the British capital. He settled at 12, Oakley Square, and here, in a little attic on the fourth floor, he spent the three years up to his arrest and final return to Russia.

G. V. Chicherin was a striking and original personality. His appearance alone attracted attention; his tall, solid figure with the brown hair, reddish pointed beard, the clever, intellectual face with the high forehead and the first signs of baldness. There was a sort of innate fastidiousness about him. His most remarkable feature was his eyes: they were bright, restless and piercing. His movements were nervous, quick and unexpected. It all somehow produced an impression of personal charm, and yet if one looked at Georgii Vasilievich one could not help thinking: What an interesting man! There is something individual and unusual about him.

And indeed Chicherin was a man apart.

In origin and education he was very different from plebeian émigrés like ourselves. He was of noble birth and aristocratic to the fingertips, though he would never talk about it. He often

70

gave me the impression that he was trying to forget it. As I was rather interested in his ancestry I did some research in various records and encyclopaedias and made some curious discoveries.

When the Turks captured Constantinople in 1453 and the last Byzantine emperor, Constantine XI, was killed in battle, his family fled to Rome. The pontiff, anxious to draw Russia into his international schemes, conceived the idea of a marriage between Ivan III, a widower, and the last Byzantine empress, Zoe Paléologue, who had been brought up in the Catholic faith. Moscow, however, considered itself the heir of Byzantium after the fall of Constantinople and was seeking some means of openly demonstrating its new position. It was under these circumstances that in 1472 Zoe Paléologue, escorted by an imposing suite, went to Russia and became tsaritsa of Moscow under the name of Sophia. One member of her suite was an Italian, Athanasi Cicerini, who was the founder of the Chicherin family.

During the centuries that followed this family produced several eminent servants of the tsars—secretaries of state, chamberlains of the royal household, clerics, warriors, judges, generals, counsellors. At the beginning of the sixteenth century, for instance, Ivan Afanasievich Chicherin, a son of the founder of the family and a member of a monastic order, had great influence with the Government. A century later, in 1611, Ivan Ivanovich Chicherin, as a clerk in the Estates Office, was one of the signatories to the edict proclaiming the election of the Romanov family as tsars. After another century we meet with Colonel Ivan Andreyevich Chicherin as governor of Poltava and losing his life in the battle near that town. In the time of Napoleon and the first Patriotic War Cavalry General Peter Alexandrovich Chicherin was present at many of the great battles of those days and in the second half of the nineteenth century Boris Nicolaevich Chicherin, professor of Constitutional Law at Moscow University, mayor of the city, jurist and philosopher, was the ideological leader of the Liberal aristocracy.

Georgii Vasilievich himself was the son of a diplomat and the nephew of the B. N. Chicherin just mentioned. He was born in 1872 in the province of Tambov: his family was rich and he received an excellent education and spoke several languages while still a youth. After taking the historico-philological course at St. Petersburg, in 1897 he followed in his father's footsteps and entered the Foreign Ministry. His wonderful memory and vast store of knowledge must have made success in that profession easy for him. It seemed that he was on the threshold of a brilliant career.

Then something suddenly happened to him. Quite unexpectedly he turned his back on everything he had been and known and became a disciple of Tolstoy. Next he left the gospel of Tolstoy behind him and became a revolutionary. I have no idea what psychological process carried him from the camp of passive resistance into that of Marxism, and often tried to find out, but he did not like talking about the subject and cleverly evaded a reply. The fact remains that in 1904 he threw up his post in the Ministry for Foreign Affairs and went to Berlin, where he was soon in close contact with Russian Social-Democrat organizations and in 1905 became a member of the R.S.D.R.P.[1] and joined its Menshevik wing.

At the end of 1905 the Prussian authorities expelled him from Germany and he settled in Paris. Here he took an active part in the French socialist movement and also became a prominent figure in Russian political émigré circles.

When I recall the spiritual figure of Chicherin I am inclined to think that there was something in his character which originated in the revolutionary seventies and eighties of the last century. Turning his back on his past, he plunged with a sort of crusading zeal into his new world. He became quite fanatical and ascetic in his actions, thoughts, conduct and way of life.

In the past he had liked to dress well and expensively; now he would never wear anything except the cheapest sort of workmen's clothes. He used to have a fine taste in food and was a connoisseur of wines; now he became a vegetarian and teetotaller. He used to like the theatre, opera and ballet; now he despised any form of entertainment. He had previously played the piano very well; now he never gave music a thought. He used to spend a great deal of money on himself; now he began to live at proletariat level and gave everything to the Party. After he joined the R.S.D.R.P. he considered that every minute of his day should be devoted to the revolution, and to the revolution alone. His asceticism was so strict, consistent and inflexible that it often

[1] Russian Social-Democratic Labour Party.

irritated us émigrés of plebeian origin. We never went to such lengths in our personal life and did not consider it necessary.

I can easily recall the Chicherin of those days. The solitary window of his dark attic looked out on the grimy roofs of London. It was damp and uncomfortable. In the middle was a plain rectangular table, without a cloth, on which there was a disorderly pile of books, papers, letters, plates, cups, half-eaten salami and half-finished bottles of lemonade. In a corner stood his half-made bed on which he liked to sit when he had visitors. On the floor along the walls there were great mounds where he had casually thrown papers, notebooks, pamphlets, circulars, fat dictionaries, bulky reference books and the many volumes of an encyclopaedia. The mounds were so high that they reached the window-ledge and so wide that you could hardly pass between them and the table. The room was literally smothered in printed material of all sorts and even his bed was all but submerged.

Of course all this was covered by a thick layer of dust and London soot which made every visitor cough. At first the land-lady had tried to introduce order into the chaos reigning in her strange lodger's room, but, finding her efforts in vain, washed her hands of Chicherin.

Georgii Vasilievich did not spend much time at home—only night and morning. Even then he had got into the habit of working very late, up to two or three o'clock in the morning, a habit which became stronger when he was People's Commissar for Foreign Affairs later on. About midday he usually left his attic and went walking in the London streets. He was very energetic, acted as secretary of the Menshevik group, was a member of various organizations and societies, always planning some-thing, helping someone or consulting the comrades on some topic or other. There was much to be done and time passed without his being aware of it. Late at night he returned to his attic, quickly had his supper and got down to his night's work.

There seemed no end to his work. It increased and multiplied spontaneously; with a nature like his it was inevitable. In his character there was a great deal of nobility and a passionate devotion to work. Whatever he put his hand to he always wanted to arrive at the best possible decision and he always tried to foresee and be ready for anything and everything.

I remember how, some time early in 1913, I was carrying out

one of those 'tours of visitation' of the émigré colonies in Belgium
and France which were fairly common in those days. Chicherin
made the necessary arrangements, as he was then living in Paris.
It is only common justice to him to say that he organized everything splendidly. My appearances at the meetings and conferences
were always timed to perfection and the halls were always full.
What a lot of energy it must have cost him! Think of all the letters
and telegrams he must have dispatched in connection with my
journey and of all the trouble he went to in looking up my ships
and trains in time-tables and finding suitable lodgings for me!
Georgii Vasilievich stopped at nothing if it was for the good of
the cause.

In London his personal specialities were more rather than less
conspicuous. Leaving his attic in the morning, he used to sally
forth wearing a long, loose overcoat which he had evidently
bought in Bavaria. Originally its colour had been a beautiful
dark green but it was now terribly faded and shabby. It was
against his principles to buy a new one. The pockets of this coat
were always stuffed with letters, bills, notes, newspaper cuttings
and other things. In addition he always carried a rather large
dispatch-case (the English equivalent of a portfolio) in which he
kept note-pads, carbons, writing-paper, a slate for calculations
and, last but not least, a 'stylo', a glass tube like a pencil which
enabled him to produce four carbon copies.

It was quite usual for him to turn up at my humble quarters,
give me some bit of news and then ask politely: 'I won't be
disturbing you, will I?'

When I replied, 'Of course not,' he used to empty his deep
pockets, open his dispatch-case and get down to work. I used to
sit in a chair reading or writing while he busied himself going
through letters and papers, using his stylo to multiply copies of
his answers, writing articles and preparing material for his
speeches and lectures. Then he got into his overcoat again and
tramped off to some other rendezvous to repeat the performance.

In those days many of the comrades used to make fun of his
astounding concentration and phenomenal capacity for work.
But what a blessing they proved later on when he was Foreign
Minister!

Of the subjects in which he was most interested during my
exile I have special memories of two.

The first was the English committee for assisting political prisoners in Russia. It owed its existence to him as it was entirely his idea. All the émigré organizations supported it. It was he who found its first English members. Among them were socialists, radicals and even liberals. He guided its activities with great skill and tact. His principal assistant was a woman, Mrs. Bridges Adams, one of those English people who somehow fail to come to terms with life and so devote all their passion and determination to some 'cause' which fires their imagination or touches their heart. In the years before the First World War Mrs. Bridges Adams was a fervent suffragette and smashed shop windows and attacked Members of Parliament. When she met Chicherin the heroic struggles of the revolutionary movement in Russia stirred her imagination. She was all fire and flame for this new 'cause' and became the moving spirit on the committee.

The official purpose of this committee was to make collections and send money to revolutionaries lying in tsarist prisons, but under Chicherin's skilful guidance it soon extended this somewhat narrow aim and gradually became a political organization engaged in systematic agitation against tsarism. It collected and published information about the brutalities of the gaolers and police, organized meetings to protest against the inhuman treatment of prisoners under 'preventive arrest' and in gaol and had questions asked in Parliament about wholesale arrests and repression in Russia. The tsarist ambassador in London got nervous and informed the British authorities of his dissatisfaction with their toleration of the existence of the committee. But Chicherin and Mrs. Bridges Adams only laughed up their sleeves and redoubled their efforts.

The headquarters of the committee was a big desert of a house, 96, Lexham Gardens, Kensington, which by some miracle had survived from the wreck of Mrs. Bridges Adams' previous life. Because its owner had not the means to keep it up the inside was cold, dusty and uncomfortable. But this had no effect on the work of the committee.

I was often at this house and certain scenes there are fixed almost photographically on my memory.

A freezing evening in the winter. In the streets outside the cold penetrated your very bones. Damp gloom throughout the house. In the drawing-room a feeble fire and near it a round table with a table-lamp burning brightly on it. It is the only decently lit spot in the surrounding gloom. At the table, huddled in their coats, sit Chicherin and Mrs. Bridges Adams compiling a new leaflet against the tsarist Government.

Another matter with which Chicherin was much preoccupied at that time was the fight against the recruitment of political exiles for the British Army, which began in 1916.

As soon as the war began, the tsarist Government conceived the 'happy' idea of taking advantage of the situation to deal the Russian political exiles a severe blow. When mobilization was in progress it proposed to extend the call-up to Russian subjects who had gone abroad for political reasons. On this excuse, which sounded so patriotic, it hoped to secure the extradition of even the emigrants who were living in countries with which it was allied. It soon appeared, however, that English and French ideas about the rights of refugees were too deep-rooted for the plan of the Police Department to be feasible.

Then the quick wits in St. Petersburg came out with another scheme: the political émigrés should make their contribution by being called up for the British and French armies, not the Russian. The idea behind this scheme was that if it materialized the majority of the able-bodied émigrés would get sent to the front and this would hamper the anti-tsarist agitation both in London and Paris.

This plan, adroitly served up with the sauce of an appeal to patriotism between allies, had an excellent reception from government circles in England. Various departments gave it their consideration and practical steps were suggested to give effect to it. The émigrés protested violently against the project. As I said before, the majority considered the 1914–18 war an imperialist war and opposed any sort of participation in it, and in particular any employment in the munitions factories.

Chicherin was a leading figure in the struggle to prevent the émigrés from being called up for the army. I supported him wholeheartedly. Once more there were protest meetings, questions in Parliament, discussions with M.P.s (I well remember Josiah Wedgwood in this connection), pamphlets, leaflets, letters to the press and so forth. For a time we managed to delay the issue of the relative orders, but ultimately they materialized. But once again history intervened. In February, 1917, came the

Russian Revolution, the émigrés went home *en masse* and the recruiting of Russian exiles for the armies of the allies ceased to be a burning question.

I returned to Russia in May, 1917. A few days before my departure I was with Chicherin in his attic and we were absorbed in discussing the great question of the course and prospects of the revolution which had just begun. We were both longing to go home, but I was luckier than he, as I was leaving in a few days, whilst Georgii Vasilievich, by a decision of the émigré organization, was to remain in London for some time to arrange the speediest possible repatriation of the Russian exiles. Chicherin's words remain in my memory:

'In a time of revolution you must be hot or cold. You can't be lukewarm and I am coming to the conclusion that the Mensheviks are the Girondists of the Russian Revolution and will suffer the fate of the Girondists. Although I was once a Menshevik our ways have parted. The war has taught me a lot and now all my sympathies are on the side of the Russian Jacobins.'

He hesitated for a moment and then added:

'I mean the Bolsheviks.'

I cannot be certain that at the time of this conversation Georgii Vasilievich was a convinced Bolshevik. It would appear so from the remarks I have just quoted. But there can be no doubt that he had moved very near to the Bolshevik position. In any case his subsequent joining the Communists seemed to be the natural outcome of the previous ideologico-psychological processes.

His Menshevism was consumed in the fires of the First World War, leaving him with his utter devotion to the cause of the proletariat and his brilliant gifts, encyclopedic knowledge, amazing memory and passion for work. It is not surprising that the Party made extensive use of Chicherin's abilities in the interests of the Soviet State.

But this did not happen straight away.

Remaining after my departure in London, Chicherin busied himself not only with the repatriation of the Russian émigrés but also with an energetic campaign among the English workers against the war and for a democratic peace. As a result the

British authorities arrested him and lodged him in Brixton gaol, the same gaol which was to become familiar to Litvinov a year later. He was confined there for several months. It was only in January, 1918, when Litvinov was accorded *de facto* recognition as representative of the Soviet Government, that he was released and given permission to return to Russia.

He arrived in Moscow at the end of that month and was immediately appointed Deputy People's Commissar for Foreign Affairs.

And so a new and extremely important page opened in his life, a page which was to record mighty happenings and changes.[1]

[1] See Appendix 3.

CHAPTER EIGHT

F. A. Rothstein

FEDOR ARONOVICH ROTHSTEIN was also an émigré and a member of the Herzen Circle, but in many ways he was very different from the majority of the Russian exiles then living in London.

As a rule these exiles had arrived only after passing through an important probationer stage in the revolutionary's career and few were less than thirty years old. Many of them, moreover, avoided contact with their English entourage and confined themselves to the self-contained Russian colony. Even when they were driven to find work somewhere in England they did no more than their jobs required of them and tried as far as possible to leave the outside world alone. Such émigrés spoke Russian only and read nothing but Russian books and papers. Quite frequently they learned of important events in England only some days later when the Petersburg or Moscow papers arrived in London.

In those days there was an old émigré, Tyeplov, who had been living by the banks of the Thames for twenty years. He kept a Russian lending library and was very popular in the Russian colony. To him the English tongue was a closed book; he found gestures better than words at the butcher's or baker's. Not all the émigrés shared Tyeplov's antipathy to the language but only a few of them were really at home with it.

F. A. Rothstein was unlike the other émigrés. The first difference was that he arrived in London in 1891 as a young man of twenty with no serious revolutionary experience behind him. The son of a provincial apothecary, he was regarded with suspicion because while still at a grammar school in Poltava he was in touch with local Narodovoltsy[1] (Bunin, Sarpinsky, Prisyetsky and others). In due course he was faced with the choice between arrest and leaving Poltava. He decided on the

[1] Supporters of 'The People's Will'—a revolutionary radical group.

second alternative. But where was he to go? He was at the stage
when the natural question was the next step in his education. In
view of the suspicion and doubt with which he was regarded any
Russian university was closed to him. Emigration alone remained
and he went to London. Why London? Why not Switzerland,
where Russian youths of radical tendencies usually completed
their education in those days? The explanation was simply that
he was much influenced by the names of Spenser, Buckle and
John Stuart Mill and wanted to fortify himself at the tree of
knowledge in its own country.

The methods adopted by Rothstein to attain his ends were
highly original. Instead of entering London or any other English
university he spent five years at the British Museum compiling
a massive work on the history of the Roman Empire. His dream
was to produce a Marxist reply (he was already familiar with the
teachings of Marx) to Gibbon's famous work, *The Decline and
Fall of the Roman Empire*. The dream did not materialize: he
lacked time and money to finish his labours. Instead, biographies
of Cicero, Socrates and Plato from his pen figured in F. F.
Pavlenkov's popular series, *Lives of Remarkable Men*, appearing in
Petersburg. It was in this way that the path of Russian literature
opened to the young émigré.

Rothstein's next departure from the stock type of Russian
exile was his close association with English life, which resulted
from his coming into contact at an early stage with the 'Free
Russian Press Foundation', founded towards the end of the
eighties by the well-known narodnik S. M. Stepnyak-
Kravchinsky. People of all political persuasions supported this
society but Stepnyak saw to it that its general line remained left
wing.

'Stepnyak was a great man,' Rothstein often told me, 'clever,
gifted, a genuine revolutionary. . . . Yet he alone of the old
revolutionaries managed to develop into a good socialist. Most of
the others just became liberals.'

In 1895 Stepnyak died, however, and other people came to
the top in the Press Foundation. In Russia Marxism prevailed. In
1896 and 1897 there were the famous weavers' strikes at St.
Petersburg. All this contributed to the process of stratification
going on in the London émigré colony. Rothstein had joined the
Marxist camp at a time when the majority of the Foundation were

not to be wooed away from the doctrine of the Narodniki. This alienated him from the Foundation and led him to join the English Social-Democratic Federation, which at that time was the only socialist organization in England sharing the views of Marx and Engels. He actually joined the Federation in 1895.

The leader of this organization was Hyndman, one of those highly individual figures which the end of the last century alone produced. The child of a substantial bourgeois family, he was attracted to Marxism in his youth and in 1884 founded the Social-Democratic Federation. He was a gifted and energetic man and a political careerist who did a great deal to expose the ulcer of capitalism inside England, but retained many relics of the conservatism in which his family had been brought up. Always immaculately dressed and wearing a silk hat, he made himself a dictator in the Federation and brooked no opposition. His comrades in the organization christened him the 'Tory-Socialist', an apt description, as on many questions he was barely distinguishable from his bourgeois contemporaries and in the sphere of foreign affairs he was a true-blue British nationalist. Engels, in a letter of the 30th August, 1881, to Bebel, described him as 'an arch-conservative and extreme chauvinist',[1] and so he remained to the end of his days. How significant it is that it was Hyndman who suggested to Disraeli, that pillar and prophet of British imperialism, that he should adopt a socialist programme.

On joining the Social-Democratic Federation, Rothstein very soon proved himself one of Hyndman's strongest opponents. This was shown very clearly during the Boer War, 1899–1902. For the first two years of this piece of brigandage the Federation carried on a doughty struggle against it. Its lectures and meetings were frequently broken up by mobs of jingo hooligans, its leaders, speakers and organizers set upon by frantic 'patriots', its publications burned and destroyed by imperialist head-hunters. Its heroic members cheerfully bore all these tribulations.

Then in July, 1901, Hyndman wrote a letter to *Justice*, the Federation paper, in which he proposed that the anti-war agitation should be abandoned and recommended a return to the Federation's ordinary work of quiet socialist propaganda, as it had done its international duty. Rothstein made a sharp reply to him in the pages of the same paper and this started a fierce struggle

[1] K. Marx and F. Engels, *Works*, vol. 27, p. 9.

F

on this question within the Federation. It soon appeared that the vast majority of its members backed Rothstein and Hyndman found himself in such a difficult position that he was forced to withdraw his candidature for the executive at the next elections. Rothstein was himself elected, receiving the maximum number of votes, and thereafter was re-elected several times.

Fedor Aronovich had now become the acknowledged leader of the left wing of the Federation and when it was incorporated in the British Socialist Party on the latter's formation in 1911 he became the leader of the left wing of the new organization.

He worked hard and productively in the years preceding the First World War. He published articles in the English and foreign socialist press, in 1906 edited the *Socialist Annual* (a compilation of valuable political information and statistics relating to the international Labour movement), was London correspondent of *The Egyptian Standard* (the organ of the Egyptian nationalist movement), took part in the Egyptian Youth Conference in Geneva in 1909, published in English in 1910 his well-known book, *Egypt's Ruin*, and led the fight against Hyndman when he backed the agitation for 'a Big Navy', to foment the rivalry between British and German imperialism.

At the beginning of the First World War he organized the revolt of the local branches of the British Socialist Party against the executive and its leader, Hyndman, which was taking up a 'pro-war position'. The result of this revolt was that at the party conference in 1916 eighty per cent of the votes were cast in favour of Rothstein's 'internationalist' stand. Hyndman then left the Socialist Party and soon afterwards disappeared from the political scene. Rothstein played a very great part in the preparations for and coming into being of the Communist Party in England and the settlement of its constitution.

In these circumstances can anyone be surprised that Fedor Aronovich kept in the closest touch with his English milieu and English life?

There was another contributory factor. In 1907, having to earn his daily bread, Rothstein got a technical job with the Liberal paper the *Daily News*, a journal which had been started by Dickens. Here he read the foreign press and made extracts from it for the staff on international questions. How useful this store of information and knowledge was to prove to him later on when he was Soviet ambassador in Teheran and subsequently served as a member of the collegium of the People's Commissars for Foreign Affairs! The *Daily News* naturally brought him into contact with left-wing radical circles in Great Britain.

Rothstein was at the height of his powers when I was living in England. He had an acknowledged position on the left wing of English public life and belonged to the small group of Russian exiles who were quite at home in London and making what, by our standards at the time, was a very comfortable living. He lived in Highgate, rented a little house (53, Whitehall Park), had a good library and was bringing up his three children, two boys —Andriusha and Zhenia—and a girl—Natasha.

I sometimes went to visit him on Saturdays or Sundays. When I first emigrated I made up my mind to profit from my residence abroad by acquiring a thorough knowledge of the political and trade union organizations in Germany and England. The four years (1908–12) I spent in Germany taught me a lot. Now I wanted to learn all about the British Labour movement and from that point of view Rothstein seemed to me a real find. From him it was always possible to get much unusual information on subjects in which I was interested and he also gave me valuable introductions to various leading figures in the English proletariat. At his house I always met an Englishman of some sort, whether socialist, left-wing labourite, radical journalist or prominent figure in the trade unions. This helped me to get a better view of the multifarious aspects of British life and naturally drew me to the little house in Highgate.

There was another factor at work in the same direction.

However busy Fedor Aronovich was with English affairs, he never took his eyes off what was going on in Russia. In 1901 he had joined the R.S.D.R.P., and after the split at the second party conference in 1903 he identified himself with the Bolsheviks. Subsequently he was associated with the work of the Russian Social-Democratic organizations and I deal later on with the outstanding part he played in the financial crisis arising out of the fifth R.S.D.R.P. conference held in London in 1907.[1]

---

[1] See Chapter Fifteen, 'Lansbury's Story', p. 134.

He was also a living chronicle of events in the history of the London political émigrés for about a quarter of a century and liked talking about the more interesting happenings in which he had been involved and the unusual people he had met. Of his stories I particularly remember one in which Lenin figures.

Meeting Rothstein one day in the Reading Room of the British Museum, I asked him:

'You were in London when Lenin was living here, weren't you?'

'Yes, indeed,' he replied; 'Lenin was living here somewhere about 1902 or 1903 when *Iskra* was being published here.'

'How did you come to meet him?'

'I generally met him in the Reading Room,' he promptly answered. 'Lenin, like any other conspirator, lived very much to himself in London; but as we were both working in the Reading Room we were bound to run across each other quite frequently.'

Rothstein took me into the room and showed me the place where Lenin usually sat. Then he said:

'I was always greatly struck by Lenin's amazing capacity for work; he was a quick as well as a hard worker, certainly three times quicker than I was. . . . The Museum staff always treated him with great respect and the attendants often remarked in some surprise: "This reader simply swallows books; no one else asks for such vast quantities." '

I was interested in the question whether Lenin worked at home as well.

'Oh yes,' Rothstein replied, 'but far more at the British Museum. For two reasons: only here had he the books and materials he needed, and his lodgings and surroundings were quite unsuitable for serious intellectual work.'

'What do you mean?' I asked in some surprise.

'It calls for rather a long explanation,' he answered. 'Let's go out. We can't talk here; there's supposed to be no talking in the Reading Room.'

He continued with his story a few minutes later when we had moved to one of the public rooms of the Museum and were seated opposite some marble antiquities from ancient Rome.

When Lenin was in London he lived at 30, Holford Square, Clerkenwell, in the northern part of the City. He did not use his own name but called himself 'Mr. Richter'. He took two little rooms on the ground floor of an ordinary English house. One room looked out on to the street, the other on to a backyard. He took the rooms unfurnished at a pound a week and furnished them himself. Apparently some of the comrades helped him. At his request Rothstein took him some materials one day and so had an opportunity to see his lodgings. Everything was of Spartan simplicity—a table, a few chairs, two iron beds, a little cupboard for crockery and kitchen utensils. There was hardly room to move, let alone for books and writing materials, and, above all, the surroundings were certainly calculated to paralyse any idea of serious work.

'What sort of surroundings?' I asked, somewhat taken aback.

'You know,' Rothstein explained. 'Clerkenwell, a citadel of petty bourgeoisie and to some extent the aristocracy of the working-class world. The way of life, outlook and psychology of the inhabitants of this district are particularly petty bourgeois. The landlady from whom Lenin rented the rooms was a typical representative of Clerkenwell and, at long range, heiress of the "Victorian tradition". She had the curious name of "Yeo". The family consisted of the mother, Emmy Louisa, a daughter in the dressmaking business, and three sons employed in printing works. This was the family, and particularly the "Victorian" mother, who now and then butted into the private life of Lenin and his wife. There were several odd encounters. Here's one of them. . . .'

Rothstein laughed and continued:

'One Sunday, soon after Lenin's arrival at Holford Square, Mrs. Yeo, looking out of a window, saw something that made her shiver—Mr. Richter [i.e. Lenin] was coming up the street with a loaf of bread, not wrapped in paper, under his arm. Next day she explained to Nadezhda Konstantinovna that in their district it was not considered proper to buy anything on Sunday, shopping should be done on weekdays and in any event anything one bought should always be carried wrapped up. She begged Nadezhda Konstantinovna and her husband to observe this custom in future.'

'Well, I'm blest!' I burst out.

'Here's another case,' Rothstein continued, smiling. 'After quite a short time Mrs. Yeo noticed that in the rooms occupied by Mr. Richter and his wife the windows had no curtains. Her Victorian heart was shocked and she explained to Nadezhda

Konstantinovna that in this district windows always had curtains. Mrs. Richter promised to comply with the landlady's wishes. Next Sunday Mrs. Yeo suddenly heard the sound of hammering in the Richters' room—Lenin was fixing up the curtains. Mrs. Yeo was horror-stricken, immediately asked Nadezhda Konstantinovna to come and see her and explained that hammering on Sunday, the day of rest, was most improper. The curtains must be hung another day.'

I could not help laughing; such Victorian 'respectability' was enough to drive one mad.

'Mrs. Yeo,' Rothstein continued, 'was extremely worried because Mrs. Richter did not wear a wedding ring. But she could not make up her mind what to do. Ought she not to turn the Richters out? But they always paid the rent very promptly and she did not want to lose such good tenants. Finally she decided that "they are foreigners and who knows what the law is in their country", and the thought reassured her, all the more because Mrs. Richter's sweet nature and kindness had meant much to her. One of the standing topics of conversation in the Yeo family was Nadezhda Konstantinovna's fondness for their cat which she had taught to shake hands and miaow good morning. But Mrs. Yeo did not altogether approve of her taking so little interest in her kitchen and spending so much time writing.'

Rothstein smiled again and added by way of explanation:

'You probably know that Nadezhda Konstantinovna was secretary of *Iskra* at the time.'

He was silent for a moment and then concluded:

'The Yeo family were much perplexed by the fact that despite the Richters' obviously modest means they were often invaded in the evening by a lot of people, and very unusual people at that, people "in heavy top coats with fur collars" (in Mrs. Yeo's own words).[1] What worried the family even more was that on these occasions they never had anything to eat or drink but simply talked.'

I laughed again, thinking how strange and incomprehensible the ways and customs of Russian revolutionaries must have seemed to English folk of the Victorian breed. It was a case of two worlds being worlds apart.

Rothstein resumed:

[1] They were comrades who had come straight from Russia.

'So if you really can visualize Lenin's surroundings at home (of which he was always being reminded) it will be quite clear why he was only too glad to spend whole days in the Reading Room of the British Museum.'

Many years later I was reading N. K. Krupskaya's book of recollections of Lenin and came across a sentence relating to his residence in London in 1902 and 1903:

'How strong these petty-bourgeois prejudices were we had an opportunity of observing in the case of our landlady's family— a working class family.'[1]

I often think of the stories Rothstein told me during the years of my exile.[2]

---

[1] N. K. Krupskaya, *op. cit.*, p. 73.

[2] Rothstein's story about Lenin's lodgings in London was confirmed from other sources. At the beginning of the forties, when I was Soviet ambassador in England, my wife, who was working as London correspondent of the Institute of Marxism-Leninism, looked up Mrs. Yeo's children (she herself had died some time previously) and invited them to the Embassy where a shorthand note was taken of their recollections of 'the Richters' when they were living at their house. My wife sent the typescript to the I.M.L. In all essentials their story agreed with what F. A. Rothstein told me so many years earlier. For Rothstein's history after his return to Russia, see Appendix 4.

CHAPTER NINE

A. M. Kollontay

ALEXANDRA MIHAILOVNA KOLLONTAY was not one of the established émigré colony in London. She paid only flying visits to England. Yet whenever she happened to come our way she could not help attracting our special attention. There were very good reasons for this.

The first was the fact that she was a very brilliant and gifted personality. By birth and upbringing she represented one of the rare exceptions in our revolutionary circle. Her father, Domontovich, was a general in the Tsar's army. Her mother, a very beautiful woman, came from a bourgeois family with connections with Finland. The Domontoviches had a small estate near Vyborg. They did not come from the top strata of the aristocracy but could certainly not be regarded as members of the middle-class intelligentzia.

In her childhood Alexandra Mihailovna was educated at home. She was sixteen before she went to a high school. From early years she could speak French, German and Russian. She was quite young when she married an engineer, Kollontay, but the drab philistine life of a housewife could not possibly satisfy so lively and gifted a woman and they were divorced after three years.

This was about the middle of the nineties. A mass working-class movement in Russia was beginning to raise its head. Marxism was winning its first victories among wide circles of the Russian intelligentzia.

Living at home with her parents, Alexandra Mihailovna drew on much of the spiritual arsenal of the progressive thought of the time. By the standards of those days and considering his position her father was a Liberal; he certainly opposed tsarism. Her governess, M. I. Strahova, was a radical—a radical of the seventies. Alexandra Mihailovna was instinctively attracted to the working-class movement. At first she interested herself in various cultural and educational organizations engaged in spreading knowledge amongst the industrial population. But the celebrated strikes of the Petersburg textile workers which broke out in 1896 and 1897 set her feet on the path to revolution. Her training and education were inadequate for this new field of activity and in 1898 she moved to Zürich where she went to the University and attended the lectures of the well-known Professor Herkner, a specialist in social-economic questions.

She spent nearly eighteen months abroad, learning about Marxism and familiarizing herself with the proletarian movement in western Europe. She lived in England, where she met those famous figures in the Labour world, the Webbs, and in Germany where she got to know Bebel, Kautsky, Karl Liebknecht and Rosa Luxemburg. In Switzerland she came into contact with several of the leaders of the Russian Social-Democrats.

All this had a great influence on her spiritual development, so that the daughter of a general was converted into a revolutionary Social-Democrat. When she returned to Russia in 1899 her further course was definitely set.

Another, and indeed the main, reason why all eyes were fixed on Alexandra Mihailovna was connected with her revolutionary activities which now passed through two separate periods, one in Russia and the other in Europe. She worked in Russia from 1898 to 1908. What was she not doing all that time? She carried on propaganda among the working classes, drafted proclamations, spoke at unlawful assemblies at the Nevsky Gate, took part in organizing clandestine newspapers, was treasurer of the Petersburg Committee of the Party and published articles in the Russian Social-Democrat journal *Zarya* and the German Social-Democrat organ *Neue Zeit*. She also co-operated in the production of the legal Marxist monthlies *Obrazovanie* and *Nauchnoe Obozrenie*[1] and in 1903 produced a work of serious research, *Life among the Finnish Working Classes*, which had cost her three years' hard work.

The 1905 revolution opened up a wide field of activity to her. As she was a very good speaker she was soon highly popular in democratic and working-class circles. Her appearances at meetings often turned them into political events. She made a particularly strong impression on the women workers. In no time

[1] *Education: Scientific Review.*

she had established the first working women's club in Petersburg.
Her closest ties were with the textile industry in which women
played a very important part. She led a determined fight with
bourgeois feminism and always strove to draw the women
workers into the Party. In 1906 she was Russian delegate at the
International Conference of working women in Mannheim.

The breaking of the revolutionary wave and the ever-
increasing reaction put an end to Kollontay's activity in Russia.
Her brochure, *The Class Struggle*, which challenged Bernstein
'revisionism', was confiscated. Another brochure by her, *Finland
and Socialism*, was made a ground for prosecution on a charge of
inciting to armed rebellion. She began to find it hot underfoot.
In 1908 there was held in Petersburg an All Russian Equal-Rights-
for-Women Conference which had been organized by the
bourgeois feminists:[1] a working-class group, led by Kollontay,
took part in it. After she spoke, the police made a raid and tried
to catch her in *flagrante delicto*. Thanks to help from friends and
comrades they failed. But it had become abundantly clear that
she must leave Petersburg. Immediately after the Conference she
had to make a clandestine flight over the frontier.

Then commenced the second, European, period of her
activities. Once over the frontier she plunged headlong into
revolutionary agitation among foreign workers. How useful her
gift for public speaking and knowledge of foreign languages now
proved!

The first stage was Berlin. There she renewed her acquaintance
with the German Social-Democrats and at the suggestion of
Kautsky and Wurm toured the Rhine Province and Westphalia,
giving lectures on the Russian Revolution.

Next year she and Clara Zetkin were sent by the German
Social-Democrats to London to support the left wing, led by
Hyndman, of the English Feminist movement. During six weeks
they attended countless meetings, both indoors and in the open
air—the Albert Hall and Hyde Park—at which they campaigned
stubbornly against the conservatism and limited range of English
suffragism.

[1] 'Feminism' was a movement to gain equal rights for women which was widespread
in bourgeois circles at the time. It deliberately drew aside from the women workers'
struggle for equal rights which was part of the general working-class struggle for its
freedom. The women workers strove to use the conferences and meetings organized by
the Feminists to push their own views.

Kollontay next devoted herself to agitation amongst the German proletariat which at that time was playing a leading role in Europe. On the invitation of local socialist organizations she also frequently visited France, Belgium, Holland, Switzerland, Sweden, Denmark and the Balkans. In 1911 she took part in organizing the French women workers' strikes against militarism and the high cost of living, and shortly afterwards she was helping to direct the strike of the Belgian mineworkers in the Borinage. And on the 8th March every year she appeared on the platform of the women's international meetings and made a glowing appeal to millions of workers all over the world.

Thus passed nearly three years. Then in 1912 an unexpected storm burst. She published a book, in Russian, *Labour in Europe*, in which a number of lively and interesting essays summed up her views on the proletarian movement in the West. In this book there is a strong attack on German opportunism, the predominance of which in the German Social-Democrat Party was becoming increasingly obvious. The full effect of this process was to be revealed on the 4th August, 1914.[1] Two years before that she drew attention to some symptoms of that political gangrene which ultimately destroyed Social-Democracy in Germany.

There was an enormous scandal. The opportunists, beside themselves with rage and screaming that they had been harbouring a snake in their bosom and that Kollontay was 'no social-democrat but a Russian chauvinist', ended up by demanding that she should be expelled from Germany. Scheidemann and Legien[2] were particularly furious. Kautsky washed his hands of her and only Karl Liebknecht and Clara Zetkin defended her. Of course, the opportunists failed to get her out of Germany but her work for the German Social-Democrats was over.

She now paid more attention to affairs in Russia. True, she had not forgotten them and earlier on had met Lenin several times. While working in Germany she sometimes toured the Russian émigré colonies and made reports and gave lectures on various current themes. In 1907, 1910 and 1912 she was one of the Russian delegates to the international socialist congresses at Stuttgart, Copenhagen and Basel. In 1912 she was a 'Russian

[1] The day on which the Social-Democrat party in the Reichstag voted in favour of war and for the military budget.

[2] Trade-union leader, president of the General Committee of the German Trade Union Movement.

guest' at the British Trade Union Congress in Cardiff. After the breach with the German Social-Democrats, however, her connection with the Russian émigrés and the Russian revolutionary movement in general became particularly close. And just at that moment her outlook underwent a great change which was to have important consequences in the future.

By nature Alexandra Mihailovna was a very emotional, perhaps too emotional, woman. This was shown in her relations with other people and also in her political activities. In 1903, when the Russian Social-Democratic Labour Party was split between Bolsheviks and Mensheviks, she threw in her lot with the former under Lenin's guidance during the '1905' period. As was mentioned previously, at one time she also acted as treasurer of the Petersburg Bolshevik Committee. But in 1906 and 1907 she had differences with the Bolsheviks on the subjects of the Imperial Duma and the trade unions.

During her exile she at first favoured the Mensheviks, but as the international situation grew ever more tense and the danger of a European war clouded the horizon she became increasingly dissatisfied with the position of the Russian opportunists. Her battle with the German opportunists hastened this process and when the First World War began she took her place under Lenin's flag.

On the day of the outbreak she was in Berlin. Together with other members of the local Russian colony she was interned but, thanks to the intervention of Karl Liebknecht, released and allowed to go to Sweden. Here she immediately threw herself into the campaign to expose the true character of the war which had been organized by the left-wing Social-Democrats of Sweden. She was arrested and imprisoned, at first in Stockholm and then in Malmö. This aroused great indignation in progressive circles of Swedish society. A question was asked in the Riksdag. To avoid embarrassment the Swedish Government expelled her to Denmark.

In Copenhagen she found herself in a very difficult position; the police kept a sharp eye on her and hotels and lodging houses refused to let her have a room. At the risk of finding herself in a Danish gaol she had to keep on the move.

But by now her political line was clearly settled, and this fortified her courage and determination in facing the daily tribulations of life. In September, 1914, she began to correspond with Lenin who was then living in Zürich. Under his direction she worked hard among the left-wing elements of the Scandinavian Social-Democrats defending Lenin's attitude towards the war. She helped him in his preparations for the Zimmerwald Conference, organized the Scandinavian part of the lines-of-communication between him and the Petrograd Bolsheviks.

Twice during the war—in 1915 and 1916—Lenin sent her to the U.S.A. to expound Bolshevik views to the American socialists. On the second occasion she toured eighty cities, giving lectures and making speeches, and in Boston she encouraged the foundation of the left-wing 'Zimmerwald League'. Her activities drew the attention of the American reactionaries to her and there was an angry campaign against her. But in 1917, immediately after the February Revolution, she arrived in Moscow as Lenin's messenger, carrying his directives to the Petrograd Bolsheviks.

Is it surprising that such a woman, with such a history, was always the centre of attention in the Russian colonies abroad?

During the years of my exile Kollontay was in England only once—for the winter and spring of 1913–14. I have already mentioned that the main purpose of her stay in London was to work at the British Museum in connection with her forthcoming book, *Society and Motherhood*.

She started by renewing her old contacts with English socialists and was often at their houses. She took an active part in the anti-tsarist campaign then in progress in England in connection with the Beilis[1] affair and I heard how she appeared on the plinth of Nelson's Column in Trafalgar Square and made a vigorous speech to the thousands of English people who had assembled to protest against the savagery of the tsarist régime. She also used to give lectures on the Feminist movement on the continent at the Herzen Circle. Soon she became the life and soul of our émigré community. Many members of the colony used to

---

[1] In 1913 the tsarist Government staged a sensational trial at Kiev, falsely charging a Jew, Beilis, with ritual murders. All the progressive forces in Russian society united to show up the Government. The well-known writer, V. G. Korolenko, went to Kiev to undertake Beilis's defence. The anti-tsarist campaign spread beyond the frontiers and more especially to England, where it was organized by the socialists and radicals. A. M. Kollontay appeared on the platform at one of their meetings.

visit her at home ('home' being the cheap little *pension* at 2, Grenville Street, Guilford Street, near the British Museum, where she lived) for lively discussions and debates on various current topics. I visited her several times myself and there I met Litvinov, Kerzhentsev and other well-known comrades. Alexandra Mihailovna was a sort of bright, friendly flame which to some degree dispelled the gloom of our London life and to which we all went for a little warmth and encouragement.

There is one vivid scene from our lives in those far-distant days which will always remain in my memory.

In the north-western district of London there is a park, Hampstead Heath, which covers a vast area. It is a piece of unspoiled nature with fields, groves, hills, ponds and plenty of small animals and birds. On Saturdays and Sundays thousands of people come here, most of them poor, working-class folk, from neighbouring districts. Near Hampstead Heath in those days there were many Russian émigrés also living in the narrow streets.

In the south-eastern corner of this park there is a pretty little hill, called Parliament Hill. Tradition has it that during the revolution in the seventeenth century Cromwell's army, fighting for Parliament against the King, encamped here; hence the name. I must admit that in my years of exile there was nothing to remind one of the hill's revolutionary past. It was then the London children's favourite playground and the Russian colony's Riviera.

We used to go there on Saturdays and Sundays, seeking fresh air, sun and natural beauty. Whole families came, bringing sandwiches and beer, chessboards and books. We amused ourselves for the whole day. The children ran around and played while their elders, sprawling on the grass, read, exchanged news or simply lay on their backs gazing at the sky and the fleecy clouds crossing it. When they felt like it they nibbled at their food or snoozed, their hats pulled over their eyes. Afterwards they strolled about, feeding the birds on Highgate pond, listening to some orator, lingering under the trees and enjoying the marvellous view of London to be had from the top of the hill. From this vantage point the eye takes in the whole panorama of the vast city of seven million people, its red tiles and smoke-begrimed houses, its towers and steeples, its narrow streets and green parks, St. Paul's and Tower Bridge, the crenellated Houses of Parliament. The huge ocean of brick and stone stretches away to the horizon.

Towards evening the grown-ups also started to amuse themselves by running races, playing *gorelki*, *piatnashka*, *lapta*[1] and various other simple Russian games they had known since childhood. Men and women, many of them fathers and mothers of families, who had been working hard in English offices and businesses all the week, now behaved like noisy and happy teenagers, scampering about, shouting, romping, roaring with laughter. Such moments often brought back clear memories of the loved and distant homeland. As the sun went down a hush descended on the scene, they collected their belongings and started for home. This improvised open-air club became a permanent feature in the life of the London émigrés, who loved it, talked about it and prepared for it during the working week.

One Sunday Alexandra Mihailovna put in an appearance on Parliament Hill. It was a warm, peaceful day. There was a white-streaked, low sky, and a pale sun lazily scattered its bright but not very warm rays. Our émigré 'club' was carrying on as usual, the children running about and playing and the grown-ups talking and chatting. Alexandra Mihailovna very soon became the centre of attraction; everyone gravitated towards her and she was involved in all the liveliest and most interesting discussions.

Towards evening the games began. We ran races. She always came in one of the first. We paired off on the slope of the hill and ran down like lunatics, singing:

> 'Burn bright, burn bright,
> And lest it grow dim
> Look up at the sky
> Where the little birds fly'

at the tops of our voices. Then we played catch, alternately finding and losing one another before reassembling on the slope of the hill. We spent quite a time in this way.

And then something happened.

I had run down the hill with my partner and, after catching

[1] Russian games involving running and playing with a bat and ball.

her, was waiting at the bottom, recovering my breath and wiping the sweat from my forehead. Alexandra Mihailovna was in the next couple. At a given signal she ran down very fast, pink in the face and her arms waving like wings. Her wide skirts fluttered and the light of the evening sun, which she was facing, bathed her figure, flowing hair and extended 'wings' in a sort of ruddy glow. The apparition was so fairylike that another émigré at my side could not restrain himself and, pointing to Kollontay, burst out:

'Look! Look! The sun has set her on fire!'

Since then many years have passed. At various turning points in life and in stormy times I often met Alexandra Mihailovna again and on every occasion that faraway scene has come back to me—the gentle slope, the evening drawing on, a woman running downhill and waving her arms like wings, the fairy-tale figure all bathed in golden light, the exclamation 'The sun has set her on fire!'

In my mind's eye that scene is indissolubly associated with the name of Alexandra Mihailovna Kollontay.[1]

[1] See Appendix 5.

CHAPTER TEN

Petro Zarechny

WHEN I was at the Herzen Circle one day I noticed what seemed to be an unfamiliar figure reading the paper in a corner. He was sitting with his back to me and I could not see his face. I was just about to leave when the stranger suddenly turned round, flung out his arms and fell on my neck.

'Ivan! You!'

For a moment, but only for a moment, I was quite taken aback.

'Petro! You?'

We embraced vigorously in Russian fashion. Then it all came back in a flash.

1903. The Volga. Samara. I was nineteen, just beginning my revolutionary career and full of youthful enthusiasm. The whole world seemed veiled in a lovely pink mist and full of unusually interesting people. I was a member of the local Social-Democrat organization, leader of study groups among workers and students and writing proclamations (reproduced by hectograph) and performing all the other multifarious duties involved in 'underground' activities in those days.

One fine summer morning a stranger suddenly appeared in Samara. His name was Petro. By trade he was a turner. He looked about twenty-three years of age. Who was this stranger and where did he come from? He told us nothing about himself and local members like ourselves did not think it proper to ask him. The laws of conspiracy forbade such curiosity, all the more so because we knew Petro was an outlaw, i.e. a professional revolutionary using a name not his own. It was only from his accent that we guessed that he came from somewhere in the south.

Very soon he became the central figure in our little underground world. He was no theorist (though anything but an ignoramus in politics) but a practical, born organizer. He knew everything, was ready for everything, coped with everything and

—what was most important of all—had the rare ability to keep the organization in his hands and assure the smooth working of all its parts. He was helped by the fact that he already had an extensive experience of party activities elsewhere. Most of us in Samara were novices and this greatly increased his standing in our eyes.

Under his influence the Samara organization underwent a series of internal 'reforms'. We had a new, carefully selected Social-Democratic committee (of which Petro and I were members) to direct and control it; a system of 'zones' was established and the workers were organized in branches according to their occupations—flour-mill employees, railwaymen, metal-workers and so forth. Agitation and propaganda were entrusted to a separate department.

The result of all this was that our morale rose. We worked quickly and enthusiastically, there was close contact with the factories and industrial establishments and proclamations, the despair of the gendarmes, appeared regularly every week.

My personal relations with Petro became ever closer as our revolutionary activities progressed. Despite the differences in origin, character and education, we easily found a common tongue. It was true that he sometimes mocked at me as a 'theorist' and pitilessly destroyed my rosy illusions about people and affairs in general, and equally true that I in turn made fun of his 'practicality' and persistently proved that there could be no revolution without theory. But in various inter-organizational disputes, of which there were many at that time, he and I nearly always found ourselves on the same side as if visually demon-strating how necessary it was for theory and practice to keep in step. We often discussed matters not directly connected with our work for the Party and discovered that our tastes, opinions and aspirations had much in common.

Occasionally, when we had some free time we used to go to the banks of the Volga to swim, catch fish, make fish soup and sun-bathe. I grew to like him more and more and found myself thinking how good it would be if we were brothers!

And then he suddenly vanished from Samara—as suddenly as he had arrived some months before. The police were after him. He had received orders from the Party to lose no time in altering his papers and changing his place of work. He told me all about it on the day he left. I was very worried and saddened. Petro too was much upset. But there was nothing to be done, so we fervently clasped hands, embraced and promised not to forget each other.

Since then ten years had passed. Now, quite unexpectedly, fate had brought us both to London. It seemed almost a miracle.

Next day, sitting in Petro's big, dimly lit room somewhere in Bayswater, I heard my friend's story of the years between. It was very typical of those days.

After leaving Samara, he continued to wander as an 'underground' worker from town to town. In 1905 he was at Ekaterinoslav where, in the Bolshevik ranks, he took a very active part in the revolutionary outbreaks and fought at the barricades in the rising at Gorlovka. After the triumph of the counter-revolution he was arrested and sent to Siberia. Here he married a local peasant girl. He escaped from Siberia, and, once more an 'outlaw', again wandered from place to place working in the Bolshevik underground, but eventually came under police observation. The ring closed round him and arrest seemed inevitable; but at the last moment he succeeded in tricking the hunters, and early in 1912 got across the frontier. He had gone to Switzerland first, then Paris and now he was in London.

He had with him his wife, a quiet, friendly woman whose time was fully taken up with housework and two little children, a boy and a girl. His immediate concern was to find work and earn enough to keep his family.

I sounded out all my friends and contacts and three weeks later he found employment as a turner in a London engineering works. As he was a highly skilled man he was soon getting ahead and after three months was earning three pounds a week, a considerable wage in those days. He removed to a better apartment. The family had good clothes and shoes and always enough to eat. After so many years of privations and want fortune had smiled on him to such good effect that he could be expected to cling closely to her wheel.

But Petro was not that sort of man. Calling on him somewhere about the beginning of 1914 I found him extremely worried and depressed. His children were asleep and his wife was out visiting an émigré family she knew. We were alone and I asked him the reason for his unhappy frame of mind.

'I can't go on like this!' he replied bitterly. 'Of course I'm doing very nicely; I have money, two rooms and no trouble at all in keeping the family. All this is all very well. . . . But it's suffocating me; I'm becoming a philistine. Every day I ask myself what I'm doing for the proletariat and the cause of revolution in Russia. Devil take it! I can't find a satisfactory answer.'

I began to tell him that he had not gone abroad of his own free will, that there were off-duty periods in the life of every revolutionary which should be used to sharpen his ideological weapons and I added that he had such an opportunity now. He listened to me with obvious impatience and then interjected in a tone of considerable irritation:

'You judge everyone by yourself. . . . You're a theorist, a bookworm, a writer. I'm sure you remember our squabbles over this subject in Samara. It's a very good thing that you are using your emigration to develop yourself theoretically. That will benefit the Party later. I'm made of other stuff! I'm a practical man, not a theorist. I'm made that way. I have a little education and no experience with books. But I can put my capacity for organization to the service of the Party and the proletariat; I understand the workers and can talk to them. That's a very different job and so far it has not been my job here. I cannot get down to it in London. That's why I'm not myself. I feel I'm on wrong lines.'

'What do you propose to do?' I asked him.

'What am I going to do?' he retorted. 'Why, find out how to serve the cause of revolution, even while I'm living in London!'

Simple and modest as ever, he said all this without the slightest ostentation; but it was plain that his mind was wholly absorbed in this ticklish question.

On my way home I reflected that it would be fine if Petro found what he was seeking. But would he find it?

It seemed almost impossible but he found it all the same.

A few weeks later he unexpectedly turned up at my rooms and asked if I could lend him five pounds. My financial condition was relatively sound (I was then London correspondent of *Kievskaya Mysl*) and I willingly complied with his request. Then

he told me his plans. He was going to throw up his job at the
factory and find work in the Port of London. From the money
point of view he was losing (which was why he needed a loan),
but the problem of serving the revolutionary cause would be
solved to his satisfaction. Russian ships often arrived in the port.
He proposed to get in touch with the crews of these ships and
develop the Bolshevik work among them.

A few days later I visited him in his new quarters. He had
moved to the dock district to facilitate his task. It was a poor,
dirty region in the east of London, and living conditions were
far worse than in the district he had left. But what did that matter
to him, now that his conscience was satisfied?

His purposes soon began to take practical forms and he could
give full rein to his great gifts for organization. Within two or
three months he had not only got in touch with the crews of
Russian steamers arriving in England but established Bolshevik
cells among many of them, supplying them with revolutionary
literature and carrying on propaganda among them. He also took
the lead in their fight for better working conditions. While he
was living in the Port of London, on several of the ships there
were strikes which were linked with the great wave of strikes
then going on in Russia.

Petro's house gradually became a real 'nest of revolutionaries'
where one could never fail to find Russian sailors getting
encouragement and leadership in their struggle with the tsarist
authorities. He became unrecognizable. Where were his irritabil-
ity, dissatisfaction and self-reproach now? He seemed to be
dominated by some inner force, his voice boomed and inspiration
flashed from his eyes.

'Do you remember, Ivan,' he once remarked, 'how I led the
"flour-mill zone" in Samara? Now I'm in the "sailors' zone" and
my work here will be on a bigger scale than on the Volga.'

Before long he had taken a further step; he began to use his
sailors to send into Russia the revolutionary literature published
abroad. Great quantities of it were carried in Russian ships to the
Baltic and Black Sea ports. He was triumphant and burst out on
meeting me one day:

'No one can say that I'm not serving the cause of revolution
now!'

The 1914 war put an end to all this activity in one fell swoop.

German submarines blockaded England and her communications with Russia were almost interrupted. Russian ships no longer arrived in London and Petro had to close down his 'nest of revolutionaries'.

In his attitude to the war he immediately adopted the pure Lenin line. Working in a munitions factory he carried on anti-war propaganda among the English workers, and often had to put up with reprisals.

When the February Revolution broke out he was one of the first to return to Russia, where he soon left Petrograd and made tracks for his dearly loved south. In those stormy times it was not possible to follow all the vicissitudes of his career. I seldom heard from him. Then his letters suddenly ceased.

Long afterwards I learned that he had died a hero's death in battle during the civil war in the Ukraine.

CHAPTER ELEVEN

F. M. Stepnyak

WHEN I looked at the well-built, energetic, active woman with the clever black eyes and halo of ash-grey hair I was always reminded of the ancient Greek myth about the Moirai (Fates) who often played cruel tricks on the human race.

Fanny Markovna's husband, Sergei Mihailovich Stepnyak-Kravchinsky,[1] was one of the most brilliant figures among the revolutionaries of the seventies of the last century. In his youth he was an artillery officer, but he soon joined the revolutionary movement of that time. In 1872 he became a member of the well-known 'Chaikovsky Circle'.

In 1873 and 1874, working as a sawyer, he 'went to the people'. He impressed village folk enormously with his great physical strength and rare ability to talk to simple people. He knew the New Testament by heart and was fond of demonstrating that the proper interpretation of passages from St. Matthew and St. Luke proved that revolutionary activities were indispensable. This made an extraordinary impression on the peasants. He had a most fascinating personality. The police hunted the 'agitator' indefatigably but could not catch him. When they occasionally arrested him he was always freed by the peasants. Ultimately the police got so hot on his heels that he had to slip abroad.

At the beginning of 1875 he arrived in Switzerland, just at the time when there was a Slav uprising against the Turkish yoke in Bosnia and Herzegovina. He joined the insurgents as a volunteer and fought side by side with them for many months. When the rising was suppressed he fled to Italy and there, with a Bakunist group, organized a revolt in the province of Benevento. Caught in possession of arms, he was thrown into an Italian prison, where he spent ten months mastering the Italian language.

[1] His real surname was Kravchinsky, but he was much better known under his literary *nom-de-plume*, Stepnyak.

103

A court martial condemned him to death, but he was saved by a great slice of luck; just before the sentence was carried out the Italian king, Victor Emmanuel, died. The new king, Humbert, proclaimed an amnesty and, greatly to Kravchinsky's surprise, he was released. There was no one he knew in Italy, and he had no money, so that he had to make the journey from Benevento to Switzerland—several hundred kilometres—on foot.

He appeared in Geneva at the very beginning of 1878. Here, with Dragomanov, Zhukovsky and others, he took an active part in the revolutionary paper *Obshchina*[1] which had just been brought out. But on the 24th January, 1878, a shot rang round the world when Vera Zasulich fired at Trepov, the governor of Petersburg, who had ordered the flogging of Bogoliubov, a political prisoner. Kravchinsky could stay abroad no longer and returned clandestinely to the capital. In July, 1878, began the hunger-strike of the political prisoners in the Peter and Paul Fortress in protest against the repressive measures taken by Mezentsev, the Chief of Police. Kravchinsky decided to act. On the 4th August, in one of the busiest squares in the capital, he stabbed Mezentsev to death and made his getaway.

This exceptionally audacious assassination stirred up the whole governmental machine. The police and gendarmerie were beside themselves with fury and a savage hunt for Kravchinsky was organized. The net round him was drawn ever tighter. But he not only refused to leave Petersburg but walked about the streets as freely as before. It was three months after the murder that his friends got him over the frontier. Even then they cunningly contrived that he should be sent to Europe to find out the simplest way of preparing dynamite.

By November, 1878, he was back in Geneva. Here there was a sharp turn in his life which was to have a decisive effect on his future career. At that time much was said and written in the West about Russian 'nihilism'. Even then lies, calumnies and distortions were the usual weapons of the European reactionaries whenever the revolutionary movement in Russia was mentioned. Kravchinsky's fighting nature could not tolerate such a state of affairs; he decided to give blow for blow and went to Italy where he wrote in Italian his first book, *Podpolnaya Rossia*,[2] which

[1] *The Community.*
[2] *Underground Russia.*

was a luminous portrait gallery of the Russian revolutionaries and gave a true account of their heroic struggle against tsarist absolutism. The book had an enormous success and was immediately translated into several European languages. His literary venture proved of the greatest service to the revolutionary movement and opened new possibilities for him. For the first time he realized that he had a gift for writing, and he decided to use it for the benefit of the revolution.

He removed to London at the beginning of the eighties and made it his object to create a trend of thought in society hostile to tsarism. In the dark night of reaction which set in with the accession of Alexander III to the throne Kravchinsky devoted himself wholly to literary and propaganda activity. He made the Russian revolutionary movement a familiar subject in European and Anglo-American countries, arranged meetings and gave lectures, published articles, pamphlets and books and established personal contact with the best representatives of radical and socialist thought at the time. He succeeded in founding a 'Society of Friends of Russian Freedom' in London, and it was thanks to his efforts that the Free Russian Press Foundation came into being. Simultaneously he produced a number of clever books about the affairs and personalities of the revolutionary movement in the eighties, books such as *A Cottage on the Volga*, *Stundist Pavel Rudenko*, *Andrei Kozhukhov*, and others, which came to be part of the 'basic stock' of revolutionary literature on which the advanced youth of my generation was brought up. There are solid grounds for saying that it was Kravchinsky who continued the tradition of Herzen and at the close of the last century did in London—allowing for the passing of time and changed conditions—what Herzen had done thirty years before.

This bright, gifted, promising life came to a sudden end—and in what absurd fashion!—at the early age of forty-three. On the 23rd December, 1895, at Bedford Park station in west London, he was run over and killed by an express train when crossing the permanent way in a thick fog.

To survive years of desperate struggle with the tsarist, Turkish and Italian governments and then die in the prime of life in an unlucky accident in peaceful, kindly London—what a shocking, ironical trick of fate! What mockery of common sense and logic!

.   .   .   .   .   .

After her husband's death Fanny Markovna was left alone. She never married again and did not leave London. When I was an émigré she lived in a north-west district (747b, Finchley Road), jealously preserved her husband's rich store of papers, kept up her old English friendships (especially with the Peases, a Labour family) and often put in an appearance at meetings and evening parties of the Herzen Circle. In her youth she had taken an active part in the *narodnik* movement but had parted company with it and been drawn, instinctively as it were, towards the Social-Democratic camp. She never became an actual member but her sympathies were with this Party: and I shall tell hereafter how in 1907 she helped the band of émigrés who made the preparations for holding the 5th R.S.D.R.P. Congress in London. In my émigré years there she was one of those 'non-party left-wingers' in our colony whom I have mentioned before.

To relieve the monotony of her lonely widowhood she educated the daughter of a London exile who had married an Englishwoman. I used to see quite a lot of her, often visiting her at home, rummaging in the library her husband had left and only too glad to hear her stories about personalities and happenings of bygone days. One of these tales of an old revolutionary I particularly liked. It was about her meetings with Friedrich Engels and is worth reproducing here.[1]

I can see her modest little rooms at this moment. There is a subdued crackle from the low fire, and in the semi-obscurity of the room my hostess, in her pensive and unhurried fashion, quietly tells the arresting story from days of long ago.

'One day after we had come to settle in London,' she recalled, 'my husband received a letter from G. V. Plekhanov, who was then in Switzerland and knew him well, in which he wrote that Engels was living in England and advised us to visit him. We decided to take Plekhanov's advice, if only because we ourselves were quite anxious to meet Engels. It was easy to arrange it, as he was extremely accessible. He worked a lot and kept to himself during the week but liked seeing people on Sundays. On holidays his house was open to all comers. Callers turned up

---

[1] Many years later, in the thirties, when I was Soviet ambassador in England, my wife, who was the London correspondent of the Institute of Marxism–Leninism, invited Fanny Markovna to the Embassy, where she repeated her account of her meetings with Engels. It was taken down and transmitted to the I.M.L. Part of it appears in the book *Memories of Marx and Engels* which was published in 1956.

without ceremony and simply took their places at the long table in the biggest room.'

Fanny Markovna poked the fire and when it blazed up again resumed:

'It was one of those Sundays that my husband and I went to visit Engels. We had with us Marx's daughter, Eleanor, who was married to Aveling, an English Social-Democrat. The Avelings were "part of the family" at Engels' house. When we arrived some twenty people—all socialists, writers and politicians—were seated at the table. The company was very international and there was a rich variety of languages. Engels, presiding over the proceedings as it were, occupied one end of the table. A first glance was enough to show that I should like him very much. He was the life and soul of the party. There were some hot disputes going on and amidst a lot of noise and shouting could be heard voices appealing to Engels for a decision. He was always ready with his answers. Sometimes in English, sometimes in German, sometimes in French.

'At the other end of the table sat Engels' housekeeper, Lenchen,[1] a buxom German with a very kind and pleasant face who made it her business to see that the plate of each new arrival was piled up with meat, salad and other comestibles. Nor was Lenchen stingy with the wine. The whole atmosphere was simple, friendly and slightly bohemian but at the same time intellectual to the highest degree. We all felt we were the guests of a great man who was living with great problems and utterly absorbed in them.'

Fanny Markovna paused for a moment and then, with a gentle smile, continued:

'At that time I did not know a single foreign language and it made me feel very embarrassed and timid. It so happened that Engels, wanting to show his respect for Stepnyak, made us sit by him, myself on his right and Sergei Mihailovich on his left. I was quite desperate and tried to squeeze up against Eleanor Marx, who was on my other side. What terrified me most was the thought that Engels might talk to me. What on earth should I do? He suddenly turned towards me and began an impassioned

[1] 'Lenchen' was that Helene Demuth who for many years kept house for the Marx family and is buried at Highgate Cemetery in the same grave as Marx and his wife. After Marx's death she went to keep house for Engels. She died on 4th November, 1890.

recitation in Russian. It is a very long time ago but I still remember what it was that he recited:

> ' "We all of us of education
> A something somehow have obtained.
> Thus, praised be God! a reputation
> With us is easily attained.
> Oniegin was—so many deemed
> (Unerring critics self-esteemed)
> Pedantic although scholar like."[1]

'Engels recited two more stanzas,' continued Fanny Markovna and, with a sly look at me, suddenly wound up:

> ' "But Adam Smith to read appeared,
> And at economy was great;
> That is, he could elucidate
> How empires stores of wealth unfold,
> How flourish, why and wherefore less
> If the raw product they possess
> The medium is required of gold.
> The father scarcely understands
> His son and mortgages his lands."

'Engels' pronunciation was splendid,' she continued, 'and he recited Pushkin marvellously. I clapped and exclaimed: "Why, you know Russian very well; please talk in it." Engels shook his head, however, and replied with a smile: "That's the beginning and end of my Russian, alas!" '

She paused again and for some time sat in silence as if her thoughts were far away from the workaday world. Then she shook her head, as if dispelling some enchantment, and resumed in a more ordinary voice:

'Fancy all that being nearly thirty years ago, yet I can see our first visit to Engels as if it had taken place yesterday!'

I asked her what happened afterwards.

'Afterwards? Well, not long after Engels returned the visit. It was plain that the friendship could ripen and it certainly did.

---

[1] From Pushkin's *Eugen Oniegin*, translated by Lieut.-Col. Spalding. Macmillan and Co., 1881.

He and my husband often met. They talked, sometimes quarrelled and even had their misunderstandings. I myself saw less of him, but I have a vivid memory of our last meeting. It must have been much later—somewhere about the middle nineties—and not long before his death.'

She threw some coal on the fire again, poked it and then resumed her place.

'When Lenchen died,' she continued, 'the question arose as to who would look after Engels. He was nearly seventy, often ill and needed a lot of attention. Lenchen's place was soon taken by Luisa Kautsky,[1] who was then divorced. When I first met her I at once took a dislike to her. My feelings were fully shared by Vera Zasulich, who was then living in London and often at Engels' house. We regretfully came to learn that she fully deserved what we felt about her. She had none of the sweetness and delicacy which Engels needed. She thought too much about herself and too little about him. This became all too plain when she married again at the beginning of 1894. She soon had a daughter. Engels, the husband, wife and child all lived together, but her thoughts were far more for her family than for Engels.

'One fine day she decided that the house where they lived[2] was much too small and he ought to move elsewhere. Engels loathed the idea. He had lived in the same house for twenty-five years, was used to it, knew every corner of it and exactly where to find anything—books, writing materials, manuscripts—he wanted. But the most important thing of all was that it was to this house that Marx used to come to see him. It is easy to imagine his feelings at the thought of living anywhere else. But he was a sick man, helpless and sensitive, and in the end Luisa got her own way and somehow persuaded him to remove to another house.[3] He tried to affect unconcern but it was clear to Zasulich and me that the removal had only upset him and made his serious illness worse. He had cancer of the throat. We could have wept but there was nothing we could do.'

Fanny Markovna sighed, paused again and then finished her story:

'The last time I saw Engels was under very sad circumstances.

[1] Luisa Kautsky was the wife of K. Kautsky. They were divorced in 1888. In 1894 she married the Austrian doctor Freiberger.
[2] At 122, Regent's Park Road, N.W.
[3] At 41, Regent's Park Road, N.W.

Luisa came to us one day to tell us that she had to go out that evening and as there would be no one at home would I sit by the sick man's bedside? Of course I gladly agreed.

'I went to his house that night. He was very glad to see me and began to talk about many things dear to his heart. He pointed out the chair in which Marx had usually sat, gave me some of the latter's letters to read and got out some photographs in which he appeared with Marx. It was clear that his whole existence was inspired by the deepest affection for Marx, and he poured out endless recollections of their work together, their meetings, talks, outings and strolls through the great city. I heard him out almost reverentially, but my heart was almost bursting because I saw that he was very ill and not getting the care and attention he so badly needed. That night I left him with tears in my eyes. A few weeks later he was dead. Sergei Mihailovich and I were at the funeral.'[1]

I listened to Fanny Markovna's story holding my breath. It seemed as if her voice were that of history itself.

[1] See Appendix 6.

CHAPTER TWELVE

P. A. Kropotkin

PETER ALEXEIEVICH KROPOTKIN was certainly the most popular figure among the London émigrés of my time. He was then nearly seventy years old and had behind him a long, interesting and eventful life.

He was born in 1842 into an ancient princely family the foundation of which goes back to the beginnings of the Russian State. The revolutionaries of the middle seventies used to say in jest that Kropotkin had a better right to the throne than Alexander II himself. As the son of a high aristocrat he entered the Corps des Pages at Petersburg, where he spent five years (1857–62). He was extraordinarily quick in learning and in 1861, as the outstanding candidate, was appointed page in waiting to the Tsar himself, promotion which opened an easy, brilliant military and court career to him.

But then occurred the first of the 'freakish twists' which were to mark his career. Against his father's wishes, and to the consternation of his friends and acquaintances, he enlisted in the Amur Cossack Army, which had just been formed, and went off to the Far East.

How did this happen?

The end of the fifties and the beginning of the sixties of the last century witnessed the first signs of the revolt of the Russian revolutionary democracy. Herzen, Chernishevsky, Dobroliubov and also Nekrassov and Pisarev were the leaders of thought of the time. Even in his Corps des Pages period Kropotkin avidly devoured what they wrote. He was particularly attracted by the Decembrists and almost worshipped them. Then he began to take a deep interest in Voltaire and the other French Encyclopaedists. It is not difficult to imagine that the result of all these influences was to kindle a flame of protest against tsarist autocracy and that is why he threw up his court career and went off to the Far East, where he calculated that he could devote all his powers to what he deemed the great revolution of the age which had opened with the abolition of serfdom.

But on his way to Siberia the old world, as if wishing to keep its hold over the future revolutionary, sent him the most potent of its enticements—love. It was just like a fairy story. Before he left for the Far East he spent a few days at the family estate. Here he made the acquaintance of a young girl, the daughter of a rich neighbouring landowner, and fell violently in love with her. His feelings were reciprocated and the romance took wings. Day followed day, but he made no move to leave. Treasonable thoughts assailed him. Why seek solitude so far away? Was it not simpler to meet fate halfway, and, best of all, marry this charming girl and settle down with her like anyone else?

Then came the second 'freakish twist' in his life. In his diary under the date 3rd July, 1862, he wrote:

> 'But for the troubled yearning of this unquiet mind,
> I'd dwell obscure and hidden,
> The sweetest joys to find:
> All cares and fears forgotten,
> The world itself a dream,
> That voice my only music,
> To kiss those eyes all life.'[1]

The 'unquiet mind' won in the end. With a sorrowful heart he burst the tender bonds and went off to the Far East.

There he found grievous disillusionment in store for him. As aide-de-camp of the Governor-General of Trans-Baikal and secretary of the committees charged with reorganizing local government and reforms in the prisons and convict settlements, the young enthusiast soon felt that the old world would not at any price give up its hold.

He was almost reduced to despair and sought relief from his ill-fated administrative activities in geographical investigations. Escorted by a few soldiers and with a little volume of *Faust* in his pocket, he made a series of bold expeditions along the Lena, the Olekma-Vitim basin, the Ussuri, the Sungari and in northern Manchuria, travelling seventy thousand kilometres in all. These

---

[1] Translated by Andrew Rothstein from *The Diary of P. A. Kropotkin*, published by Tsentroarchiv, 1923.

journeys enabled him to accumulate a rich store of data about the orography and geology of the Far East, enabling him a few years later (1873) to publish a new physical map of Asia which shook the authority of the celebrated Humboldt.

But geographical research could not reconcile Kropotkin to the cruel realities of tsarist Russia, particularly as during his wanderings in Siberia he had come into close contact with the 'world of outcasts', and had seen with his own eyes the merciless exploitation of the workers at the Lena Goldfields and the deliberate encouragement of drunkenness among the 'natives'[1] by Russian traders. He was utterly revolted by all this and in 1867 decided to return to Petersburg. There he went on half-pay and pondered deeply on the question of his future.

The old world again reminded him of its allurements. He was invited to take the post of secretary to the Imperial Geographical Society, an important post in the scientific world and likely to prove valuable in his service career as the honorary president of the society was the Tsar's cousin. The gifted twenty-nine-year-old aristocrat was once again offered the prospect of a distinguished career as a man of learning and one which carried no risks and at the same time gave some meaning to life.

But here intervened that third and last 'freakish twist' in his life which finally determined his future course. He declined the offer.

Why?

The decisive factor was the Paris Commune and its fate. What happened then deeply affected him and fired his imagination. His reflections led him to the following conclusions:

'Science is a very important thing. I know and appreciate the joys it brings if only because many of them have been mine. But what right had I to all these higher joys when all around me I could see utter beggary and a heart-rending struggle for a stale crust of bread, and when all I spend in order to live in the world of high intellectual achievement must inevitably be at the expense of those who grow corn for others but have not enough bread for their own children?'

At the beginning of 1872 Kropotkin went abroad for the first time and spent several months in Belgium and Switzerland, absorbing vast quantities of socialist and anarchist literature and becoming a follower of Bakunin.

[1] The original inhabitants of Siberia.

H

On his return to Petersburg his double life began. As Prince Kropotkin he continued to work hard for the Geographical Society, write learned works and move in aristocratic circles. But he also took part, under the revolutionary alias of Borodin, in the activities of the recently founded Chaikovsky Circle and, wearing a workman's blouse, carried on propaganda in the secret workmen's groups at the factories behind the Nevsky Gate. The news of this new and remarkable propagandist spread among the Petersburg proletariat. The police too heard about him and a fierce hunt for the elusive Borodin began. For a long time all the efforts of the tsarist *Okhrana*[1] were in vain but ultimately its *agents provocateurs* had their reward and in 1874 Kropotkin was arrested and lodged in the S.S. Peter and Paul Fortress. He stayed there more than two years. The rigorous conditions of the Tsar's dungeons affected his health, and in the spring of 1876 he was transferred to the prison wing of the Nicolaiev Military Hospital. From here, on the 30th June, 1876, he was helped by friends to make a most audacious escape. After many tribulations and adventures he succeeded in passing the frontier. So began his long exile, which was to last for more than forty years.

In contrast to many other refugees, who seemed to wither away when uprooted from the home soil, Kropotkin became a figure of international significance. He established a close association with the European anarchists—and especially with a man of his own stamp, the well-known French geographer and anarchist, Elisée Reclus—edited an anarchist paper, *Le Revolté*, and published many articles, pamphlets, brochures and so forth. He spent three years in French prisons.

In 1886 he eventually reached London, where he finally cast anchor. He lived in England more than thirty years, indeed right up to the 1917 revolution. It was during this period that most of his important works appeared, *Speeches of a Rebel, Memoirs of a Revolutionary, Notes, In Russian and French Prisons, The State and its Role in History, The Great French Revolution* and others.

In this period, too, he emerged as the recognized leader of world anarchism and at the same time became—what at first sight must seem very strange—very popular in bourgeois-liberal circles in England.

·   ·   ·   ·   ·

[1] Security police.

During my émigré years he was at the height of his fame and his influence in England was very great. Even His Majesty's ministers listened to him. He lived outside London, by the sea at Brighton, and kept somewhat aloof from our émigré colony, appearing only occasionally at meetings of the Herzen Circle. His authority was universally admitted but, fundamentally, the attitude of different groups and individuals towards him was not always the same, being dictated by their party-political standpoint. But everyone admitted that he was a great man and a great revolutionary.

With the recommendation of the old member of Narodnaya Volya, A. I. Zundelevich, I got to know Kropotkin and several times visited him at Brighton. He had a rather big house of English type and spent his time working hard in his well-stocked library. I was immediately struck with his appearance—the vast bald head with side-curls, the mighty forehead, the big nose, the bright, sharp eyes under well-marked eyebrows, the fine grey moustache and the great white beard projecting from each side of his face and descending to his chest. The whole impression was of a strange blend of savant and prophet.

His house at Brighton was like a Noah's ark. Who could not be found there? A revolutionary émigré from Russia, a Spanish anarchist from South America, an Australian farmer, an English radical M.P., a Presbyterian minister from Scotland, a famous savant from Germany, a liberal member of the Imperial Duma from Petersburg and even some bold general in the Tsar's service —all these found their way to Kropotkin's house on Sundays to pay their respects to their host and discuss all sorts of matters.

The amazing variety of the company which gathered round was primarily due to the world fame of the old revolutionary and the vast range of his interests. But not exclusively. His social views also played a great part. In my personal relations with him they operated in two ways.

In one way I liked him very much. I was much impressed by his vast knowledge, the variety of his talents, his world fame, his courage, noble character and the magnificent story of his life. I particularly enjoyed looking at him when he talked.

It so happened that I never saw him at big meetings and only heard from others of the power of his words on those occasions.

A big audience always intoxicated him and made him exceptionally eloquent. My own meetings with him were under much more modest circumstances—at home, over the tea table or by a blazing fire in the drawing-room. Yet even here his talk was exceptionally inspired and enchanting. He had the particular gift of so setting forth a question, so anticipating all possible objections and somehow touching a chord in the heart of his hearers that it was extraordinarily difficult even for those who disagreed with him to resist the power of his ideas and feelings. Listening to him at Brighton, I well understood why Borodin's lectures in the Nevsky factories had had such huge success among the workers.

On the other hand I never could resist a vague feeling of distrust, a feeling for which there were two main sources.

First and foremost, between Kropotkin and myself was the barrier of the contradiction between anarchism and Marxism. It is well known that this contradiction was particularly fierce in the years of the First International; and although Kropotkin, Reclus and other champions of anarchism subsequently tried to refashion their programme to some extent, the fact remains that when I was an émigré in England the conflict of principle between the two camps had in no way diminished.

I remember one day when I called on him with Zundelevich and found him expounding his credo to a small company of Russian and English visitors. He was sitting in a chair by the fire depicting with broad strokes of the brush the main contours of his ideological conceptions, like a prophet preaching to the heathen. I sat down near him and listened. His line of thought was typically anarchist and the exposition was saturated with extreme hostility to Marxism. It even seemed to me that his polemical fervour increased considerably when he noticed me among his audience. When he had finished he turned to me with an ironical smile and remarked:

'Now you're going to attack me, I suppose.'

I did not take much pressing and, not without some trepidation—after all I was challenging a world-famed celebrity—began my reply. For a few moments he listened in silence like Jupiter watching a barking puppy, and then my words seemed to irritate the god of thunder. A shadow came over his face and he somewhat rudely interrupted me, calling out:

'What about a cup of tea?'

The visitors noisily got up and the discussion was at an end.

But the gulf between anarchism and Marxism was not the only ground for my lack of faith in Kropotkin. There was another—the feeling that, for all his break with his own class and the remarkable story of his life, he had never really turned his back on the 'old Adam' of his origin and education. It always seemed to me that, despite all the conscious efforts of his intellect, he always retained something of that 'We-are-the-Masters' attitude against which he had fought so strenuously in his youth. In this respect he reminded me forcibly of Leo Tolstoy.

The presence of the old Adam showed up in his manners, tastes, habits and whole way of life. None of that mattered, of course; but what was much more dangerous was that it also showed up in his attitude towards the most important problems of a political order, the chief of which were the wars at the beginning of the twentieth century.

Consider what he was in theory—anarchist, prophet of world revolution, rejecting all State and national frontiers and dreaming of the universal brotherhood of mankind.

But what about him in practice?

During the Russo-Japanese War of 1904–5 he was an ardent 'Russian patriot', though at that time not only socialists of every stamp but even many liberals opposed the war and fought hard against the tsarist Government.

What about his attitude towards the 1914–18 war?

I well remember one particular episode. Somewhere about the summer of 1916 G. V. Chicherin and I were visiting Kropotkin on behalf of the Committee for the Relief of Political Convicts in Russia, which I have mentioned previously. The Committee wanted to enlist the help of a few English notabilities and was asking Kropotkin to write to them about it. Peter Alexeievich willingly agreed and we were just about to leave when his evening paper arrived. He glanced at it and suddenly swore loudly.

'What is it?' I asked.

'More defeats on the Russian front!'

This was the spark and a violent dispute developed. Chicherin remarked, somewhat ironically:

'Surely you don't want Russian tsarism to win?'

'What do you mean—Russian tsarism?' Kropotkin heatedly

retorted. 'It is not tsarism which is at stake but the fate of humanity. I know very well all the evils of capitalist society—after all, I've done a good deal in my time to expose them. But if German imperialism triumphs the work of freeing humanity from capitalist beastliness will be held up for years. So I am all for the victory of England and France, even if for the moment they are allies of tsarism.'

At that time Chicherin was not yet a Bolshevik and had not broken formally with the Mensheviks; but he strongly opposed the war, which he considered imperialistic. He started to reply to Kropotkin, urging that a true socialist and revolutionary was bound to fight against Anglo-French imperialism no less vigorously than against German. Kropotkin's face turned red, as did Chicherin's, their voices rose and the light of battle came into their eyes. I intervened, and, in the spirit of my ideas at that time, said:

'The proletariat is not interested in either a German or an Anglo-French victory, but solely in its own; that is the starting-point in determining our strategy and tactics.'

Kropotkin was boiling with rage and sharply retorted:

'You are all suffering from Marxist dogmatism. Of course the proletariat is interested in its own victory, but it won't get its victory unless England and France beat Germany first. It's an inevitable and inescapable preliminary, so I'm all for the war to the bitter end, the end of German militarism!'

There was no point in continuing the quarrel and Chicherin and I said a frosty goodbye. Yes, we had seen the real 'anarchist-chauvinist', as Lenin called him in those days.

Now what did all that amount to? Simply that the dead were at the throats of the living, to use the picturesque French expression. The past and the future were in some fantastic way changing places inside him and thus producing those sudden oscillations peculiar to man when he finds himself between two fires.

Kropotkin was that sort of man.

I realized this and understood it and that is why there were two sides to my personal relations with him and acquaintance with this truly remarkable man.

When the February Revolution broke out Kropotkin immediately returned to Russia. The journey from London was difficult, dangerous and quite impossible without official co-operation. But as he did not want to get any help from the Russian Embassy in London (the old leaven was still at work!) he applied directly to the British Government. His request was quickly complied with. The English ministers did everything possible to facilitate his return. They considered that his presence in Petrograd at such a critical moment could be advantageous only to the Entente, paralysing, or at least neutralizing, the 'internationalist' influence of Lenin and his supporters.

His behaviour in 1917 was in fact the logical outcome of his attitude towards the war. He supported the Provisional Government and took part in the August Council of State where he called on 'the whole Russian people' once and for all to break with 'Zimmerwaldism' and fight on 'until final victory'. He advocated a close alliance with England and France.

The October Revolution faced him with a terrible dilemma. He had too much nobility of character to sink, like many of the other anarchists, to participation in anti-Soviet conspiracies and risings. But he could not fully understand and accept the dictatorship of the proletariat either. Why should he have done? All his politically conscious life had been one long struggle against the very nature of such a dictatorship and at seventy-five people do not change their whole outlook. But all the same, though he had called the Bolsheviks the 'Jacobins' of the Russian Revolution, and reprobated many of their actions and methods, he considered that the revolution, the Russian people and humanity in general owed a great deal to them.

These opinions grew stronger, in particular when the 'fourteen Powers' intervened to give aid to the Russian counter-revolution. He was a fierce opponent of such intervention. In June, 1920, at the request of the British Labour delegation then visiting Moscow, he addressed an 'open letter' to the workers of Europe in which he set forth quite clearly what he thought at the time.

'First of all,' he wrote in this interesting document, 'the working men of the civilized world and their friends in the other classes ought to induce their governments entirely to abandon the idea of armed intervention in the affairs of Russia—whether open or disguised, whether military or in the shape of subventions to various nations.'

After pointing out that historically speaking the Russian Revolution was a continuation of the English Revolution in the seventeenth century and the French Revolution in the eighteenth he went on:

'Russia is trying to make a step now in advance of where France stopped when it came to realize in real life what was then described as real equality (*egalité de fait*); that is real equality; Russia is trying to establish political economic equality.

'The Russian Revolution,' he wrote further, 'is not a mere accident in the struggle of parties.' No, it was the product of 'nearly a century of Communist and Socialist propaganda, since the times of Robert Owen, Saint-Simon and Fourier'.[1] The idea of councils of workmen and peasants controlling the political and economic life of the country appealed greatly to him. But he was not prepared to accept the position—and here the anarchist in him came out—when the councils themselves were dominated by only one party.

The letter concluded with another appeal to the workers of Europe to do everything humanly possible to put a swift end to interference in Russian affairs.

This was the last flight of the great spirit. Death was already tapping on his shoulder. At the beginning of 1921 the old revolutionary went down with pneumonia. At first there were hopes of recovery, but a crisis soon followed; nor was this surprising considering that he was seventy-eight. Lenin sent to Dmitrov, where the sick man was, a group of the best doctors, with the People's Commissar for Health, N. A. Semashko, at their head. There followed a long and stubborn duel between science and death. Fortune changed sides frequently but ultimately Kropotkin's heart gave out and on the 8th February, 1921, he died.

A special train bore his remains to Moscow. The coffin lay in state in the House of the Unions and the Moscow Soviet gave the old revolutionary a great public funeral.

I was in Omsk when he died. I was then working full time with the Siberian Revolutionary Committee, but at night I took on the additional job of writing articles for *Soviet Siberia*.

[1] British Labour Delegation to Russia 1920. Report. (London, 1920, pp. 89, 90.)

They were hard times. Civil war and intervention had only just ended. The October Revolution had triumphed, but throughout the country there was economic chaos. We were starving and freezing. The staff of *Soviet Siberia* could not keep themselves warm as there was no wood. The ink froze in the inkpots. The journal was printed on wrapping paper, the type knocked about and the print faint and smudged. But what did we care? We had spring in our hearts and an intoxicating vision before our eyes—the revolution had triumphed over all its enemies!

On the evening of 9th February I went to the newspaper office as usual. I was at once sent for by E. Yaroslavsky, then the editor, who silently handed me a Russian Telegraph Agency cable—the news of Kropotkin's death.

'I believe you knew Kropotkin personally,' he said. 'Perhaps you would write something about him.'

I went back to my own room and sat down at my table. It was icy cold but my head was hot. Thousands of images and memories flashed through my mind. For a long time I could not get down to work. At last my hand reached out for the pencil (the inkpot was frozen) of its own volition. Half an hour later I returned to Yaroslavsky's room and handed him a well-covered sheet of paper. He ran through what I had written and sent for the make-up man.

'To the composing-room at once,' he said.

Next morning, the 10th February, on the front page within a black frame the following article appeared:

'Kropotkin is dead.

'In the world revolutionary movement of the second half of the nineteenth century, which prepared the way for the great socialist rebirth of our era, he was one of the most gifted, interesting and picturesque figures. A Russian prince of ancient lineage, Cossack officer, eminent geographer, daring traveller, brilliant writer, outstanding revolutionary and the leader of European anarchism, he passed through many stages and took up many points of view but always and everywhere remained a great man and a bold fighter for the downtrodden and oppressed.

'We have disagreed, and still disagree, with Kropotkin on

many things. Our idea of the final goal to which the great movement now embracing the whole world is leading differs from his. We do not share his views about the ways and means of ensuring the triumph of this movement. During his lifetime we often had long and heated disputes with him and his supporters about ideological questions, programmes and tactics. At times these disputes became bitter and almost hostile. But even in moments of the fiercest polemics we knew that we were dealing with a great spirit, the spirit of a revolutionary even when he most disagreed with us.

'Now Kropotkin is dead. The great spirit is no more. One of the most brilliant figures of the nineteenth century has disappeared from the scene. And before the open grave of the old revolutionary, we, his ideological opponents, involuntarily bare our heads because, despite his illusions and errors, he remained to his last days a brave soldier in the battle to free humanity from the yoke of political and social tyranny. . . .'

Moscow immortalized the memory of P. A. Kropotkin by giving his name to one of the great streets of the capital.

CHAPTER THIRTEEN

A. I. Zundelevich

'OLD ZUND' the émigré colony affectionately called that well-known revolutionary of the seventies, Aron Isakovich Zundelevich, to whom Stepnyak Kravchinsky devotes such touching lines in his *Underground Russia*.

In his youth he was a fanatical devotee of the underground press. His object was to establish an effective secret printing-press in Petersburg. His friends and comrades mocked at him and considered him a dreamer, so remote seemed the possibility of regularly turning out revolutionary literature in the capital under the noses of the police and gendarmerie. But he did not agree and stubbornly stuck to his point of view. After much argument and controversy he managed to get hold of four thousand roubles to set up his secret press—and did set it up. This was in 1877.

For four years his press operated without a break, at first turning out quite large pamphlets and then an illegal newspaper also. The police spies were reduced to despair; despite all their efforts, they could not discover its whereabouts. A stupid accident proved its undoing. Owing to some confusion over the names of the tenants the police came by mistake to the very flat where the press was working. As a result of this disaster he had to flee abroad. He settled in London and remained there to the end of his days.

When I met him at the Communist Club he was already an old-established Londoner. His outward appearance was remarkable. He was rather short and stocky: with a huge grey beard descending to his waist, sharp little eyes, and kindly smile, he resembled the legendary gnome in some fairy story. But there was something wonderful about his heart: it was kind, responsive and crystal clean. He was always helping or worrying about someone or other. I found that out for myself.

'Old Zund' was a bachelor and roosted in a damp, dim room

in the vicinity of Charlotte Street. I do not know what age he was—he always quietly evaded that question—but he must have been well on in years, undoubtedly over sixty and possibly seventy. Nor do I know what his political views were in his youth; at the time I met him he was 'non-party left wing' and represented the incarnation of a sort of opportunism which was shown in small things as well as big.

When he and I discussed Russian affairs I could never find out what he felt about existing parties or currents of opinion. He believed that all of them—Bolsheviks, Mensheviks, Socialist-Revolutionaries, Anarchists—were equally valuable, that each was an essential element in the revolutionary movement and that the new order in Russia would develop out of a compromise between their various beliefs. So he looked on with a superior smile at the political and ideological struggles then in progress between the Social-Democrats and the Socialist-Revolutionaries and between the Bolsheviks and the Mensheviks.

When he and I turned to British affairs, with which he was so familiar that he was able to give me a great deal of useful information, I found myself in the presence of a typical 'Labour' man, and not very left wing at that. In all his thoughts, feelings and opinions he seemed to be saying: 'Why all this unnecessary excitement and impatience? Life goes its own remorseless way. It cannot be hurried. One must wait and hope for the best and meanwhile get on with the daily round and common task.'

Such was Zundelevich in big things. And in small?

One day I found him with his face in a bandage. It turned out that he had bad toothache. I advised him to see a dentist I knew, but the old man answered:

'Why? Leave it to nature. She's the best cure. I must just wait until she does her work.'

Whatever argument I used was unavailing. He utterly refused to see a dentist. After two weeks the pain ceased. Meeting me at the Communist Club he cried triumphantly:

'I was right, you see! Nature did her job. I only had to give her time.'

'But why put up with all that pain when you need not?' I retorted.

'How do you mean, "put up with pain"?' he said, assuming a philosophic tone. 'Our whole life is pain. If I hadn't had

this pain I should have had something else unpleasant, perhaps something worse than toothache. Nature abhors a
vacuum.'

I made no reply, but could not help wondering: Can he ever
really have been an ardent revolutionary? And then involuntarily
I recalled something once said by F. A. Rothstein to the effect
that by the beginning of the twentieth century almost all the
surviving *Narodovoltsy*[1] had become ordinary liberals.

Be that as it may, my friendship with 'Old Zund' continued
and became ever closer. I liked the fairy-tale gnome as a man—
and in addition he had a wonderful gift for talking about the past,
in particular the events and personalities of the seventies, which
always revived a sense of history which I had possessed to a very
high degree in my early youth.

Of his stories one drama of long ago, which has become
almost legendary, springs to mind, and I should like to reproduce
it here.

I visited him one day in his shabby, old-man's bed-sitting-
room. There was the usual disorder characteristic of bachelors—
the half-made bed, papers and kitchenware piled up on the table,
books and newspapers, covered with a thick layer of dust,
stacked in the corners. I bent over one of these mounds and began
to rummage in it. I soon came across a small grey brochure with
the words: 'Nikolai Ivanovich Kibalchich, St. Petersburg, VI.
Raspopov, 1906, price 12 kopeks', on the title-page.

'What's this?' I asked.

The name of Kibalchich was well known to me from the
history of our revolutionary movement, but I had never seen
anything in print specially devoted to him.

'Interesting stuff,' Zundelevich replied. 'Reminiscences about
Kibalchich, extracts from his trial and his closing speech. . . .
Someone managed to bring this out during the 1905 revolu-
tion. . . .'

The old man sighed, and a look came into his face which I
knew from experience was the prelude to an interesting story. To
hurry him up I asked:

'You knew Kibalchich, I suppose?
'Yes indeed, I knew him very well.'
'Tell me about him.'

[1] Members of 'The People's Will' (Narodnaya Volya).

He smoothed his great beard, for some reason moved the papers on the table and began.

'Kibalchich's story is the story of how tsarism destroyed scientists of genius——'

'Not only scientists,' I interrupted, 'but writers, artists, great thinkers. . . . We know all about that. . . .'

'Yes, but now we're concerned with a scientist, a scientist of genius, whose premature death was a great loss not only to Russia but to the whole world. . . .'

The usually unruffled Zundelevich was visibly upset and twice rose from his chair and paced up and down his little room, awkwardly colliding with the meagre furniture.

'Out with it!' I exclaimed, my impatience aroused by his actions and words.

'Here goes!' he said, resuming his chair and obviously settling down to a long story. 'I first met Kibalchich either in 1874 or at the beginning of 1875, when he was a student at the Medico-Surgical Academy in Petersburg. At first he made no great impression on me. His appearance was quite ordinary—dark-red hair and a little beard, pale face, medium height, nothing striking about him. As they say on passports, "no special peculiarities". There was nothing special about his background and education either. The son of a priest living in the Chernigov province, he was born in 1854, educated at a seminary, entered the Institute of Railway Engineering at seventeen and two years later became a medical student——'

'So he was a rebel *popovich*.[1] Just a *popovich*!' I interrupted.

'What do you mean?' he asked, quite taken aback.

'I'm referring,' I replied, 'to the curious fact that in the fifties, sixties and seventies of the last century there were many sons and daughters of priests who turned their backs on their own milieu and joined the progressive, and even the revolutionary, camp. . . . Don't you remember that both Chernyshevsky and Dobroliubov were *popoviches*? My own uncle, M. M. Chemodanov, the radical caricaturist of the seventies, was a *popovich*. . . . But please go on.'

'As I have said,' he went on, 'at first sight Kibalchich looked a very ordinary sort of person and also absent-minded and unpractical. He knew nothing about organization and did not want to. When I first knew him he had no definite political views.

[1] Literally: son of a 'pop' (priest).

He certainly joined several educational groups among the students
but none of them had any specific political character: the students
simply discussed the sort of problems in various branches of
knowledge, and particularly the natural sciences, which interested
the young at that time. I remember lots of arguments over
physiology, Moleschott, Virchow and Pasteur.

'Putting it shortly, for several months I took little interest in
Kibalchich. I could not help noticing that he was poor, ascetic
and much interested in questions of a theoretical character—a
field in which he was much stronger than most students.'

Zundelevich once again stroked his beard, and continued:

'In 1875 he was suddenly arrested. As I learned later, it was a
paltry affair. He was spending the summer with his brother in the
country and gave a peasant a banned pamphlet, *Tales of Four
Brothers*, which was very popular at that time. The little book
passed from hand to hand and eventually came into the possession
of the police. He was put in gaol. The position was complicated
by a fortuitous circumstance. As he was not interested in politics
the revolutionaries considered his lodgings a "safe place" and just
before his arrest a girl whom he knew had asked him to take care
of a package, which in fact contained "underground" literature
just arrived from abroad. Kibalchich was quite unaware of the
fact. This package was to prove a damning piece of evidence
against him.'

'What happened next?' My impatience was too much for
me.

'Exactly what happened so often in those days. He spent nearly
three years in prison while the investigation was going on, and
was then given a sentence of . . . one month! Just imagine! In
the spring of 1878 he was freed, and we met again. But he was a
very different Kibalchich! He had travelled far in those three
years, read an enormous amount (including Marx's *Kapital*),
thought a lot and had many discussions and disputes with other
prisoners. His views had radically changed; I was in the presence
of a fully fashioned socialist and revolutionary.

'Of the revolutionary groups of that time he favoured most
the terrorists who at the end of 1879 founded "The People's
Will". He had given the matter careful thought while in prison
and now he decided to help them. But how? Not as an organizer,
or even as a bomb-thrower or expert with a revolver, but as a

scientist. . . . I mean exactly what I say, as a scientist. How characteristic it was!

'How did he start? With a thorough enquiry into the theory and practice of explosives. He first got hold of and digested all the Russian literature on the subject, then he learned English, French and German and read everything on the same subject in those languages. He followed this up by carrying out a whole series of experiments with explosives at home. His particular favourite was nitroglycerine. Ultimately he became such a great expert in the subject that when he had to argue on technical questions with the tsarist experts at his subsequent trial he had no difficulty at all in flooring them.'

While he was speaking 'Old Zund' got so worked up that his face turned red and his eyes, usually so quiet and somewhat sceptical, flashed fire in a manner quite foreign to him.

'In 1879,' he continued, 'when his preparatory work was done, he offered his services, "technical" services, to the executive committee of the "People's Will" through Kvyatkovsky, a member of that organization. The offer was accepted, and during the next two years Kibalchich was the head of the laboratory engaged in turning out the explosives, bombs, mines and other deadly weapons of the revolutionary struggle. He became a real virtuoso in this sphere. He always carried in his head dozens of chemical and technical combinations, he could easily apply his mind to all conditions and knew what could be got most easily, what took up the least possible space, what was best for use on water, on land, etc. To prevent unnecessary loss of life he took great pains to ensure that the violence of the explosion should be no more than was required for the attainment of its object. As a "technician" he took part in a whole series of attempts on the life of Alexander II—at Odessa, Alexandrovsk, Moscow and finally Petersburg where the Tsar was killed on the 1st March, 1881. What is most remarkable about the whole story is that, though the conditions in which he lived were about as unsuitable as possible for pure scientific work, the fact is that he did a great deal of such work!'

'Do you really mean to say,' I interrupted incredulously, 'that he had the time and tranquillity of mind to be interested in anything but bombs and nitroglycerine?'

'Just imagine,' Zundelevich retorted with unusual warmth. 'I
had occasion to find out. Some time in 1880 I happened to meet
him in the street. Usually we avoided contact as we were both
engaged in very secret work, I with my illegal printing press and
he with his secret laboratory. But here we accidentally ran into
each other. There were no police spies about so we got into
conversation. Among other things I asked him what he was
doing. What was my surprise when he replied that he was
designing a flying machine! I remember thinking: "Is he a bit
lightheaded?" It seemed to me that he was rather *distrait* and put
it down to the difficulties of a hunted life and the revolutionary
struggle. But that was not the cause, as became quite clear at his
trial a year later for his part in the affair of the 1st March. Let me
tell you what happened.'

He grew red in the face again, and a hard metallic tone quite
unusual with him came into his voice.

'On the 17th March, 1881, Kibalchich was arrested and on
the 3rd April he was executed, along with Zheliabov, Perovskaya,
Mihailov and Rysakov. He died with philosophic composure.
How did he occupy himself during those fateful sixteen days in
the Peter and Paul Fortress? With his own affairs? Preparing his
defence for his trial? Not at all! Those fateful days he passed
wholly absorbed in his design for the flying machine of which he
was telling me. Gerard, the lawyer who defended him at his trial,
said afterwards that Kibalchich took no interest whatever in the
forthcoming proceedings, and when he [Gerard] asked him any
questions in connection with the preliminary investigation
Kibalchich impatiently waved him aside and said: "You can
decide this any way you like without me." He had no thoughts
for anything but his flying machine and did not want to waste
a minute on other things. One can't help thinking of old
Archimedes and his circles. And what do you think? He did finish
his design. He handed it to the prison authorities and asked them
to submit it urgently to technical specialists. But what became of
it no one knows.[1] I myself am quite convinced that his design
embodied a great invention, which the Tsar's *Okhrana* kept from
the world. Mankind was simply robbed.'

'Old Zund' got up and went to the little window, the only
window in his room, opened it and put his head out, as if he

[1] See Appendix 7.

I

wanted a breath of air. Then he came back to his chair and finished
his story:

'There is no getting away from it; tsarism alone was to blame.
It drew Kibalchich from his real bent as a scientific man of genius.
Tsarism deprived the world of his invention. Tsarism killed it.'

'Tsarism must be destroyed, and it will be destroyed,' I replied.

He sighed, and there was a note of passion in his voice as he
said:

'May we be living then!'

CHAPTER FOURTEEN

P. B. Karpovich

PETER VLADIMIROVICH KARPOVICH was the hero of the assassination of the Minister of Public Instruction, Bogolepov, which made a considerable stir at the time. The beginning of the nineteenth century marked a swift expansion of mass revolutionary energy which led to the outbreak of 1905. One of the manifestations of this energy was the wide development of the student movement. There were constant students' strikes which paralysed the work of the higher schools for weeks and months. The streets of Petersburg, Kiev, Kharkov and Odessa witnessed student demonstrations which were ruthlessly suppressed by Cossacks and gendarmes. The mass flogging of students in Petersburg on the 8th February, 1899, was particularly serious. Hundreds and thousands of students were arrested and sent to 'distant parts of the Russian Empire'. This duel between the students and tsarism attracted the attention of the whole world and won increasing support for them in the nation itself. The stream of protest grew from month to month. The struggle got fiercer and because the representatives of the intellectual movements are always apt to resort to the weapon of individual terror it is not altogether surprising that the students took the same line, especially as the Socialist-Revolutionary Party, which was coming into existence about this time, officially included in its methods the killing of prominent figures in the Tsar's Government.

The first clear indication of the adoption of the new method was Karpovich's deed. On the 14th February, 1901, in the guise of a student presenting a petition, he was received by the much-hated Minister of Public Instruction, N. P. Bogolepov, and mortally wounded him with several shots from a revolver. Karpovich was arrested on the spot, sentenced to twenty years' imprisonment and incarcerated in Schlüsselburg where he spent several years under terrible conditions. The 1905 revolution brought an amnesty and his sentence was substantially reduced. He was transferred to Akatui (Siberia) and in 1907 released for settlement in exile. On his release from prison he at once escaped abroad and joined the 'Fighting Organization' of the Socialist-Revolutionary Party. But the exposure of the *agent provocateur* Azeff, who was the life and soul of its terrorist activities, made a shattering impression on him and he turned away from terror and the Socialist-Revolutionaries. After many adventures he reached London and settled down as an émigré.

Tall, square-shouldered, with dark hair and brown eyes, he was the incarnation of physical health and strength. He could not be called handsome, but there was something very noble and intellectual about his face. A bachelor, living in a cheap lodging house, he earned his living by working as a masseur. When I met him he was getting on towards forty, and his old love for terrorism had withered. He did not break officially with the S.R.s and he had many friends among them, but he criticized the party a great deal and showed distinct understanding of Social-Democratic ideas. In particular he considered that the basis of the revolution must be a mass movement of workers and peasants. He was one of those left-wing 'odd-men-out' to which I have referred previously.

As a man, I liked Peter Vladimirovich very much; he was straightforward, honest, modest, hardworking, with a pleasant dash of kindly, Ukrainian humour. He sang very well and had an undoubted gift for acting. I well remember how in 1917, almost on the eve of the February Revolution, the Herzen Circle staged a then popular comedy-farce, *Ivanov Pavel*, which was all about the misfortunes at college of an overgrown ninny. Karpovich played the part of Ivanov with such brilliance that he kept his audience in fits of laughter.

As I have said, I was fond of him and we often met at the Herzen Circle, at home or the houses of mutual friends. Sometimes we used to go for expeditions into the country or to the seaside. We got so intimate that I secretly cherished the hope that I could win him over to Marxism, and very probably I should have achieved my object but for a fatal chance.

When tsarism collapsed in Russia the one passionate desire of all the émigrés was to return home to Russia, anyhow, at any cost. But how? At that time England was blockaded by German submarines and her communications with other countries were limited and dangerous. But the émigrés were not to be thwarted; they stubbornly persisted in finding some way of getting back. But they did not always arrive, alas! In this terrible lottery Karpovich drew an unlucky number, and lost.

I well remember my last meeting with him. It was in the middle of April, 1917, and the warmth of spring was in the air. The fogs had been left behind and London saw blue skies more frequently. I ran into Karpovich one morning at the junction of Oxford Street and Tottenham Court Road. He cheerfully told me that he was leaving for Russia next day.

I asked him how he had managed to fix things and he told me that through one of his English patients he had contacted the captain of a tramp steamer which was sailing from London to Norway. The captain had agreed to take him as a casual passenger and put him off at Bergen. The ship in question was sailing at its own risk, without any escort, and was armed with nothing but a small gun.

What he told me made me very dubious, and I began to dissuade him from going, pointing out that in the very near future he would have another and much more reliable opportunity of getting home (I say more about this later on), but he simply would not listen to me. A fervent patriot, he was longing for Russia with all the passion of his rare nature. He considered it almost a crime to waste another moment in a foreign country after a revolution had broken out at home. In answer to all my urging he merely repeated:

'How can I sit with folded hands in London when in Petersburg the people have risen? Come what may, I'm off!'

We embraced fervently on parting. He sailed from London next day.

A week later a telegram arrived from Bergen; his ship had been torpedoed by a German submarine and gone to the bottom. None of the crew and passengers had been saved.

CHAPTER FIFTEEN

Lansbury's Story

SOME time about the beginning of 1914 I entered the restaurant of the Communist Club. At one of the tables sat old A. I. Zundelevich entertaining an Englishman I did not know. They were both laughing heartily about something. Zundelevich got up and introduced me to his companion, who was George Lansbury. I moved to their table and for a quarter of an hour we were absorbed in a free and easy conversation on various current topics. Then Lansbury got up and left us. When Zundelevich and I were alone he said:

'A very interesting figure, and purely English at that.'

He went on to tell me such curious things about Lansbury that I decided to get to know him better. In the months following I realized my hopes and found I had no reason to regret them. My meetings and talks with him greatly helped me to understand the real spirit of the English Labour movement which I was then studying.[1]

At that time Lansbury was over fifty, although he looked quite young. Tall, broad-shouldered, with a frank, open face and bright, piercing eyes, he gave the impression of a kind-hearted bear masquerading as an English preacher. Nor was this accidental.

Of middle-class origin, he was a Radical in his youth, turning socialist at the beginning of the nineties and subsequently joining the Independent Labour Party, which in 1900 joined the Labour Party which was formed that year. He was an ardent supporter of the suffragettes in their struggle for votes for women. The poor of the East End sent him into Parliament where his voice was passionately raised on their behalf from the Labour benches. During my time in London I often heard him speak at Labour meetings and was always much struck by his manner; his speeches were not so much political as socialist moral homilies. At first this was a surprise, but afterwards I realized that it could not be other-

[1] See Appendix 8.

wise, for when I knew him better the sources of his faith became
more obvious to me.

'Faith' is the right word! He was an unusually brilliant representative of the emotional strain in English socialism. He was
ruled less by his head than by his heart, and his heart was big and
noble. All the sufferings of the London poor were his sufferings,
and he was prepared to do everything humanly possible for them.
But he did not know what was required (how can the heart
know?). So his outlook was extraordinarily muddled and his
actions were often strange and inconsistent.

He was deeply religious and drew his inspiration from
primitive Christianity. If one tried to trace the original source
of his socialism, it would be found in the New Testament, 'Love
thy neighbour as thyself'. He attacked the bourgeoisie; had not
Christ driven the publicans and money-lenders from the temple?
He demanded an end to social inequality and the liquidation of
large-scale capitalism; had not Christ said that it was easier for a
camel to pass through the eye of a needle than for a rich man to
enter the kingdom of heaven? These and similar images had a
great influence on Lansbury's psychology and determined the
aims and methods of his struggle.

His ideas of struggle, however, were certainly his own. He
did not admit the class principle. Revolution frightened him.
He was a consistent pacifist both in international and in home
affairs. The Tolstoy principle of non-resistance came naturally
to him. What then was left for him? The only way to convince
those who did not agree with him was by his own word and
example. In his parliamentary life he particularly appreciated the
opportunity of winning over opponents from such an august and
authoritative platform. In his private life he tried to be the model
of all the virtues which particularly appeal to the imagination of
the masses. He neither drank nor smoked and was the perfect
family man. The doors of his modest home were always open to
anyone seeking help or advice and there was never a moment
when he was not aiding or worrying about somebody or going
to powerful friends to get help for someone.

It is superfluous to say that in the sphere of theory there was
a wide gulf between Lansbury and myself. We often argued, but
neither ever came round to the other's point of view. But that
did not prevent our remaining good friends, for in current

affairs he often took up a very left wing position—a fact which
came to Lenin's notice. In his article on the 'Congress of the
English Social-Democratic Party', which was published in
Zvezda in 1911, Lenin wrote very sympathetically about him:

'George Lansbury, a Member of Parliament, sharply criticized
the policy of the parliamentary "Labour" group for its dependence
on the Liberals and its reluctance to "endanger" the Liberal
Government. "I often felt so ashamed of the behaviour of the
Labour Members," he said, "that I have considered resigning. . . .
I sit in the House of Commons and see before me the working
people, men and women slaving day in and day out in the slums
of Bow and Bromley, who have sent me to Parliament. They
have gone on working and electing me because they think I am
different from the Liberals and Tories. They have sent me to
bring up one thing only, the question of poverty. I call upon
you"—here the speaker turned to the delegates[1]—"to think of
yourselves as a solid party utterly independent of either the
Liberals or Tories. The poverty-stricken working classes expect
nothing from them; their sole hope, their sole salvation lies in
organizing their own strength."'

I was particularly indebted to Lansbury for the willing help
he gave me in learning all about the British Labour movement
and I frequently went to him for any information I needed.

'Would you like to see a Socialist church?' Lansbury asked
me one day.

I was only too anxious to see it, as at that time I wanted to
see and know anything that was in any way connected with the
English working-class movement. Our visit took place next day.
The church in question was in Southgate Road, in the north-
eastern part of London, and was called the 'Brotherhood Church'.
We had a long walk through the dim and dirty streets of the
working-class quarters before we arrived. I took in the building
at a swift glance. It was like dozens of similar buildings in the
capital—soot-begrimed walls, high, narrow windows, a grimy
roof with a short steeple pointing to the sky. We entered through
a small side door, and were met by one of the leaders of the
socialist group to which the church belonged. He warmly shook
hands and led us into the vestry. This was a simple, bare room
which would hold about two hundred people. In one corner

[1] It was at a congress of the Independent Labour Party.

was a small platform and in the other a painted wooden table with a few chairs. Lansbury was at home here, and at once got into a lively conversation on matters of common interest with the socialist friend who had met us. We sat down for a rest, and then I began to question the latter about the church and its purpose.

I found out that the church was owned by a socialist body of considerable size, which maintained it at their own expense and held regular religious services there. Attached to it was a Sunday School which was attended by the children of the members. The purpose of the church, as indicated by its name, was to inculcate the idea of brotherhood between people of all nations, religions and convictions and to convert human society to socialist principles by peaceful means. When I was given this explanation I could not help reflecting what an enormous hold religion had on the English working class. You could not get away from it.

When we had finished talking our friend offered to show us round. We went from the vestry to the main hall where the services were held. It was big enough to hold three to four hundred people. In the body of the hall were rows of benches for the congregation. To right and left were galleries, with long benches divided by narrow aisles. There was a pulpit from which the sermons were delivered. It was just like any other church except that everything was simpler, poorer and more austere. We went up to the galleries and I looked down at the pews, the pulpit and the lectern.

Lansbury, standing by me, suddenly laughed and said:

'Would you believe that I once spent three hours in those pews at your party Congress?'

'What Congress?' I asked, taken aback.

'The 1907 Congress,' he replied. 'It's a remarkable story! I'll tell you about it.'

Here I must indulge in a little digression, so that my readers can understand what follows.

The 5th Congress of the R.S.D.R.P. took place under very difficult circumstances. The revolutionary tide in Russia was ebbing and tsarist reaction raising its head. The parties were torn by quarrels between the various sections, particularly between the Bolsheviks and the Mensheviks. It was absolutely essential to call a party congress but quite impossible to hold it in Russia; the police would never have allowed it. So it was decided to hold it in Scandinavia. After all, the 4th Congress had met at Stockholm. Copenhagen was now proposed and the Danish Social-Democrats promised their full co-operation.

In April, 1907, nearly three hundred delegates and guests who had illegally passed the Russian frontier and come through Sweden arrived in that city. A great disappointment was in store for them. The political situation in 1907 was very different from what it had been in 1906 when the revolutionary tide was at its height, tsarism was still unsure of itself and Sweden thought it could safely permit the holding of the Congress on its territory. Now the position in Russia had changed to the disadvantage of the revolution, and Denmark (and the other Scandinavian powers) did not wish to annoy their 'eastern neighbour' too obviously. A further consideration was that at that time Denmark was closely connected with Russia by dynastic ties (Maria Fyodorovna, the mother of Nicholas II, was a Danish princess) and the Russian Government's influence was very strong. The result was that the Danish Government not only refused to allow the Congress to be held in Copenhagen but actually threatened to hand the delegates over to the Tsar's Government. An attempt to transfer the Congress to Sweden or Norway failed for the same reason.

Then it was decided to hold the Congress in England, where all the delegates arrived during the first half of May. The meetings were held in London from the 13th May to the 1st June (New Style) and at them appeared almost all the party leaders and very many of the outstanding figures—Lenin, Stalin, Voroshilov, Litvinov, Yaroslavsky, Lyadov, Nogin, Rosa Luxemburg, Markhlevsky, Potressov, Deich and others. For nearly three weeks there were long and stubborn debates between the various factions and eventually a series of resolutions emerged.

For more information about those resolutions I must refer my readers to the history of the party. I am not concerned here, however, with the political work of the Congress. My purpose is to throw a little light on some personalities and matters of organization.

When the delegates arrived in London their financial position was extremely difficult. The party had raised a special fund to meet the expenses of holding the Congress and this would undoubtedly have proved adequate if, as proposed, it had met in Copenhagen. But the unexpected delay and subsequent transfer from one place to another exhausted the fund and there was little prospect of raising much in the way of money in the short time available. So while still in Copenhagen the leaders sent word to London that the expense of holding the Congress there must be kept down to the absolute minimum. The technical arrangements there were in the hands of a number of Russian émigrés (non-Social-Democrats among them) living in the English capital, among whom I should mention F. A. Rothstein, F. M. Stepnyak, R. Nadel, B. I. Kagan, A. I. Zundelevich, N. A. Alexeyev and others. On receipt of these instructions the London comrades naturally tried to do everything at the lowest possible cost, and they had a great measure of success. They managed to secure the 'Brotherhood Church' for the meetings, and to find large numbers of well-wishers among the émigrés and English socialists who were prepared to put up Russian revolutionaries. Unfortunately the number of such well-wishers was less than the number of delegates, so that many had to find quarters in cheap and uncomfortable East End lodgings.

And so it came about that on the 13th May, 1907, the 5th Congress of the R.S.D.R.P. opened within the walls of that very 'Brotherhood Church' to which Lansbury had taken me.

Despite all the efforts to economize (the delegates were allowed two shillings a day for their expenses) it soon appeared that the Party, which had already spent nearly a hundred thousand roubles on the Congress, could not make ends meet. The sum of at least twenty thousand roubles was needed to enable it to continue to the end, to cover all the costs of organizing it and to get the delegates home (the average cost of the return journey was calculated to be sixty roubles a head). The financial position got worse every moment. The delegates had to pull in their belts tighter. Some of the factions ran out of funds altogether and had to help themselves out with small loans from the more fortunate among the émigrés. Among the Mensheviks it was being said that in view of the financial position the Congress should be wound up, whether its work was finished or not, and they should all go home. The delegates became more and more gloomy and irritable.

It became necessary to take heroic measures to save the situation and the leaders ultimately commissioned the Finance Committee to find some way of borrowing two thousand pounds[1] in English bourgeois circles. The Finance Committee in turn considered all the possibilities, and applied to the group of sympathisers who had made the arrangements for the holding of the Congress.

It very soon appeared that there would be no chance of a loan unless it was guaranteed by some member of the Congress whose name was widely known—Gorky or Plekhanov, for example. These two were both brought into the search for money. These searches followed various lines, led to various people and at length found the path which led the Finance Committee to the golden fountain. It happened in this way.

I have already said that the émigré group which made preparations for the Congress included F. A. Rothstein, who made his living by providing summaries of the foreign press for the liberal paper, *Daily News*. There was an English journalist working on that paper, H. N. Brailsford, who was then a left-wing radical and later went over to the socialist camp. Rothstein, who was on good terms with him, told him of the difficult position in which the Congress found itself and asked him whether he could find someone prepared to lend the Party the money it so urgently required. Brailsford lent a sympathetic ear, and after some reflection replied that he knew of only one person who might possibly help the Congress—a substantial soap-manufacturer, Joseph Fels.

Here I can conclude my digression and let Lansbury get on with his story.[2]

'One morning at the very end of May, 1907,' he continued, 'I was rung up by Joseph Fels and asked to go straight to his office. I had often met him before. He was a very original sort

[1] At that time a pound was approximately ten roubles. Two thousand pounds would cover the deficit of the Congress.
[2] Some curious details of the financial troubles of the Congress and the measures taken to meet them can be found in the *Proceedings of the 5th Congress*, published by the Institute of Marxism–Leninism in 1935.

of person. His parents, Polish Jews, took him to the United States when he was a boy. He grew up in America and had a brilliant career, becoming head of a large soap-manufacturing concern. He was a complex character, a combination of the purely American, ruthless business man and the philanthropist wishing to help his fellow men. Despite his wealth, he considered the world anything but perfect and in fact badly in need of reform. But how to reform it? On this point he was not very clear. He was attracted by the doctrines of Henry George, and at one time thought that the "Single Tax" would be the salvation of humanity. He wrote and published pamphlets on the subject of the "Single Tax", kept a stock of them on him and always handed a copy to every visitor.

'But when he came to England he began to have doubts about the healing powers of the "Single Tax". It was true that force of habit made him continue to hand out one of his tracts to anyone coming to see him, but he also started to give money direct for various social and philanthropic purposes. He did this in quite haphazard fashion, often on the spur of the moment and without any consistency. One day he would give a donation to a temperance society, or the Salvation Army, or to establish colonies for tuberculous children, and the next—to the Independent Labour Party or even the Social-Democratic Federation. As his expenditure on "humanitarian" causes ultimately became very large indeed he used to invite me to assist him in the capacity of adviser. When he was thinking of giving money to some cause he first asked me whether it was worth doing.'

He sat down on a front bench and I followed his example. Then he continued:

'When I joined Fels that morning I found Brailsford and Rothstein with him. They had just been telling him about the difficulties with which your Congress was faced and asked him to lend the money it needed. Fels was in two minds and asked me my opinion. Of course I advised him to do so. This impressed him greatly, but he still hesitated. Suddenly he said: "Before I finally decide I want to see these people." No sooner said than done. All four of us immediately left his office and came here to the "Brotherhood Church". There was a session in progress. They brought us up to this gallery and we sat where we are sitting now and looked down at the scene. Rothstein gave the necessary explanations. Fels was all attention. He did not understand a word of Russian, but for all that his eyes devoured the scene before him. He was very interested in it and at one time called out: "How young they all are!" though without giving us any idea whether the youthfulness of the assembly appealed to him or not.[1] Later on he said: "How absorbed they are," and again we did not know whether he was praising or criticizing them.

'We were in the gallery for three hours, Fels making no move to go. At length he got up and said: "I'll give them the money." Rothstein quickly informed the leaders of his decision. Several people came up to us and began to thank Fels. One of them was Plekhanov, whose appearance and manner made an excellent impression on him. Of course he remained in character and promptly thrust one of his "Single Tax" pamphlets into Plekhanov's hand. Then we adjourned to Fels's office and two hours later a delegation from the Congress arrived to collect the money. At the last moment there was an unforeseen complication; he suddenly demanded that the Congress should give him a promissory note signed by all the members of the delegation. I never could understand why he wanted this, though sudden whims and caprices were not altogether unknown with him. I tried to dissuade him, but in vain; he categorically insisted on his conditions. Then the delegates said they must consult their comrades and went away. After some time they returned and said that the Congress was prepared to meet his wishes. Fels at once cheered up and the business was concluded in a few minutes.

'Thus was the financial crisis of the 5th Congress satisfactorily solved. Fels handed seventeen hundred pounds to L. Deich, who on this occasion was accompanied by F. M. Stepnyak and B. I. Kagan, and received in exchange a document of the following tenor:

' "The Russian Social-Democratic Party. The London Congress. May, 1907. The Brotherhood Church, Southgate Road, London, the 31st May, 1907.

' "We, the undersigned delegates of the R.S.D.R.P. Congress, promise to pay Mr. Joseph Fels on the 1st January, 1908, or earlier seventeen hundred pounds sterling—the amount of a loan kindly made without interest."

[1] The average age of the delegates was under twenty-eight (see *Proceedings of the 5th Congress*).

'This was followed by the signatures of all the three hundred and more participants in the Congress.'

A few hours before the agreement with Fels three hundred pounds was received from the Central Committee of the German Social-Democratic Party. Thus did the Congress acquire the two thousand pounds it urgently needed to finish its work and enable the delegates to get home.

The story which Lansbury told had the following remarkable conclusion.

When the 1st January, 1908 came and went, and the promissory note given by the Congress was not met (how could it be having regard to the growing strength of the reaction in Russia?) Fels suddenly got worried and began to complain to Lansbury and Brailsford about the unreliability of the Russians in matters of business, threatened to start a campaign in the press and asked them to bring appropriate pressure to bear on the leaders of the R.S.D.R.P. What his motives were I have never understood. Perhaps it was a flash of the ruthless business man in him of which Lansbury had spoken, as it must have been clear to him that his loan had nothing in common with an ordinary commercial transaction. Be that as it may, it was the capitalist in Fels which came to the fore when the note became due. Lansbury and Brailsford did their best to persuade him not to make a public scandal of it, but were not very successful.

Then Rothstein wrote to Lenin about the position which had arisen. On the 29th January, 1908, Vladimir Ilyich, then living in Geneva, replied that an immediate discharge of the debt was extremely difficult and ended his letter thus:

'The Englishman ought to be told this. It should be explained that conditions at the time of the 2nd Duma, when the loan was made, were quite different, that the Party will of course pay its debts, but to demand payment now is impossible and unthinkable and would be downright blackmail. You must convince the Englishman. He can hardly get his money now, and a scandal will not help him.'

Rothstein was in a very difficult position but got out of it quite skilfully, instinctively anticipating the actual course of historical events. Seeking to calm Fels down, he assured him that

when the Russian Revolution came and the R.S.D.R.P. seized
power the loan would promptly be repaid. Rothstein's assurances
obviously impressed Fels, as the latter ceased to worry about
repayment and confined himself to boasting to his friends about
the remarkable promissory note, 'the only one in the world',
which he kept in his safe. At that time Fels, of course, never
suspected all the historical significance of that document.

After the triumph of the October Revolution and when
relations with England had been restored, L. B. Krassin, who had
arrived in London as official representative of the Soviet Government, was instructed by the Central Committee of the Russian
Communist Party to get in touch with Fels and pay back the
seventeen hundred pounds which the 5th Congress had borrowed
in 1907. Fels was then dead, but Krassin gave his heirs the money,
and received the promissory note in exchange. It is now carefully
preserved in Moscow as one of the Party relics.

Whenever my thoughts return to that romantic episode in the
early history of our Party my heart fills with a feeling of un-
wonted pride—pride in the great and victorious path which the
Party has travelled since the 5th Congress, pride in its fidelity to its
word, as was so effectively demonstrated by that remarkable
incident.

CHAPTER SIXTEEN

Sic Transit . . .

ALL these and many other scenes crowded into my mind when I visited Charlotte Street once more in the autumn of 1932. Here the passage of twenty years had brought little change; there were the same old soot-begrimed houses, the same dirty pavements and the same pale sky above one's head. Here was the familiar house, No. 107. . . . But what is this? The familiar house has an unfamiliar look about it; it has been altered and painted, its windows have been converted into show-cases for tables, chairs and beds, and over the entrance is the shop-sign of a furniture emporium.

I was overcome by curiosity and went inside. Here everything was changed. Where the old restaurant used to be stood counters and safes. The big room where we used to hold our meetings and dramatic performances was a furniture depository. The room used by the Herzen Circle was the counting house. *Sic transit . . .*, I could not help thinking.

An obliging salesman approached me and asked what he could do for me. There was nothing I really wanted, but to spare him embarrassment I said I was looking for a good writing-table. He came to life and began to make some suggestions. I examined five tables, but did not like any of them. He began to get desperate, and was particularly upset because I rejected a big mahogany writing-table which he seemed to think extremely handsome and comfortable. When I turned away to leave he barred the way and said, with the air of a gambler throwing his last but undeniable trump card on the table:

'Do you know, sir, that you are turning down a table which will be a museum-piece in a hundred years' time?'

It was all so English, but I was inexorable.

Before taking my leave I stopped for a moment and asked him:

'Have you any idea what this place was used for before?'

He came to life again and replied, as if to end on a friendly note:

'There used to be some sort of German club here but it was closed by the authorities when the war started. Then it was empty for several years and afterwards my employer took it for a furniture shop.'

So that was what had happened to our émigré headquarters! And again the thought assailed me: *Sic transit* . . .

Yes, indeed, the glory dies, but is born again too!

I left the furniture shop and slowly wandered through the streets. Dusk was falling and there was a light mist in the air. The outlines of houses, churches, street-lamps and hoardings seemed to be fading away in the grey gloom. I walked on and thought:

The Communist Club. It was, and is no more. But does that mean that it died and left nothing behind it? No! A thousand times no! It had not existed for eighty years without purpose for humanity. Yes, indeed, for humanity! I am not afraid of that big word! In 1847 did not Marx and Engels give their lectures and make their reports within these walls? Was it not here that in hard debate and argument with their comrades they prepared the famous *Manifesto of the Communist Party*—the corner-stone of all Marxist ideology? Was not its first edition printed at the club press? Did not Marx frequent the Club during those long, slow, hard émigré years in London when he was hammering out that mighty weapon, the theory with which the revolutionary proletariat was to conquer the world? Was it not here that he so often inspired his followers, and got involved in frequent dispute with his opponents? Was it not from the clashing of these intellectual blades within his head that there sprang the sparks of those new thoughts, speculations and ideas which afterwards inspired the great work of all his life, that work which has definitely changed the course of history? Yes indeed, how much that was important and precious to humanity came to birth within the walls of the Communist Club, which has now ceased to exist!

As I continued my walk my thoughts took another turn.

Twenty years after Marx's death another man appeared here

on the banks of the Thames, a man from a different country and of a different people, but treading the same path as he did— Lenin. He seized the torch which had burned so fiercely in Marx's hands and bore it onwards. Living in another, maturer age, when the seed sown by Marx was beginning to produce a rich harvest, Lenin did more than hammer out the weapon of theory for the revolutionary proletariat. He set before himself another goal, a goal of nothing less than world-historical importance—to lead that proletariat to make an immediate reality of the ideas first set forth in the *Manifesto of the Communist Party*. And he achieved what he intended—in the great days of the October Revolution in Russia!

I do not know whether Lenin ever visited the Communist Club, but even if he did not he had the closest spiritual ties with it—through the Manifesto, through Marx's teaching, through Marx's very life. And how many of Lenin's disciples, fellow-soldiers in the battle, fellow-workers in the creation of the first socialist State in the world, were for years habitués of the Communist Club, visited it from time to time to meet their comrades, spar with their opponents, find out something about England, discuss Russian affairs, read the papers, learn languages, listen to music and see amateur plays and shows! Did not the thoughts, visions, feelings, moods, hopes and expectations born within the walls of this Club afterwards go to fertilize the seed of the greatest of all great revolutions, the October Revolution?

When the aphorism I have quoted was in vogue, the Romans were great pessimists, and had good reason to be. They said '*Sic transit gloria mundi*' and put a full stop. But we Soviet people are, on the contrary, great optimists and have good reason to be. Where the Romans put a full stop we put a comma and continue: 'but is born again'. And this 'new glory' we find more interesting and fascinating than that which has passed.

CHAPTER SEVENTEEN

The Socialist Congress in Copenhagen

IN THE very centre of London, in one of the crooked little lanes opening out of Fleet Street, there is an old, smoke-blackened inn with the picturesque name of Ye Olde Cheshire Cheese. Dickens was very fond of it, and inside they show you the place where the great writer usually sat. I frequently went there in my émigré days.

Twenty years later I paid it another visit. After ordering an English dark beer I sat down in a remote corner of a small room which was getting black with age and smoke and at once a whole series of pictures and scenes passed before my eyes. It was on this very spot that at the beginning of 1914 I had spent a whole evening engaged in a lively talk with an émigré comrade about the International Socialist Congress in Copenhagen which we had both attended as journalists. Let me record what I remember.[1]

It was the autumn of 1910. I was then an émigré in Munich studying economics at the University and the working-class movement outside it. I knew that at the end of August the 8th International Socialist Congress was to be held in Copenhagen. I was very anxious to see a world meeting of socialists for myself and made up my mind I would get to Copenhagen somehow. But how? In my pocket I had a few correspondents' visiting cards from Russian newspapers and journals for which I was then working and this to some extent provided the answer to the problem. Mobilizing all my modest pecuniary resources, I set out for the Congress in the capacity of journalist. My pen

---

[1] In writing this chapter I have fortified my memory from the official account of the Congress published in 1910 by the International Socialist Bureau in Brussels and from Lenin's article, 'The Co-operative Question at the International Socialist Congress in Copenhagen'. (See V. I. Lenin, Collected Works (4th Russian edn.), vol. 16, pp. 249–57.)

had rescued me as it had done, and would often do, during my life—both before and after Copenhagen.

I quickly crossed Germany from south to north, arrived in Copenhagen on the 27th August and found accommodation in the attic of a third-class hotel near the assembly hall.

The Congress opened next day, Sunday, the 28th August. The fact that it was a holiday enabled the local workers to take part in the mass demonstration with which the Danish Social-Democrats greeted their comrades from other lands. For the sessions they had taken the fine big 'Concert Palace', the walls of which were now adorned with socialist slogans and posters. Nine hundred delegates, in addition to over a hundred press men, assembled in the great hall. The public packed the broad galleries.

Sitting in the balcony in the midst of a crowd of journalists of all races and tongues, I devoured the spectacle opening before my eyes. I had a splendid view and could easily see the prominent delegates—Kautsky, Ledebour, Ebert, Legien, Bemelburg, Klara Zetkin from Germany; Victor Adler, Otto Bauer, Karl Renner and Pernerstorfer from Austria; Jaurès, Guesde and Vaillant from France; Keir Hardie, MacDonald, Ben Tillett and Quelch from England; Vandervelde, de Brouckère and Huysmans from Belgium; Troelstra and Wibaut from Holland; Hillquit from the U.S.A.; Iglesias from Spain; Rosa Luxemburg, Karski and Daszynski from Poland. The Russian delegation, numbering thirty in all, included not only Bolsheviks and Mensheviks but also Socialist-Revolutionaries and representatives of the trade unions.[1]

Among the Russian delegates I saw Lenin with Plekhanov, Lunacharsky and Kollontay a little further away. Martov, Maslov and Chernov were also present.

There were vacant seats which attracted considerable attention. Bebel was absent through illness and Katayama was missing because the Japanese Government would not allow him to come. A telegram of greeting sent by him was received with loud applause by the assembly and there were vociferous shouts of 'Down with Japanese militarism!'

[1] Independently of the number of delegates each country had a fixed number of votes which had been agreed upon in advance: England, France, Germany, Austria and Russia 20; Italy 15; U.S.A. 14; Sweden and Belgium 12, and so on. At Copenhagen the Russian votes were divided as follows—Social-Democrats of all shades 10, Socialist-Revolutionaries 7, trade unions 3.

Next came the music. The orchestra of the Copenhagen opera played a cantata specially written for the Congress by the socialist poet and deputy, Meier. Then a Danish workers' choir, five hundred strong, appeared and gave an admirable performance of several socialist and national songs. It was followed by artistes from the Copenhagen opera, and then Vandervelde mounted the platform and thundered out:

'In the name of the International Socialist Bureau I proclaim the 8th International Socialist Congress open!'

The speeches of welcome were the next item. The first, from the Danish Social-Democrats, was made by Stauning. He recounted the successes of his party in the thirty years of its existence and pointed out with some pride that at that moment it was publishing thirty-three newspapers, had twenty-eight deputies (out of 114) in Parliament and half the town councillors in the Copenhagen municipality, while the number of Danish workers organized in trade unions amounted to 120,000. He concluded his speech with the cry:

'Capitalism stands for slavery and war, socialism for freedom and peace!'

His speech was loudly applauded. I took a good look at this tall, heavily built, level-headed Dane with the long, flowing beard and could not resist an uncomfortable feeling. The speaker's revolutionary words and bourgeois exterior did not seem to go together. Nor was my feeling at that time without foundation. He subsequently proved to be one of the greatest Social-Democrat opportunists in Europe.

Then came Vandervelde, one of the orators of the 2nd International, who greeted the Congress in its name. In his opening he was very liberal with compliments to the various parties of the International and he ended up by announcing that at that moment there were thirty-three countries and eight million people in the socialist world-organization.

In these days, when the World Federation of Trade Unions has nearly one hundred million members and the number of members of all the Communist Parties of the world exceeds thirty-six millions, the 1910 figures may seem very modest. But half a century ago they were most inspiring.

Next came Huysmans, the Belgian secretary of the International, who produced a number of proposals relating to organization and administration. The Order of the Day for the Congress, comprising eight points, was passed unanimously, five committees were appointed and it was decided that the representatives of Sweden (Branting), Norway (Jeppsen) and Denmark (Clausen) should take the chair at the Congress sessions in turn. This was by way of thanks to the Danish comrades for allowing Copenhagen to be the meeting place.

This concluded the first session of the Congress and everyone rushed off to the restaurants and cafés to refresh the inner man.

At four o'clock there was a mass demonstration. A huge procession of workers assembled in the Western Boulevard, not far from the congress hall. There was a forest of red flags. The men wore red carnations in their buttonholes and the women had red posies pinned to their blouses. There were thousands of young girls wearing red hats, and masses of huge banners with bold slogans: 'Long live the International Proletariat!' 'Hail to the international brotherhood of workers fighting against Capitalism!'

Then fifteen big bands started up and the great procession got on the move. At its head were the two Social-Democrat burgomasters of the Danish capital, Knudsen and Jensen—a spectacle unthinkable in any other capital in those days. Still more remarkable was the fact that many soldiers were to be seen in the procession. In these days, of course, when mighty armies march under the red flag of socialism, the idea of soldiers taking part in popular demonstrations seems perfectly natural and obvious. But in Europe half a century ago that sort of thing was never seen. It is hardly surprising that the foreign delegates went out of their way to clap every group of soldiers. Along the route thousands of heads appeared at windows and thousands of hands waved a welcome.

For over an hour the streets of Copenhagen resounded to the tramp of marching feet and then the procession reached the great Sondermarken park on the outskirts. Here a vast crowd was waiting. A mighty sea of heads made everything else indistinguishable. There must have been at least a hundred thousand people. The famous leaders of international socialism addressed them from four high platforms. The bands gave of their best, and the din of boisterous clapping and shouting rose to the distant blue sky. The atmosphere vibrated with excitement, joy and

exultation. At length the official part of the demonstration concluded and the jollification began. The crowd took to drinking,
dancing, throwing confetti, tossing up coloured balls. There was
much laughter everywhere, much noise, much of a purely
youthful enthusiasm.

It was late that night before I got back to my tiny attic, but
my heart was filled with elation and an unshakable faith in
the future. I seemed to have had a glimpse of a new world
to come.

On the following day, the 29th August, the business sessions
of the Congress began. The meetings of the working committees
came first and the plenary sessions—from the 1st to the 3rd
September—followed.

I have already mentioned that the Congress accepted the
eight points of the Order of the Day, but in fact the attention of
the Congress was concentrated on three basic groups of questions:

    1. Strengthening the forces of the international proletariat.
    2. The danger of war.
    3. The fight against international political reaction.

Today, long afterwards, it is abundantly clear that by far the
most important problem at that time, the really critical problem,
was the fast-approaching danger of war. Yet in Copenhagen,
strangely enough, it took second place. Not that it was formally
under-estimated. Far from it. It had its due place in the principal
speeches. None the less, it is remarkable that consideration of the
problem of war took up less of the Congress's time, and aroused
far less emotion and passion, than the discussion of such a comparatively minor matter as unity in the trade-union movement
in Austria. I am not in any way exaggerating. Here are the facts.

At that time Czech social democracy was split into 'Centralists' and 'Separatists'.[1] The Centralists, led by Tusar, considered
that in the struggle against united capital in Austria the working
classes should themselves be united, and therefore the Czech
workman should join the combined trade unions which had
been organized by the Austrian Social-Democrats at the end of
the last century. The Separatists, headed by Nemec, on the other

[1] At that time the Austrian Social-Democratic parties were divided on national lines:
the German Social-Democratic Party, the Czech Social-Democratic Party and so on.

hand, maintained that as long as there was a separate Czech Social-Democratic Party there must be separate Czech trade unions—otherwise how could there be that close contact between the Party and the trade-union movement which had been called for by a resolution of the International Congress at Stuttgart in 1907? Such was the official justification. But in fact the real position was this: the Czech Social-Democrats needed money for their work; they could look only to the trade unions for it and they would look in vain unless there were separate Czech trade unions in Austria. The Separatists did not confine themselves to words. They proceeded to create Czech national trade-union organizations and maintained at the Congress that they had forty-five thousand members.

Their opponents, the Austrian-German Social-Democrats and the Czech Centralists, argued with considerable force that the policy of Nemec was splitting the working class, and ran counter to the Stuttgart resolution demanding that the unity of the trade unions should be maintained at all costs. Nemec's adversaries further maintained that the majority of the Czech working class was on their side, and to prove it emphasized the fact that despite all the efforts of the Separatists there were a hundred and eighteen thousand Czech workers in the Austrian trade unions.

The struggle inside the Austrian trade-union movement ultimately became so acute that the Austrian-German Social-Democrats decided to bring it up for consideration by international socialism. At Copenhagen the Austrian situation was studied from every point of view. The committee concerned with the trade-union movement devoted four long sittings to it. Twenty-three speakers from thirteen countries addressed it. There were some hot debates and very hard words. The Nemec group found itself entirely isolated. The Russian delegate on this committee to consider the Czech trade-union question was G. V. Plekhanov. He took a very active part in the enquiry, speaking himself, questioning the other speakers and suggesting the contents and wording of the official resolution. He found himself in direct conflict with Nemec, in which he was supported by the majority of the committee. As he was a Slav himself, it was not easy for the Czech Separatists to ascribe his attitude to nationalist motives, as they invariably did when dealing with their German, French or English opponents. This was the real reason why the committee asked Plekhanov to act as *rapporteur* on the Czech question at the plenary session of the Congress.

Plekhanov's report produced one of the most critical moments at the Copenhagen conference. In perfect French he made a most powerful speech in which he showed that the logical application of the principle which Nemec defended would mean 'the suicide of the trade-union movement'. By way of illustration he pointed out that there were eight separate nations in Austria and if each of these eight nations insisted on having its own trade unions the Austrian proletariat would be completely without defence against the united forces of Austrian capital. Even worse would be the position in Russia where the adoption of the Separatist point of view would mean the establishment of not eight but scores of separate trade-union movements. So in the name of the whole committee, with the exception of Nemec, he proposed that the Congress should pronounce in favour of a sole and undivided Austrian trade-union movement and that it should be given sole authority at any international gathering.

Nemec was allowed to present his point of view and he spared neither time nor effort in trying to convince the assembly that he was right. But in vain. The debates followed, with a multitude of speakers, much passion and many heated exchanges.

Ultimately the assembly passed to the resolution, which was worded in the sense of Plekhanov's report. The tension reached its highest pitch, and even spread to the journalists' tables. Each nationality voted separately. When the result was announced it emerged that there were 222 votes in favour of the resolution and five against, with seven abstentions. The five were Nemec's group and the seven abstentions comprised five Finns and two representatives of Turkish Armenians. There was a loud burst of applause. The thorny question had been settled, and settled justly and in accordance with principle. But what a vast expenditure of passion and time it had cost the Congress!

What about the question of war?

Here there was a very different story. This matter was also referred to a committee. But this committee held only two short and formal sittings and then formed a sub-committee to frame a resolution which was accepted, practically without discussion, at its third and last sitting. At the plenary session of the Congress to discuss the war question there were eight speeches, in none of which was there anything of the urgency and passion which had distinguished the debate on the Czech question.

What can be the explanation?

It is to be found in the balance of power in the Congress at that time, the fact (not entirely obvious to a contemporary) that the opportunist wing of socialism was clearly gaining the upper hand.

What was the actual position?

There were two distinct lines of thought in the Congress on this question. They were conveniently labelled the 'German-Austrian' and the 'Anglo-French'. The tactics of the Germans and Austrians were to hark back to the resolutions of the 1907 Stuttgart Congress on the subject of war and militarism and insist that there was no reason whatever to go beyond those resolutions.

The Anglo-French (whose chief speakers were Keir Hardie, the leader of the Independent Labour Party, and the Frenchman, Vaillant), on the other hand, maintained that as the danger of war which had inspired the Stuttgart resolutions had manifestly increased it was imperative to take further steps. But in fact they never got beyond empty talk because at heart they were just as much opportunists as their German-Austrian partners.

Behind the scenes there was a welter of hot debate among the delegates, some of whom, particularly the Reformists, were prepared to prove that a great war had now, generally speaking, become impossible. They had two main arguments: that the fabric of world economy was so tightly woven that it would be torn to shreds by a war and that the psychology of contemporary man was so refined that it could not bear the horrors of war.

To think that such views were possible on the very eve of the First World War!

When the debate on the war question ended, the time for decision arrived. What happened?

Vandervelde, speaking in the name of Belgium, put forward the following formula: 'The Congress decides to refer the Keir Hardie-Vaillant addendum to the International Socialist Bureau

for examination and instructs it to report on the proposals in
this addendum at the next international socialist congress.'

Belgium was supported by Germany, Holland, Austria, the
United States and Poland. England ultimately sided with them.
The Congress welcomed Vandervelde's formula. Unity had been
preserved. But to what purpose?—the purpose of evading a
decision.

This was very remarkable. Four years later the fruits of the
Copenhagen mentality ripened. When the great historical
balance-sheet was drawn up in 1914 both lines of thought—the
German-Austrian and Anglo-French—proved bankrupt. Vaillant
in particular came out as one of the most ardent Socialist
Chauvinists.

I happened to have kept a letter which I wrote to my brother
in Moscow a few days after the close of the Congress. I will
quote part of it:

'I have been much struck by the methods of work at the
Congress. I had supposed that all business would be done at the
plenary sessions. I knew of course that such congresses set up
committees and sub-committees, but I thought that these had
merely technical and auxiliary functions. Now I see that I was
greatly mistaken. In actual fact all the real work of the Congress
is done in the committees; it is here that the real clashes of
opinion take place (if some controversial subject comes up) and
the nature of the resolution to be passed is decided. The plenary
session? As a rule it merely confirms the proceedings of the
committee and serves as an arena for a contest in eloquence by
the orators.'

From such methods some practical results emerged. I noticed
that all the more active of the delegates, those who wanted to
have a real influence on the decisions of the Congress and not
merely shine as orators before an international audience, made a
bee-line for the committees, choosing the committee or committees which they considered particularly important.

So it is hardly surprising that at Copenhagen V. I. Lenin
concentrated his attention on the co-operative committee. Why
the co-operative? For the simple reason that at that moment the
co-operative question had great importance for the fate of the

international working-class movement, from both a practical and theoretical point of view. This was clear enough to anyone familiar with the position inside the socialist International at the time and equally clear from the composition of the committee selected by the Congress to draft the resolution on the co-operative movement, which was regarded as one of the most essential elements in strengthening the international proletariat. The committee consisted of seventy-five members, representing twenty countries, among whom were Jaurès and Guesde (France), Vandervelde and Anseele (Belgium), Elm and Wurm (Germany), Greulich and Grimm (Switzerland), Rosa Luxemburg (Poland), Karpeles (Austria), Balabanova (Italy), and Wibaut (Holland). Russia was represented by Lenin and Lunacharsky, who was using the name of Voinov at the Congress. Victor Chernov, of the Socialist-Revolutionaries, was also present but kept very much in the background.

We were much struck by the fact that England—the birth-place of the co-operative movement and the country where a powerful co-operative movement already existed—played a very modest part when the subject came up. Her leading representative, Whitely, spoke only once in the debate and even then was quite noncommittal. The obvious explanation was that the English delegates in the committee were of the co-operative 'business man' type who had no liking for theoretical argument on matters of principle and were not cut out for it. Yet it was those very questions of principle and theory that dominated the debates on this particular problem.

Two main points were involved:

1. The role of the co-operative movement in the class struggle of the proletariat.

2. The relations between the co-operative movement and the party.

Two main currents of thought were at once revealed in the committee. They were known for convenience as the 'Belgian' and the 'German'. The Belgians, represented by the leader of the Belgian co-operatives, Anseele, maintained that the workers should be socialist-co-operators and not co-operator-socialists, i.e. should not regard the co-operative movement as a sort of independent means of deciding social questions but as one of the weapons which, if properly used, could prove of considerable advantage to the proletariat in its class struggle (improving the workers' conditions, giving them business training, etc.). The Belgians therefore considered that while in every way supporting the co-operative movement socialists should saturate it with their own teaching, while the co-operatives for their part should maintain the closest possible contact with the socialist parties. At times their speeches lacked precision and showed a want of hard thought but it was felt that on this question the substance of what they said was thoroughly sound and that they were on the right track.

The Germans, whose chief speaker was Elm, the leader of the German co-operative movement, and who were supported from the start by the French Reformists and their leader, Jaurès, had a very different standpoint. Rejecting the clear definition of the role of the co-operative movement as one of the weapons of the proletariat in the class war (and a more auxiliary one than the trade unions) Elm and Jaurès circulated hazy and suspicious formulae to the effect that the co-operative movement was 'a means to the democratization and socialization of society'. Simultaneously they pronounced against close ties between the co-operative movement and the Party because, as Elm said, the former was interested in roping in 'all consumers, without regard to their political, economic and religious views'. It was perfectly clear that the Elm-Jaurès programme was sheer opportunism and akin to the theories of various bourgeois 'reformers' who dreamed of saving society by world-wide, co-operative self-help.

The battle between these two lines of thought—the Belgian and the German—raged in the committee and the Congress. All those furthest to the left and the revolutionary elements (Guesde, of the French minority, Wurm, of the German minority, Wibaut, of the Dutch Marxists, Rosa Luxemburg and others) supported the Belgians. Those furthest to the right, the Reformist elements (Thomas, of the French majority, Spargo the American, Modracek, of the Czech Separatists, Sestrem the Swede, Chernov, on behalf of the Socialist-Revolutionaries), backed the Germans. Karpeles, the Austrian, made a speech trying to compose their differences. Hot debates continued throughout three days and passions rose to such a pitch that, as had happened in the case of the committee considering the Czech Separatist question, the position of the various nations became absolutely clear.

The position of the Bolsheviks at the Congress was very difficult. The greatest influence was naturally exercised at Copenhagen by countries like Germany, England, Belgium, Austria and France, where there was a well-developed working-class movement. Russia at that time was not among them. The revolution of 1905 to 1907 had just been put down. Thousands of revolutionaries had been executed, exiled or thrown into prison. Party organizations had gone underground and trade unions, much enfeebled, had become semi-illegal. Not a sound could be heard from the countryside, suffocated by the reaction. For the moment tsarism was triumphant. True that it was celebrating its last victory, but who could have foreseen in 1910 that seven years later the red flag would be flying over the Neva? The situation at the time complicated the position of the Russian Social-Democratic delegates at the Congress, including the co-operative committee. Because Lenin firmly adhered to the logical, revolutionary point of view in relation to the co-operative movement he found himself up against a double opposition, as he clashed not only with the right-wing Reformists, of whom there were several on the committee, but with the wavering Centralists who were only too inclined to make concessions to the defeatist Elm-Jaurès line. But Lenin was not the man to flinch before obstacles. Great political strategist that he was, he showed outstanding skill in coping with the difficult position.

He began by clearly setting forth his own principles and producing a resolution elaborating the Bolshevik point of view, which he had drafted himself. In it he demonstrated that although proletarian co-operatives 'improve the position of the working class' and can 'prove of great importance in the economic and political mass struggle of the proletariat by giving aid to the workers during strikes and lock-outs and periods of political persecution', none the less their role under a capitalist régime was very limited. The benefits derived from the co-operative movement had been 'quite insignificant'. Not being 'organizations engaged in the direct struggle with capital', moreover, the co-operatives were apt to give rise to the illusion that they provided a way of solving the social problem 'without class war and the expropriation of the bourgeoisie'. Starting from this enunciation of principle, the resolution called upon the workers of all countries to do everything in their power to promote the development of proletarian co-operatives and carry on active propaganda among them 'of the ideas of the class war and socialism' and strive to ensure 'the closest ties between all sections of the working-class movement'. It was specially noted that producers' co-operatives were useful to the working class only if they were a 'component part of consumers' co-operatives'.

Of course it was clear to Lenin from the start that with the existing balance of power in the committee his resolution had no chance of being accepted. He considered, however (I heard him explaining this to our comrades behind the scenes), that if we were to have the greatest possible influence in the committee we should not adapt ourselves to its mood but bring out our own point of view as sharply as possible. Only thus should we succeed in bringing over waverers and wring concessions from the opportunists.

Lenin also began to seek for allies and he did so in a remarkable way. Sitting at the committee table he followed the course of the debate with close attention. No point of substance, no shade of meaning in any speech, escaped him. Occasionally he would lean across the table and put his hand to his ear to catch every word of some speech in which he was particularly interested. Sometimes, with a sly smile, he made a quick note on a pad in front of him, as if saying to himself: 'You've slipped, my boy! Now I've got you!' And indeed it was very difficult for an opponent to deal with a Lenin *riposte*. He had a rare gift for finding the weak spot in his adversary's armour and then beating on it mercilessly. During the debates in the committee he got to know which were his friends and which his enemies.

He always maintained close contact with his friends or even any potential sympathizer. On several occasions he encouraged and inspired Guesde, Rosa Luxemburg, Wibaut, Wurm and several others to speak. Little notes were constantly passing between then. Vladimir Ilyich could often be seen sitting in a corner and gesticulating energetically or, with his thumbs stuck into the armholes of his waistcoat, eagerly trying to convince some European left-winger on some point.

All this effort was not in vain. He succeeded in creating a solid *bloc* with the Polish Social-Democratic delegates and winning friendly support from the Guesdists and Dutch Marxists. He did not fare so well with Wurm, who at that time was considered a left-winger, or at any rate a left-centre Marxist in the ranks of German social democracy. Under Lenin's influence Wurm tried to rouse opposition to the Elm-Jaurès combination, but showed such a lack of backbone that he fully justified his name ('Wurm' means 'worm' in German).

The real fight in the committee raged round the fundamental question of the role and importance of the co-operatives. Elm categorically rejected the proposition in Lenin's resolution that the social problem could never be resolved without the 'expropriation of the bourgeoisie' and asserted that this was a 'controversial' question and that the programme of German social democracy spoke not of 'expropriation' but of 'overcoming capitalism', without exactly indicating how that would be done.

Jaurès in his turn insisted by way of ultimatum on a formula to the effect that the co-operative movement was preparing the way for the 'democratization and socialization of the means of production and exchange'. Lenin vigorously denounced these opportunist theories.

'What do you mean,' he said, 'by "the democratization of the means of production and exchange"? Peasant production is more "democratic" than large-scale capitalistic production. Does it mean that we socialists want to set up small-scale production? And what's this talk about "socialization"? It can mean a change to ownership by the community as a whole, but it can also mean any half-measures you like, any reforms within the framework of capitalism, beginning with friendly societies for peasants and ending with municipal baths and lavatories.'

Wurm, who also disliked 'socialization', hovered helplessly between the right and the left. He tried to weaken the force of the formula somewhat by transposing the paragraphs, but Elm promptly threatened to reject any compromise. Wurm was frightened to death and quickly withdrew his suggestion.

Then a sub-committee of ten persons was appointed to draft the resolution. In this sub-committee Lenin, supported by Wibaut, fought a stubborn battle for improvements in the text and obtained an important success. In the final draft it was emphasized that the co-operative movement was of itself 'powerless to reach the goal which socialism had set before itself—to conquer social power for the purpose of achieving collective ownership of all the means of production'. The resolution went

L

further, with a special warning to the workers against the influence of 'those who consider that the co-operative movement
is sufficient in itself'.

All the same, the Elm-Jaurès combination managed to retain
their 'socialization', and in the question of the relations between
the party and the co-operatives it was decided that although the
proletariat was intimately concerned to ensure that the three
sections in which the working class was organized—parties,
trade unions and co-operatives—should work harmoniously
together, nevertheless 'each country should decide for itself to
what extent the co-operatives should give direct aid to their
party and trade-union allies from their resources'.

Lenin did not confine himself to the results obtained in the
sub-committee. When the draft resolution was put before the
committee he once more showed unusual energy in attacking the
position of the opportunists. He did this very skilfully, not in
the name of Russian social democracy alone but always trying
to get the backing of sympathizers from other nations. He and
Guesde put forward two amendments, one in connection with
'socialization' and the other with the relation between the parties
and the co-operatives. These amendments, as might be expected,
were rejected by the majority of the committee.

But Lenin did not lay down his arms. He consulted with
Wurm and the latter proposed a new formula recommending,
in more ambiguous language, close contact between the parties
and the co-operative movement. Elm and Jaurès categorically
rejected this new formula. Wurm got very confused and withdrew it. Then Lenin exchanged a few words with Wibaut and
the Dutchman quickly took up Wurm's formula and put it
forward again in his own name. The committee threw it out
again. The resolutions on 'socialization' and the relations between
the parties and the co-operatives remained as left by the opportunists. All the same, there could be no doubt whatever about
the great political importance of the struggle which Lenin had
carried on.

Next came the question of what line to take at the plenary
session of the Congress. Lenin consulted with Guesde and both
came to the conclusion that, though the resolution was admittedly
imperfect, it put the proletariat on the right lines as regards the
co-operative movement: so there was no question of starting a

big controversy on this particular matter at the plenary session. The Bolsheviks and the Guesdists both voted in favour of the resolution, and the decision with regard to the co-operative movement was accepted unanimously by the Congress.

I took the very greatest interest in the battle over the co-operatives. I attended every meeting of the committee and sub-committee, followed the affair at every stage and picked up everything I could from conversations and discussions behind the scenes. There cannot be the slightest doubt that if the resolution on the co-operatives ultimately turned out to be not altogether unsatisfactory, it was very largely due to Lenin, and this despite the difficult position of the Russian delegation at the Copenhagen Congress! Considering the times, the resolution was certainly not too unsatisfactory. In his article 'The Co-operative Question at the International Congress at Copenhagen' Lenin wrote: 'With regard to the work of the Congress on the question of the co-operatives we must say, without concealing its imperfections from ourselves or the workers, that the International, broadly speaking, properly defined the problem of proletarian co-operatives.'[1]

It was at the Copenhagen Congress that I first saw G. V. Plekhanov at closer quarters. He was then fifty-four and at the very height of his powers. His name was widely known in the International and most European socialists regarded him as the personification of Russian social-democracy. Inside our party his authority was by no means so undisputed as in the international arena. The controversy between the Bolsheviks and Mensheviks had not been without effect on his prestige. At the time of which I am writing, however, he was the leader of the 'Party Menshevik' group[2] and therefore often lined up with Lenin in his controversy with 'liquidators' like Dan and Potressov. At Copenhagen, in fact, they worked closely together, and it is known that at the time of the Congress Lenin wrote a letter to the International Socialist Bureau asking that Plekhanov should be made a member of it as well as himself. Plekhanov made his most serious political mistakes later—in 1917, during the First World War.

I have already said that he took an active part in the question

---

[1] V. I. Lenin, *Collected Works* (4th Russian edn.). vol. 16, p. 257.

[2] That is, those Mensheviks who were against the policy of dissolving the 'underground' Social-Democratic Party, put forward by the official Menshevik leaders—Tr.

of trade-union unity in Austria. It was interesting to watch him in those days. At the committee table he usually sat quite still. He had nothing of the liveliness and dynamism which so struck one in Lenin nor had he Lenin's attractive simplicity and democratic outlook. One felt that he was rather condescending towards those around him. Even when he wanted to be charming (and he knew how to be) it seemed as if it was specially in honour of the person he was talking to at the time.

He was a very fine speaker, rather in the French style, perhaps because he knew French best and often made speeches in that language. Yet he showed a reserve on the platform which always seemed to keep him and his audience apart. He was also fond of impressing his hearers with the erudition, wit and eloquence he undoubtedly possessed and accepted the most vociferous applause as nothing more than his due.

In contrast to Lenin, who in the debates at the Congress showed tremendous initiative, concentrated on all possible adherents and himself sought and found allies, Plekhanov was distinguished by a certain passivity and he usually waited for his friends to approach him themselves.

I have vivid memories of another debate at the Copenhagen Congress which was concerned with the position of tsarist Russia in international affairs.

At that time the autocratic régime was on the brink of ruin. But for that very reason it was seeking salvation in an orgy of cruelty and imperialistic adventures. The revolution of 1905 had just been drowned in blood. The country had become one vast realm of the gallows. Bobrikov, the Governor-General of Finland, was busy pacifying that country. Colonel Lyakhov was threatening the liberation movement in Persia. Charykov, our minister in Constantinople, was intriguing against the Young Turk revolt in the Ottoman Empire. Tsarism's tentacles stretched to Germany, France and Switzerland and the Government at Petersburg was demanding that revolutionaries who had taken refuge in those countries should be surrendered to it. Not without some measure of success, either. M. M. Litvinov in 1908 was expelled from France, but fortunately found refuge in England. Several Bolsheviks were imprisoned in Bavaria and some in

Switzerland were handed over to the tsarist Government. The reactionary forces in Europe all gave support to Tsar Nicholas II's Government, supplying money, loans, arms and paid apologists in the world press. The dark shadow of tsarist Russia was falling across the whole European scene and the Copenhagen Congress could not ignore this ominous factor in the situation at that time. The Congress in fact devoted a great deal of attention to that subject. Four resolutions dealing with tsarism were proposed—on Persia and Turkey, Finland, capital punishment and the right of asylum. It was with the questions of Finland and the death penalty that the delegates were particularly preoccupied.

Wiik, a young Finnish Social-Democrat, opened the debate on the first question. Slight and unassuming though he was, he made a powerful speech in which he hotly protested against the suppression of the Finnish constitution by the tsarist Government. This was his peroration:

'Tsarism means the oppression of all working, thinking and feeling people. Tsarism means prison, the punishment cellar, Siberia. Every victory of tsarism is a blow to civilization. . . . Tsarism means death, and so we, fighters for life, must fight tsarism to the very end.'

The Congress cheered him to the echo and afterwards passed unanimously a resolution of protest against the tsarist Government in which all socialist parties of all countries undertook to use all the means at their disposal to defend the freedom of Finland.

Twenty years later fate brought Wiik and myself together again when I was Soviet plenipotentiary representative in Helsinki (1929–32) and he was editing the chief organ of his party, *Suomen sosial-democrati*. We often met to talk of this and that and exchange reminiscences of Copenhagen. His position was very difficult. In those days rabid reaction was in the saddle in Finland, and within the Social-Democratic Party Tanner was becoming the strong man. None the less, Wiik maintained a stout struggle against the reactionary forces in the Party and the country.[1]

On the second question, the death penalty, the chief speaker was Ellenbogen, the leader of the Viennese proletariat. Citing

[1] During the Second World War, Wiik joined that section of the Finnish Social-Democrats which had sufficient courage and principle to raise the flag of revolt against the fascist toadies to Germany. He was imprisoned, and released only after the Soviet-Finnish treaty in 1944.

Russia as the 'classical home of the death penalty', he inveighed
with all his might against the Petersburg Government.

'At the present time,' he said, 'when three decent people meet
anywhere on earth they cannot help protesting, at any rate in
their own minds, against the curse of tsarism. From this Congress,
which is striving for freedom and a better lot for humanity,
let there go forth the spirit of passionate, irreconcilable, sacred
detestation of Russian tsarism!'

A storm of clapping interrupted him, like a mighty wave
sweeping from the body of the hall to the platform and then
falling back.

'From here,' he exclaimed in inspired tones, 'let there resound
a war-cry not only to the proletariat of all countries but to every
decent and honest man, summoning them to join in the battle
against this accursed régime which is the most faithful bulwark of
the most rabid reactionaries of all other countries!'

The hall resounded with another burst of applause. Then the
whole Congress unanimously passed a resolution branding
tsarism for what it was.

Later, on a report by Keir Hardie, the Congress vigorously
proclaimed the inviolability of the right of asylum for political
émigrés in Western countries.

But the Congress did not spend all its time on serious work.
The Danes looked after the lighter side of life as well: theatres,
concerts, circuses, exhibitions, art galleries, excursions, walks
in the country round Copenhagen—all this was organized. The
delegates made full use of the opportunities afforded.

Two particular scenes are indelibly fixed in my memory.

In the middle of the 'Socialist Week' the members made a
trip to the fashionable Danish watering place, Klampenborg.
Two large steamers were engaged, but even so the delegates
and their Danish hosts had some difficulty in packing themselves
into them. We were all in unusual high spirits, quite excited
and very garrulous on the trip. The buffet was an enormous
success; corks popped, there was an incessant clatter of plates
and the staff scuttled about. The Germans raised great tankards
of dark beer and shouted 'Prosit!' The French and Italians clinked
glasses of burgundy and chianti. The English slowly drank their

ale and whisky-and-soda. There was even vodka for the Russian comrades. It was all noisy, crowded and somewhat stuffy. Next came singing and dancing. Each delegation gave of its best. There was a competition between the nations. We Russians were far from coming in last. A. M. Kollontay was a tremendous success.

At Klampenborg the motley throng of delegates invaded the streets, parks, beaches, cafés and restaurants. The Germans were soon buying mountains of picture postcards with views of Denmark, pulling out their eternal fountain-pens, scribbling their '*Grüss von Denmark*' and dispatching ten apiece. The representatives of the other nations bathed, hired rowing-boats, listened to bands or went for walks in the surrounding country. Late at night the Congress revellers, tired out but happy and pleased with their day, returned to Copenhagen the same way they had come.

The other scene was at the very end of the Congress. On Sunday, the 3rd September, it finished its work. At the last session, as at the first, the fanfares sounded. Victor Adler proposed that the next Congress should be held in Vienna in 1913. Then Jaurès spoke. Referring to the Franco-Prussian War, he thundered out:

'In 1870 both nations suffered defeat, for democracy in both countries did not fulfil its obligations. We French lost the war but you Germans are still suffering from its consequences, because it established the reign of the jackboot in Germany.'

The Congress greeted these words with loud applause, the Germans and French being particularly demonstrative.

Then the closing speeches were delivered by Molkenbuhr (Germany), Hillquit (U.S.A.), Branting (Sweden), Clausen (Denmark) and Vandervelde (the International Socialist Bureau). At six o'clock in the evening Vandervelde loudly proclaimed: 'I declare the 8th International Congress closed!'

Two hours later all the delegates assembled for a big farewell party in the Copenhagen town hall. How unusual, how inspiring such a thing was in those days! In what other country could the representatives of the world proletariat have met together for a triumphant banquet in the official headquarters of the city authorities? Nowhere. Not in London, not in Paris, much less in Berlin!

The Danish hosts excelled themselves. The interior of the town hall was a blaze of light and all the rooms were thrown open to the guests. Long tables were loaded with deliciously smelling eatables and the famous Scandinavian hors-d'œuvres. Batteries of bottles promised a riot of jollification and loosened all tongues. By ten o'clock the motley, multi-racial crowd of delegates were thoroughly at home, drinking, dancing, talking, summing up results, exchanging impressions and swearing friendship and solidarity.

I happened to stroll into the throne-room, where on very special occasions the King met the municipal councillors of the capital. A group of well liquored-up German delegates was gathered round the gilded throne. I noticed the celebrated atheist, Adolf Hoffman, who wrote the popular book *Zehn Gebote* (*Ten Commandments*) and was accordingly known in the Party as 'Hoffman-Ten-Commandments'. He was in tremendous form, laughing uproariously and gesticulating wildly. He suddenly broke away from his group, ran to the steps of the throne and plumped himself down in it. Assuming the most kingly of airs and haughtily jerking his head up, he exclaimed:

'Adolf the First!'

This obviously struck him as inadequate and he quickly amended it:

'Adolf the Great!'

Everyone burst out laughing. Next moment, however, it seemed that some of his German comrades, brought up in the strictly monarchical traditions of Germany, were distinctly ill at ease. There was a whispered conference and then they hustled him out of the room.

In another room, not far from the entrance hall, a sort of non-stop meeting was in progress. In the middle was a small improvised platform, round which a noisy crowd, of every race and tongue, was gathered. People came and went, but there were always a hundred or two present, prepared to listen to speakers and cheer them. There was no lack of orators, English, French, German, Russian, Swedish, Bulgarian, Italian. Their hearts were full, their feelings were overflowing and they all tried to tell their colleagues at the Congress how overjoyed they were to see the growth of international socialism and to be there that evening among friends and comrades.

I remember A. V. Lunacharsky's appearance on the platform. He was in the highest spirits, excited and intoxicated by the atmosphere around him, and made a passionate, rousing speech in French, with much eloquent gesticulation. He was loudly applauded. A. M. Kollontay followed. An attractive, lively minded and gifted woman, she was immensely popular with the members of the Congress and now went straight to their hearts with successive speeches in three languages, English, German and French. She received a great ovation.

But the most moving scene occurred when Jaurès appeared on the platform. At first he spoke in his own language but then changed to German. He spoke the latter well, but all the same it was not his own tongue. It was clear that he was himself aware of his linguistic inadequacies. After speaking for a few minutes in German he suddenly stopped, a charming smile wreathed his face and, looking very like a shy schoolboy, he cheerfully cried:

'Dear friends, my heart is still full but my German vocabulary has given out!'

Here he made a gesture as if he were pressing his entire audience to his bosom, and with a great shout: 'Long live international socialism,' he jumped down from the platform. The delegates cheered him to the echo and then . . .

Lunacharsky appeared in the middle of the crowd and yelled out:

'Let's toss Jaurès! Toss him!'

Some of the Russian delegates ran up and seized the slightly apprehensive Jaurès. Some Bulgarians, Serbians and other Slavs joined in and were followed by Austrians, Frenchmen and Italians, carried away by the general excitement.

Jaurès' heavy body was suddenly raised and flew up into the air, not once but many times, to the accompaniment of loud applause. His broad face showed some bewilderment and concern. He did not understand what was happening to him, and what it all meant.

When he was perpendicular once more and had his feet on the ground he gave an involuntary sigh of relief. His forehead and temples were bedabbled with sweat.

Since then many years have passed—the most remarkable years in human history, endlessly painful and endlessly glorious, profoundly destructive and profoundly creative. The year 1917 was revealed as the great watershed between two systems, capitalism and socialism.

And when I try to see in perspective the course of events since Copenhagen and to define the most vital and fundamental changes in those years there rises before me the mighty figure of Lenin. The last half-century can indeed be called the Lenin era!

Nor is it over. On the contrary, with every year that passes his standard, like the sun, rises higher, rallying round it all forward-looking mankind.

PART THREE

*

Among the English

CHAPTER EIGHTEEN

'The Socialist Camp'

NUMBER 110, Peckham Road, S.W. I stood facing this big, grimy, gloomy house, then the headquarters of the Amalgamated Society of Engineers, which is so famous in trade-union history, and a place I had frequently visited twenty years before, and once more a whole succession of scenes of long ago came to mind.

In the summer of 1913 it so happened that I unexpectedly found myself with a fortnight's holiday on my hands. I decided on a visit to the seaside. But where?

I have already said more than once that I was busy studying the English Labour movement. So, when faced with the question what I should do with those few weeks, I wondered whether I could not find somewhere where the holiday itself could contribute something to my education on the subject.

I sounded out my friends, Russian and foreign, but could not get any definite lead. Each had his own ideas and I was swung this way and that. Then I decided to visit 110, Peckham Road, and have a heart-to-heart talk with a cheerful young engineer named Brown, who had worked at the central office there. During the preceding winter we had become rather close friends and he had helped me a lot in my study of English trade unionism. I had not the slightest doubt that he would help me with my new problem. I was not mistaken. When I asked him what I should do he laughed and said:

'I know where you ought to go—"Dodd's Socialist Camp" is the place for you.'

'What's that?' I asked.

'Go and find out for yourself,' he replied. 'If you want to see the English working class at close quarters you won't be disappointed.'

Youth likes adventure. I took the cheerful engineer's advice
and had no reason to regret it.

'Dodd's Socialist Camp' was held at Caister-on-Sea, near
the fishing port of Great Yarmouth, on the east coast of England.
It was a green field, with a sprinkling of trees, stretching along the
'deep-blue sea'. To be truthful, the sea, the cold North Sea, was
leaden rather than blue, but what did that matter? The sea is
always the sea. In one corner of the field there were some flimsy
barrack-like buildings—the dining-room, kitchen and stores.
All the rest of the area was dotted with coloured canvas tents in
which the guests were accommodated on arrival, men on one
side, women on another and married couples on a third. In the
centre of the field was a tall mast from which a red flag was kept
flying. The domestic arrangements of the camp were on 'semi-
Communist' lines. We slept three or four to a tent, had our
meals together in the common dining-room and took turns in
helping in the kitchen. We did the washing-up and made our own
beds. The food was simple but good and we got as much air and
sea as anyone could want. There was not much sunshine, but it is
no good worrying over that in England.

The way the daily programme was arranged was a curious
mixture of discipline and liberty. We got up at seven and had
breakfast between eight and nine. Then we went to the beach,
played on the sand, bathed, swam, sun-bathed if there was any
sun. We were always ready for lunch between one and two
o'clock. In the afternoon we rested in our tents or on the grass.
At five we had the traditional English tea, with toast and jam,
and had dinner at eight. Before tea or between tea and dinner
we went for walks in the neighbourhood—to the old castle,
or the wide estuary of the River Yare, or the sinuous Ormsby
Broad where it was so pleasant to go for a row. After dinner in
the evening there was dancing and music, general conversation
and discussion, or we simply paired off or split into small groups
and sat about, smoking, chatting, telling stories or exchanging
unusual experiences. At eleven o'clock we went off to bed and
the whole camp was soon asleep.

I liked this 'Socialist Camp' very much. The visitors were
very pleasant, friendly, simple and sincere souls who created a

cheerful and happy atmosphere. Under such conditions it was easy to relax and I certainly had a good rest and got up my strength. But that summer I was more concerned with something else, as I was mainly interested in the visitors themselves, the men and women who like myself were living under canvas by the seashore. Who were they? What did they believe in? What did they want?

The owner of the camp, Mr. Fletcher Dodd, fell into the category of those whom the English call 'reformers' and whose brains are usually in an unimaginable tangle. Although Mr. Dodd was formally a member of the Independent Labour Party, he was actually very dissatisfied with that party, and indeed with all other parties in England at that time. As a true individualist he was critical of the very idea of parties. Every party, he was fond of saying, put fetters on the free human personality and this was inimical to the true interests of society. At the same time Mr. Dodd much disliked the world around him and badly wanted various improvements in its arrangements. So he lent a willing ear to any protest against the existing order of things, from whatever source it emanated. The result was that he ransacked each party and line of thought for anything he liked—he took a little from John Stuart Mill, a little from Henry George, a little from Keir Hardie, a little from MacDonald and a little from the Fabians.

Of course, all this was not, and indeed could not be, amalgamated into a single creed. Every idea which he picked up from somewhere or other lived its separate life, and occasionally it was very entertaining to see how these various fragments came into hopeless conflict with each other or suddenly combined to produce some perfectly fantastic whole.

Yet, as so often happens with Englishmen, out of Mr. Dodd's hopeless tangle of theories emerged some distinctly useful and practical achievements. One fine day he decided that the best way of serving humanity was to organize a 'Socialist Camp' where, at a very modest charge, socialists and 'reformers' of all breeds could have a good holiday and work out a system of truth and justice by exchanging ideas in a friendly atmosphere. He acted on his impulse.

The visitors who came to this camp represented all shades and hues in the British Left Wing at the time. There were Marxists

from Hyndman's Social-Democratic Federation, socialists from
Keir Hardie's Independent Labour Party, 'Gradualists' from the
Fabian Society, political opportunists from the Labour Party,
narrow-minded 'economists' from the trade unions and, last
but not least, 'reformers' of every possible hue. I was also struck
by the number of cranks (though this was perhaps typical of
English socialism at the time). Some of them ate nothing but
raw vegetables, others refused tea or coffee and drank nothing
but water, some never wore a hat, others never wore socks and
went about in sandals in any sort of weather. I remember how
surprised I was when a young and intelligent trade unionist
came to say goodbye to me one day and said:

'Our trade union is holding a conference in Edinburgh in a
fortnight. I'm leaving for it tomorrow.'

'Why so soon?' I asked in some surprise.

'It's not too soon,' he replied. 'I don't travel by train on
principle. I always walk; it's much more pleasant and healthy.
In exceptional cases I go on horseback. If I start tomorrow I shall
get to Edinburgh in time.'

The usual number of visitors was two hundred, and they
came from all parts of the country: shipyard workers from
Scotland, textile workers from Lancashire, metal workers from
Birmingham, miners from Wales, shop assistants from London.
Sometimes you met incipient intelligentzia—journalists, teachers,
doctors, lawyers' clerks.

My cheerful engineer proved right: it was impossible to
imagine a better opportunity to study the English working-class
milieu. I was only too glad to make the most of it.

The first thing to attract my attention was the free-for-all
discussions, of which there were very many. They usually took
place before tea or after dinner. A table was brought out and
put under a tree. A chairman sat down at it and the audience
sat around on chairs brought from the dining-room or lay on
the grass. A little mound had to serve as a platform. The scene
was almost biblical.

Every sort and kind of topic was brought up for discussion,
from the system of municipal rating to the structure of the future
socialist society. Anyone could speak and say anything he or she
liked. This was in conformity with the views of Mr. Dodd who
attached such great importance to the free interchange of opinion

between 'reformers'. Yet the rules were strict and somewhat miserly in the matter of time. The chairman was allowed five minutes, the opener fifteen to twenty minutes and all other speakers five minutes, with the exception of the closing speech, which could extend to ten. The entire session lasted not more than an hour and a half. These rules were strictly observed without any reminder from the chairman, who never had to interrupt a speaker, much less shut him up. The orators seemed to have no desire to exceed the time allotted to them and yet— what surprised me greatly—managed to say all they wanted. That's what age-long training in the routine of open political life meant!

The English socialists with whom I came in contact every day were very different from the Russian socialists. They were a totally different intellectual, psychological and moral type, the exclusive product of a British soil which was so unlike the Russian. Three things particularly struck me about my British comrades: their peace of mind, their complete indifference to theory and their profound belief in evolutionary progress through the medium of parliament.

In those days the Russian word 'socialist' was almost equivalent to 'martyr'. Socialists in Russia were required to be ready to sacrifice everything—comfort, ease, health, liberty and even life—in the name of the battle for their ideals. This was bound to endow them, and did in fact endow them, with a loftiness of spirit which made them feel that nothing in life deserved a moment's consideration except 'the Cause'. It was unworthy of a serious socialist to waste time on the trifles of life; indeed it was almost a crime.

Our English socialists felt nothing of the kind. They ate and slept well, amused themselves without a care in the world and were not afflicted by 'problems', as the Russians were. They danced morning, noon and night when they felt like it and even grown-ups sometimes carried on in such childish fashion that all I could do was shrug my shoulders. That is not to say, of course, that my English comrades in the camp took no interest in serious questions. They took interest all right, but only in their own way, the English way, placid and business-like and without any sort of mental anguish. Atkins, one of my tent mates, once said:

'I very much want to see socialism in England, but I only

M

think about it on Sundays when I have a bit of spare time, or at election time when I have to decide which party I am going to vote for. During the week I am too busy with my ordinary work.'

Here on holiday in the 'Socialist Camp' the English socialists had plenty of time not merely to 'think about' socialism but also to give serious consideration to its various aspects. But, bless me, what muddle-headedness then came to light!

I remember one day when there was a discussion about the progress of socialism in England. The young journalist from the Social-Democratic Federation who made the opening speech used the twenty minutes allowed him to set forth the basic Marxist principles on this question. I was filled with admiration. How clear and unanswerable was the case he put. How could anyone doubt the rightness of our great theory?

Yet when he had finished there was a storm of objections. Only one speaker gave voice to a measure of agreement with him: all the rest (ten in all) attacked him on various grounds. They had two main arguments. The first was that the basis of progress is not the economic factor but the 'moral instincts' in the heart of every man which found their highest expression in primitive Christianity. The second argument was that revolution was unnecessary in England because the change over to socialism could be effected within the framework of the normal parliamentary system.

An odd situation developed at this point. One speaker, for instance, asserted:

'And when we have established socialism there will be no need to change the existing form of government.'

Someone in the audience called out:

'Are we going to keep the King?'

'Of course we are,' was the emphatic answer. 'In England the King does what the people want. He will be a socialist King.'

Another speaker, a workman from Yorkshire, turned to the first speaker and said:

'According to you, in a socialist State bread will be distributed from State bakeries. That won't suit Yorkshire folk at all. Our workmen like to have their bread baked at home by their wives. If socialism means that the Government is going to

compel everybody to buy their bread from it, we Yorkshiremen
certainly won't agree to socialism.'

The young journalist seemed to regard this notion as worthy
of consideration. He frowned for a moment, as if coping with a
difficult problem, and then his face lit up.

'The Socialist Government could issue flour instead of loaves
to anyone wanting it, so the Yorkshire wives could go on baking
bread at home for their husbands.'

The Yorkshire man got up, politely thanked the speaker and
said:

'In that case I have no objection to socialism.'

This discussion astounded me at the time. That evening it
was continued in the tent which I shared with three Englishmen
—Atkins, a bank clerk from London, Macdougal, a printer from
Glasgow and Draper, a teacher from Yorkshire. They were all
kind and pleasant people and treated their 'Russian comrade' in
the most friendly fashion so that I could talk freely to them. I
learned much that was interesting about England and the English.

On this occasion we had a great argument. I explained at
some length the Marxist point of view on the problem of the
future form of society and the way in which the change from
capitalism to socialism would be carried out. But we could not
understand each other. Towards the end Draper said:

'Let me tell you a story which will show you better than a
long argument how the English settle their arguments.'

I gladly agreed and Draper settled himself comfortably, lit
his pipe and began:

'Do you know the city of ——?'

He named one of the big manufacturing towns in the Mid-
lands. I replied that I had heard of it but had never been there.

'At the end of the eighteenth century,' he continued, 'on the
outskirts of this town there was a big royal park which was
surrounded by a high wall and closed to the public. With the
growth of liberal sentiments, however, the townsmen began to
voice their dissatisfaction with this state of affairs, especially as
the King hardly ever came their way and never visited the park.
The ill-feeling became more acute when warehouses and factories
had been built on one side of the park and to reach them the
inhabitants had to make a big detour, whereas it was half the
distance straight across the park. The municipal authorities

began to press for the opening of the park. For this a special
Act of Parliament would be required. Five thousand pounds—a
very large sum in those days—was raised in the town to get a
bill through; nothing could be done without "gifts" and bribes as
corruption was rampant in parliamentary circles at the end of the
eighteenth century. A special delegation was sent to London to
put the business through. A member was found to introduce
the bill in the House of Commons for the opening of the park.
The King was furious and obstinate, and started a counter-attack.
The battle went on for three years and ultimately the House of
Commons passed the bill; but the House of Lords threw it out.
The town had suffered defeat.'

Draper took several puffs at his pipe and then continued:

'But the town was not down-hearted. Two years later it
started a fresh agitation, raised another five thousand pounds and
sent another delegation to London. The controversy raged more
fiercely than before. The King would not hear of any concessions.
It took all of five years for the bill to pass through the various
stages. It was even passed by a committee of the House of Lords,
but at the last moment the King bribed several influential peers
and the House of Lords itself threw out the bill a second time.

'Once again the town was not dismayed. Three years later it
introduced a bill with the same object into Parliament for the
third time. Its representatives laboured in London several years
and spent a great deal of money. It is impossible to say how the
affair would have ended had it not been for the outbreak of the
revolution in France. The King got frightened, and reluctant to
irritate the masses. Five years after the introduction of the third
bill the town won a complete victory, and the King had to sign
an Act of Parliament, passed by both Houses, which secured the
opening of the park.'

'Was that really the end?' I involuntarily asked.

'Well,' Draper continued, 'it had taken almost twenty years
for the town to win the right to have the park open, but as a
matter of fact the matter did not end there. The law had
decided, but the King sent secret instructions to his keeper that
the park was not to be opened. Nor was it opened. The keeper
actually installed a pack of fierce dogs to guard it.

'The citizens began to get excited and protested once more.
The Town Council met, considered its powers and decided to

give the King another year in which to change his mind. The year passed but the park remained closed. Public excitement increased. Then a bold citizen called Hartley, who had a small machinery business, came forward and said: "The Law gave me the right to walk in the royal park, but the King is forcibly preventing me from exercising my right. That is illegal!"

'Thereupon he climbed over the wall surrounding the park and "trespassed" in the park. The keepers caught him, beat him and brought him before the magistrates. The latter, who were also bribed, sentenced him to three months' imprisonment. Hartley served his sentence, but when he came out he proclaimed that he would assert his right again. He climbed over the wall once more and walked about in the park. Once again he was caught, beaten and sentenced and when he came out he said: "The Law is above the King, so I intend to go on walking in the park!" By now the town was in a fury. Everyone considered that he was perfectly right and that the King and the magistrates had violated the law. When he climbed the wall for a third time he was not alone: two dare-devils were with him. The keepers caught all three and they were sentenced to a year's imprisonment. The indignation of the citizens knew no bounds, and there was a mighty wave of protest against the unjust sentence. Meetings were called, seditious speeches delivered and signatures obtained to a petition demanding that the whole matter be reviewed. The agitation reached such a pitch that the authorities found themselves forced to do something to soothe public passions. The case of Hartley and his companions was remitted to a higher court which gave a compromise judgment; the period of imprisonment was halved, so that in view of the time they had already served they were immediately released.

'That amounted to the victory of the town. There was universal rejoicing and Hartley and his companions were the heroes of the day. Next morning Hartley led several hundred citizens in climbing the wall and strolling about in the park. The royal keepers did not lay a finger on them.

'Thus was the controversy between the town and the King decided, and decided once and for all. Since those days no one has questioned the right of the citizens to use the royal park.'

'A remarkably interesting story,' I said when Draper had stoked up his pipe again, 'but what amazes me is English patience.

In Russia the people would probably have started off by pulling down the wall and killing the keepers.'

Draper gave me a very superior look and then muttered:

'We're a democracy, and you are a tsarist autocracy.'

I was stung by what he said, but it was not easy to answer. We were in 1913 and no one could have foreseen what was to happen in Russia four years later. I felt that I could not refute his contention with arguments from facts, so I took refuge in an allegory.

'We have a famous fable in Russia, the story of Ilya Murometz . . . 'and I went on to tell my friends that remarkable work of the people's creative spirit which throws such light on human nature in Russia.

'Ilya Murometz,' I ended, 'sat in one spot for thirty years without moving, but when he got up he went so fast that no one could catch him. That's what will happen in my country when the hour of freedom from tsarist tyranny strikes. That hour is near.'

At that moment I had no idea that history would bear me out so soon and so dramatically.

Draper shook his head dubiously and then summed up:

'You Russians may have other methods; it takes us English a long time to win our rights but we win them for good. We don't need revolutions; we have Parliament. We shall get socialism that way.'

There was the sound of unshakable conviction in his words and, with very few exceptions, it was like that with all my comrades in the camp. Marxist ideas just did not get through to them.

CHAPTER NINETEEN

The Trades Union Congress

IN THE autumn of that year, 1913, I went to Manchester where the 46th Trades Union Congress was being held. I was familiar with German Party congresses and trades-union conferences, and had attended the International Socialist Congress at Copenhagen. These experiences had shown me that I could learn a lot about the Labour movement—on the national as well as international scale—from each of these reviews of the proletariat's forces. So when I found out that there was to be a Congress of the British trade unions in the Lancashire city from the 1st to the 6th September it was quite clear what I must do.

Londoners like making fun of Manchester. They say that it is a wet and dirty city, very provincial, out of step with the times and living on memories of the last century, its climate is the worst in England, and much more to the same effect.

But I liked Manchester from the first glance. I liked its big stone buildings, meant to last for centuries, and its industrial activities which stimulate trade all over England and even throughout the world. Here there was no trace of the aimless sauntering so often met with in London; here everyone worked and the place was like a boiling cauldron. I liked its streets, squares, buildings and shops. I liked that gloomy pile, its Town Hall. I even liked the soot which here lay even thicker than in London. Somehow I became a Manchester patriot at once and was not in the slightest bit shocked when a local inhabitant, solemnly raising a finger, sometimes said: 'What Manchester thinks today England will think tomorrow.' This saying dates from the previous century when textile manufacture was the main branch of British industry and Manchester was the real economic centre of the country. At that time all the great social movements—the struggle for reform of the suffrage, Chartism, trade unionism, free trade and much else—usually started in Manchester or found powerful support there. In the twentieth

century, when coal, iron and steel relegated textiles to a second-
ary position, Manchester's star began to wane. But human
psychology is more conservative than the facts of economic
development, and in 1913 the citizens of Manchester were just as
confident of their intellectual hegemony as they had been in the
days of Palmerston and Canning.

After settling in at a cheap hotel where many of the Congress
delegates were staying I began to take my bearings. The Congress
was to meet at the fine big Milton Hall. It appeared that it was
to be a sort of jubilee Congress as there had been a trades-union
congress in Manchester exactly thirty years earlier. That previous
congress had been attended by 153 delegates representing 509,000
organized workers. Now 560 delegates, sent by 2,232,000
members, had assembled. The movement had more than quad-
rupled. For those days such figures were enormously impressive
and naturally promoted an enthusiastic atmosphere.

It also appeared that the representation of foreign trade
unions was both larger and more varied than it had been on
previous occasions. At Manchester there were 'fraternal delegates' not only from the United States (there had been American
delegations before) but also from Canada, Germany and France.
In the German delegation was Karl Legien himself, the greatest
leader of the German trade unions, who was accompanied by a
dozen second- and third-rankers. From France came Leon
Jouhaux, the most prominent Syndicalist leader and head of the
General Confederation of Labour. In view of the rapidly approaching danger of war their presence at the Congress was particularly
significant. I was immensely impressed by all this, which greatly
increased my interest in the forthcoming meetings.

The opening of the Congress was typically English. At the
secretary's office on the previous evening an official whom I
knew said to me:

'Come with me to Manchester Cathedral tomorrow morning.'

'The cathedral?' I queried, doubting my hearing. 'Whatever
for?'

'What for?' replied the Englishman, equally surprised.
'There'll be a service in honour of the Congress.'

I was taken aback, but, with the experience of the 'Socialist

Camp' behind me, said nothing more. Next day, in the principal church of Manchester, there was in fact a solemn service which was attended by virtually all the delegates, headed by the president, W. J. Davis, and the secretary, S. W. Bowerman. The Dean of Manchester, Dr. Weldon, officiated. Towards the close of the service Dr. Hicks, the Bishop of Lincoln, preached the sermon. As his text he took the words of the Bible: 'We, being many, are one body in Christ and everyone members one of another' and developed them into a discourse in favour of brotherly solidarity among the working class. He laid stress on the necessity of paying special attention to the support of the weaker brethren—the agricultural labourers and the women. He admitted the lawfulness of the 'collectivist ideal' aimed at overcoming the evils of the day, but solemnly adjured us to see that 'we must keep moving gently forward'. He gave us a special warning against 'stagnation', in which he saw the 'greatest danger'. In his conclusion he strongly appealed for the international solidarity of the proletariat and said:

'The greater the sense of solidarity between Labour abroad and Labour in Britain, the better for the world at large. . . . The interest of the workers everywhere is international peace. . . . I hope and pray that organized labour may reach out its hands over the sea from country to country until principles of liberty, brotherhood and, above all, of international peace, shall be recognized as essential to the welfare of all humanity.'[1]

Members of the Congress prayed fervently, either standing with bowed heads or kneeling. While Dr. Hicks was speaking it was as if a wave of exultation passed over his congregation and the further he got in developing his theme the higher rose the excitement. One felt that if his hearers had not been in church they would have interrupted him by clapping.

I listened, looked, and was much surprised . . . and had another lesson in my study of the psychology and ideology of the English Labour movement.

On the following day, the 1st September, the business sessions in the Milton Hall began. Once more everything was quite

---

[1] *Trades Union Congress, 1913*, pp. 44-6. In writing this part of my memoirs I have refreshed my memory from the official record of the Congress.

English. The proceedings opened with the addresses of welcome,
of which there was a very large number. Letters and telegrams
were read and speeches made. Arthur Henderson sent the Congress the best wishes of the Labour Party and D. Johnston and
Tom Fox did the same for the Co-operative movement and the
Manchester Corporation respectively. This was followed by
speeches from two Manchester Labour M.P.s, J. R. Clynes and
J. E. Sutton, and Dean Weldon. All of them said only what
they could be expected to say on such an occasion, and I was not
particularly impressed except by the representative of the Church
who wound up his brief speech by saying that he saw great hope
in the development of the international activities of the Labour
movement as he considered that his hearers were far more
likely than other politicians to put an end to wars between
nations.[1]

As I listened to Weldon I could not help thinking of the
flexibility of the British bourgeoisie and the peculiar role of
the Church in England, a role very different from what I was
used to in Russia and from anything on the continent.

When the greetings were over W. Mullen, a textile worker,
thanked all the individuals and institutions which had organized
hospitality in Manchester and D. Williams, a musician who was
born in the city, turned to Mullen and said:

'I want to emphasize the point that all great movements have
sprung from Manchester and that all great men were born in
Manchester.'

The audience burst out laughing and then the President,
Davis, presented each of the speakers with a good large kitchen
knife. These were a gift to the Congress from the Sheffield
co-operatives. There was another loud burst of laughter and
everyone was highly amused. Even Dr. Weldon, clumsily
handling his knife, indulged in a broad, somewhat embarrassed,
smile.

All this seemed to me very odd. But we had not finished with
it. On the third day the 'fraternal delegates' from abroad offered
their greetings and at the end of their speeches Davis suddenly
rose and said, with a kindly smile:

'I now have much pleasure in presenting to the American
delegates a case of cutlery each.'

[1] *Trades Union Congress, 1913*, p. 54.

He bowed low and handed a fine case of cutlery to the two representatives of the American Federation of Labour, S. L. Braine and Louis Kemper. The Congress cheered vociferously. Both Americans were much touched and warmly thanked him. There was another loud burst of clapping.

Then followed the gifts to the other 'fraternal delegates'. P. M. Draper, the Canadian, received a gold scarf pin and cuff-links, while Legien, the German, and Jouhaux, the French-man, got the badge in gold of the British trade-union movement. There were more speeches of thanks and more thunderous applause. But the elation of the audience reached its apogee when Davis fastened a gold chain and pendant round Mrs. Kemper's neck, and presented Mrs. Draper with a beautiful silver bag. Both ladies were quite confused and wanted to get back to their places as fast as possible but there were loud cries of 'Speech! Speech!'

Mrs. Kemper's cheeks turned very red and she hastened to hide behind her husband, but Mrs. Draper was braver. She walked on to the platform and after thanking the Congress for the 'splendid reception' given to her and her husband said:

'I have always had every sympathy for the workers of the world in their struggle for betterment of their lot and, to use a familiar expression, flatter myself that I have got a good grip of the Labour movement.'

She received an absolute ovation.

One other thing struck me very forcibly—the excessive politeness pervading the whole atmosphere of the Congress. I have never favoured lack of respect or rudeness in relations between people and have always considered that, even in moments of fiercest controversy, energy of ideas should not be replaced by energy in expression. None the less the decorous behaviour at this workers' congress frequently perplexed me greatly. To listen to the delegates one would think that all the speeches were 'excellent' or 'brilliant', that all the resolutions introduced were 'valuable' or 'profound' and that every motion was 'wise' and 'far-seeing'. And there was an absolute welter of thanks. Practically every member of the Congress was thanked for something. Sometimes the level of farce was reached, as when Davis reported to the meeting on the activities of its executive bodies during the past year. Though he spoke for half an hour and his report contained no special revelations Ben Turner, the leader of the weavers, rose up and said:

'I have much pleasure in moving that our best thanks be given to our friend W. J. Davis—the only W. J. Davis there is, one of the stalwarts of the Labour movement—for his remarkably plain and useful statement of facts.'

R. Smillie, a miner and one of the outstanding leaders at the time, got up and added:

'I have pleasure in formally seconding the vote of thanks to the President for his address.'

Then the Congress unanimously passed the vote of thanks.

I sat and reflected: 'How very odd! It is the President's duty to make a report to the Congress. What is there to thank him for?'

Obviously the English did not agree with me.

Of course all this was by the way. What about the real work of the Congress?

It presented the greatest interest, but it was all very, very English.

In accordance with established custom the Parliamentary Committee—the principal executive organ of the Congress in those days—presented a very comprehensive printed report on its activities during the past year and this was discussed, section by section, at the sessions. In addition resolutions brought before the Congress by the individual trade unions were also debated. Such was the daily agenda. There was a good deal of 'small beer' in it, petty topics which took up a lot of time, sometimes stirred up much heat and really were of no importance at all. But there were also some big questions, in two of which I was particularly interested.

The first, a matter of the highest importance, was concerned with the events in Dublin, events involving the fiercest class conflict of those years. Here is the gist of what was happening.

In the years immediately preceding the Manchester Congress the trade-union movement in Ireland had made rapid progress. The form and aims of its organization followed the English pattern but in spirit it stood far closer to French syndicalism. This was particularly true of the strongest of the Irish trade

unions, the Transport Workers' Union, the leader of which at
the time was Jim Larkin, an extremely interesting and picturesque figure. Tall, well built, with dishevelled hair, blazing eyes
and a booming voice, he was a born rebel against the dictatorship of the money-bags and the poverty and the oppression
of the workers. The Dublin transport workers worshipped him
and his word was law with them. In his mind the idea of the
contemporary class war was strangely mixed up with the traditional Irish feud with England, and in a muddle-headed and
passionate way he pursued his personal plans for bettering the
lot of the working classes. He produced in Dublin his own
paper, *The Irish Worker*, in which he made fierce attacks on the
Irish employers. He was particularly bitter against their leader,
Murphy, the president of the Irish Chamber of Commerce,
owner of the Dublin tramways and proprietor of three Dublin
newspapers. Murphy paid him back in his own coin, never
ceasing from inveighing against him and accusing him of conspiracy to overthrow the existing order. In this way the class
struggle was complicated by the personal hatred between the
two leaders and this greatly increased the tension in the relations
between capital and labour.

Larkin did not like the English trade unions either. He
poured scorn on their strategy and tactics, their enthusiasm for
the idea of peaceful mutual aid and their efforts to avoid open
collisions with the capitalists and to settle all disputes by compromise. Instead of this he preached 'a policy of offensive' against
capitalism, attacks on individual employers, solidarity strikes in
support of strikes, refusal to handle the goods of firms on the
black list, etc. He did not stop at preaching, but carried his policy
into practice. Murphy's counter-attack was no less vigorous.
He once provocatively said that he was prepared to spend three-
quarters of a million to destroy the Irish trade unions. The
Government, in the person of the Lord Lieutenant, Lord Aberdeen, sided with the employers. The police constantly threatened
the workers with severe repressive measures. The public temperature was mounting every day and only a spark was needed
to produce an explosion. This explosion took place on the very
eve of the Manchester Congress.

The tramwaymen working for Murphy joined Larkin's
Transport Workers' Union. Murphy in fury dismissed two

hundred of them, and demanded an undertaking from the rest that they would not join that union. In reply all the tramwaymen struck and they were backed by the other transport workers. The class struggle immediately became extremely bitter. On the 30th August the strikers organized a big meeting which started at a hall and ended up at Eden Quay. Larkin and several of the Dublin trade-union leaders addressed this meeting. As always at Irish gatherings, there was a vast amount of noise, excitement and strong language but, generally speaking, everything passed off quite normally. There was no violation of 'public order'. Suddenly the police appeared and set about the workers with their truncheons. Two were killed and more than four hundred injured. The 'mob leaders', including Larkin, were arrested and lodged in gaol. The anger of the masses knew no bounds. On the following day, the 31st August, in spite of official prohibition, another mass meeting was held in O'Connell Street. The police attacked again and broke it up.

These happenings raised a storm of protest not only in Ireland but also in England, where such brutally frank methods of coping with the proletariat had long been abandoned. Even the London bourgeoisie considered that the Dublin administration had been 'too zealous'. The working-class world was furious and protested loudly.

The Congress, which opened on the 1st September, was dismayed and enraged by the news from Ireland. However much the trade-union leaders disliked Larkin, the affair was getting out of hand and seemed a dangerous precedent for the British Labour movement as a whole. So even on the first day, immediately after the greetings, Smillie demanded that the Dublin affair should be brought up immediately. He was warmly supported and the debate on the subject opened that very day. It was continued on the following day when a special delegation from Dublin attended the Congress. On the third day resolutions were passed.

I followed all the vicissitudes of this affair with the closest attention and it taught me a great deal about the psychology, opinions and methods of ruling circles in the English Labour movement.

The first burst of indignation among the members was very violent, and the discussions were extraordinarily stormy. There were many speakers, the language used was strong, emphatic and sometimes revolutionary. The hall resounded sometimes with bursts of applause, sometimes with loud cries of protest. At one moment the delegates almost came to blows and the atmosphere was explosive. But what actually happened? What actually happened was that J. Sexton, leader of the Liverpool dockers and a typical trade-union opportunist, proposed a resolution protesting in the strongest terms against what had happened in Dublin and demanding the immediate restoration of the right of public meeting in Ireland and a strict enquiry into the conduct of the police. He developed his argument in a long speech apparently based on the principle: 'On the one hand we cannot but admit; on the other we cannot but confess.'

Both the resolutions and his speech met with vigorous and well-deserved criticism.

Ben Tillett, the well-known leader of the London dockers, who played an outstanding part in organizing the unskilled workers at the end of the last century, deployed all the force of his great eloquence in a fierce attack on the Government. He even compared it to Russian tsarism—the greatest insult imaginable at that time. Amidst thunderous applause he bluntly advocated that to prevent any repetition of what had happened in Ireland the people should have the right to keep and use firearms.

With his burning ardour, inspired air, vigorous gestures and flaming eyes, Ben Tillett seemed the very incarnation of revolution.

Then the miners' leaders, Smillie and Stanton, made speeches calling on the nation to 'throw respectability to the winds' and answer the massacre in Dublin with a general strike.

With that the upward flight of the 'revolutionary' spirit in the Congress reached its apogee and the descent began.

After the miners' leaders came a gas worker, Jones, who proposed that the Congress should immediately be transferred from Manchester to Dublin. This would be both a form of protest against the action of the Irish police and a reassertion of the rights of free speech and public meeting which were being denied. Then a coal-miner, Whitefield, asked for permission to speak and cautiously suggested that under existing circumstances the most practical course would be to select a small delegation from the members and send it to Dublin to make a thorough investigation on the spot.

The official leaders of the Congress such as Davis and Bower-man openly sympathized with Sexton, but it was clear that if his resolution was put to the vote it would be thrown out. Something more was wanted. So the chiefs began to manœuvre. Of the proposals put forward during the debate they selected the most harmless—to send a commission to Ireland to investigate —and officially supported it as a rider to Sexton's resolution. Davis went to great lengths to prove how essential it was for Labour, especially at such a critical moment, to preserve unity in its ranks, and therefore it was inadvisable to insist on the adoption of extreme proposals which would inevitably cause dissension among the members.

The chairman's appeal had its effect. The polemics abated and the temperature fell. When Sexton's resolution with White-field's rider was put to the vote there was no opposition. Even Ben Tillett and Smillie voted in favour although Congress had in its resolution 'forgotten' the demand for the release of Larkin and his companions, a condition on which Ben Tillett had insisted. Then a delegation was chosen, with W. Brace and H. Gosling to lead it. It arrived in Dublin on the 3rd September.

In the course of its investigation the delegation questioned Lord Aberdeen, the Lord Mayor of Dublin, Murphy and the leaders of the local Labour organizations and, as might be ex-pected, came to the conclusion that there was not a shadow of justification for the brutality of the police. By way of reasserting the right of free speech and public meeting, the delegation called a big meeting in O'Connell Street. This meeting was addressed not only by members of the delegation but also by A. Henderson, G. Barnes and other leaders of the Labour Party. Lord Aberdeen did his best to dissuade the delegation from calling this meeting, saying that he feared the dangers of fresh 'disorders', but the members stood firm and eventually the Lord Lieutenant took the line: 'I do not authorize this meeting, neither do I forbid it; the responsibility for any possible consequences is on your shoulders.' In reply the delegation demanded that on the day of the meeting the police should be kept away; its duties would be taken over by three hundred marshals provided by the trade unions. Lord Aberdeen, making the best of it, was forced to agree.

In such circumstances the meeting took place and proved a

great success. Of course there was no 'disorder' whatever. But
the delegation did not succeed in securing either the release of the
imprisoned Irish leaders or any settlement of the conflict between
the workers and the employers. Murphy categorically refused
its offer to mediate. The struggle in Dublin continued after the
Congress was over. The English trade unions helped their Irish
comrades by raising funds, sending a ship laden with food and
in various other ways, but the Dublin workers did not manage
to win. After months of struggle the dispute was finally ended
by a 'compromise' which was of little advantage to them.

Such was the 'English' way of settling serious conflicts.

The other question at the Congress in which I took a great
interest was of a somewhat different character. At that time there
was a heated controversy over the right of the trade unions
to take part in the political life of the country. In 1900 a Labour
Representation Committee was formed, out of which the Labour
Party subsequently developed. This Committee was in the main
maintained, supported and financed by the trade unions.

This Committee had a good deal of success. At the General
Election in 1900 it secured 63,000 votes and the return of two
members. In the next three elections the corresponding figures
were: 1906—323,000 votes and 29 members; 1910 (January)—
506,000 votes and 40 members; 1910 (December)—371,000
votes and 43 members. The rapid growth of the influence of
Labour was extremely distasteful to the English bourgeoisie,
and as the Asquith-Lloyd-George Liberal Government then in
power did not consider it profitable to have direct recourse to
repressive measures against the political awakening of the proletariat the reactionaries decided to use the judicial machinery
for their purposes.

In 1908 a member of the Railwaymen's Union, Osborne
(prompted and supported by the 'diehards'), brought an action
against his trade union for the return of his contribution to a
special levy for political purposes which that union had imposed
on all its members. The court of first instance rejected his claim
but the higher courts pronounced in his favour. So over the head
of the Labour Party hung the threat of being deprived of the
main source of its revenue, as the decision in the Osborne case

N

was a precedent, the effect of which extended to all the trade unions.[1] A stubborn controversy, both in and out of Parliament, started at once. It had been going on for a considerable time when in 1913, not long before the Congress in Manchester, it was crowned with success; a new law was passed legalizing expenditure for political purposes, provided that the members of each union passed a special resolution to the effect that they considered it essential. The enactment in question was hotly debated at the Congress, and one point emerged in the course of the proceedings which made a very great impression on me at the time.

'In our ranks,' said Battle, a delegate from the cotton spinners, 'we have Liberals, socialists, and Conservatives. . . . I am not a member of the Labour Party and I have stood upon scores of Liberal platforms.'

Stokes, a representative of the glass blowers, added:

'I am a socialist, but I do not believe that there are many socialists in the trade-union movement. . . . It is the Liberal expression of opinion that comes from the Trades Union Congress.'[2]

At first I simply could not bring myself to believe these statements. It never entered my head that organized labour would not vote for the political representatives of its own class. But later on I had to change my opinion. A closer look into the atmosphere of the Congress and its reactions to the various speeches made me realize that even here, in this 'Labour Parliament', there were many adherents of the bourgeois parties. Liberals of Battle's type were not in the least ashamed to confess their political faith. The Conservatives preferred to keep silent.

In the corridors of the Congress I obtained statistical proof that my impressions were correct. Jim Middleton, a member of the staff of the Labour Party whom I knew well in London, gave me the figures for the number of trade unionists represented at the Congress and the number of votes cast for the Labour Party. What emerged?

[1] How serious the judicial decision in the Osborne case was for the Labour Party can be seen from the following figures: in 1912 it had 1,895,000 members, of which 1,858,000 were trade unionists and the rest members of organizations affiliated to the Party (the Independent Labour Party, the Fabian Society, etc.). So practically the whole financial resources available to the Labour Party came from the unions.

[2] *Trades Union Congress, 1913*, pp. 229–32.

Here is a little, but very significant, table:

Year	Number of trade unionists represented at the Trades Union Congress (in thousands)		Number of votes cast for the Labour Party (in thousands)
1906	1,555		323
1910	1,648	January	506
		December	371

This was remarkable. It meant that only twenty to thirty per cent of those paying their subscriptions to the Labour Party funds were voting for it at elections. What were the rest doing?

'The rest,' Middleton explained, 'voted for the Liberals or Conservatives or simply abstained. We have working-class families which, by tradition from generation to generation, cast their votes for one or other of the two established parties. Lack of class consciousness, you will say. . . . Of course it is. But you must realize that the Labour Party as a separate political organization for the workers is only thirteen years old. For the previous thirty years Trades Union Congresses through their parliamentary committee gave their votes to those members of the Parties who at election time promised to introduce legislation favourable to them. Sometimes they were Liberals and sometimes Tories.'[1]

'What you mean,' I interjected, 'is that the Trades Union Congress sold its votes to the bourgeois parties for reforms of some sort?'

'Why "sold"?' Middleton said with a grimace. 'Congress simply came to an agreement with the Liberals or Conservatives on the basis of "you scratch my back and I'll scratch yours". Now the position has changed. We have created our own party and we need the whole working-class vote to keep it going; but the psychological habits of many years are not easily eradicated. But wait; give us time!'

[1] The Parliamentary Committee existing in 1869 had in fact complete liberty to negotiate with either of the recognized parties. The task of this Committee is defined as:
1. To watch all legislation affecting labour.
2. To initiate such legislation as Congress may direct.
3. To arrange programme for Congress from resolutions sent from Trades.
4. To verify all delegates' credentials.
5. To arrange for the meetings of Congress.
6. To ballot for position and order of the resolutions.
7. To transact the business between each Congress.
There was no political programme (of even the most general description) of either the Parliamentary Committee or the Trades Union Congress.

He raised his hand in an expressive gesture and added:
'There's a law of progress. It's no good trying to go too fast.
We can only work hard, have patience and wait.'
How English it all was! I had been given another useful
lesson.

Of course, Congress was not concerned solely with 'domestic'
issues. The shadow of the First World War was already cast over
the European scene. The war had not actually begun but frequent
ominous flashes of lightning lit up the dark political horizon
heralding a storm in the near future. The 'Parliament of Labour',
meeting at such a moment, could not fail to touch on this painful
topic. It certainly did so.
I have already referred to what was said by Dr. Hicks and
Dr. Weldon at the opening of the Congress. But this was just
a start. A much more vigorous debate on the problem of war
began on the third day when the 'fraternal delegates' from other
countries appeared on the platform. It was true that the representatives of the United States and Canada devoted their speeches
wholly to the working-class movements in their own countries.
Threats of war did not concern them, and this was very characteristic; in those days the peoples of the American continent
firmly believed that two oceans could be relied on to keep international unpleasantnesses far away, and therefore took little
interest in what was going on beyond the frontiers of the New
World. But the delegates from Germany and France did not
for one moment forget the terrible apparitions on the horizon.
What did they say about them?
Jouhaux, the French representative, made a powerful speech
in which he described in detail the programme of syndicalism—
that symbol of faith, as he called it, of 'six hundred thousand
rebels' in the General Confederation of Labour—and went on
to say:
'I rejoice to see the international bonds of solidarity, of
mutual interest, becoming stronger day by day. This is a sure
sign that "race hatred" and the "barriers" of nationality are fast
disappearing in the ranks of the workers, making place for a
sentiment of international brotherhood which, in its development, will prove the real reason for the disappearance of wars,

which always have been, and always must be, fraught with dire consequence to the future of the international proletariat.

'War, whatever the causes may be which produce it, for the working classes has always been, and will be, an occasion for sorrow and misery. A war always is a set-back to the progress of civilization. For this reason then we should not hesitate to make a stand against it. To combat the possibility of future wars all available means ought to be considered as serving the purpose well if they will prevent the horrors and sufferings of future wars.'[1]

Legien, the German delegate, was even more emphatic:

'In their thoughts and aims the German and British workers are one. Neither languages nor political boundaries shall keep us divided. In spite of all those whose personal interests are in the direction of fomenting strife between the labouring classes of our two lands, who would even commit the crime of instigating war, we are here today to loudly proclaim our mutual, our common interests, which demand our brotherly co-operation if we are to successfully combat modern capitalism. . . . We are happy to know, however, that the working men of this country want peace and you may rest assured that the German workers too are out for peace. . . . I am convinced that war will be an impossible thing as soon as the toiling classes of our respective countries are unanimous on this matter.'[2]

In conclusion he invited Congress to send a 'fraternal' English delegation to the congress of the German trade unions which was fixed for June, 1914 (it never took place). It would, he said, be one more mighty demonstration of friendly co-operation between the English and German workers and a valuable contribution in the struggle against the danger of war.

Congress gave him a tremendous ovation. All the delegates rose from their seats, cheered vociferously and banged on the tables: peace was not restored for several minutes. I have seldom seen the phlegmatic English so greatly excited. In reply to the speeches of the French and German delegates on international solidarity and peace Congress passed a resolution which had been introduced in the name of the Liverpool dockers by F. Sanderson. It was in these terms:

[1] *Trades Union Congress, 1913*, p. 339.
[2] Op. cit., pp. 254–60.

'That this Congress strongly condemns any action likely
to lead to war between nations, and pledges itself to do everything
possible to make war impossible; and further instructs the Parliamentary Committee to confer with the Miners' Federation of
Great Britain, the National Transport Workers' Federation and
the National Union of Railwaymen with a view to opening
negotiations with foreign trade unions for the purpose of making
agreements and treaties as to common international action in the
event of war being forced on us.'[1]

Sanderson made a powerful speech in support of the resolution. He was loudly applauded. Then the resolution was carried
unanimously amidst a scene of great enthusiasm.

Now, many years later, when I think back to that resolution,
the ovation Legien received, the frame of mind in which the
Congress discussed the swiftly growing danger of war and when I
remember that only ten months later the First World War broke
out in Europe and the 2nd International collapsed like a house
of cards, I cannot help asking myself a question: was all that
happened in Manchester the result of blindness or hypocrisy?

It seems to me that there was both. There was blindness,
no doubt, the result of a lack of historical experience, that something which is well expressed in the phrase 'the wish is father to
the thought'. Unquestionably, however, there was hypocrisy
also, the hypocrisy of the man who is a coward by nature but
gets used to everyone else thinking him brave and so beginning
to believe it himself. In his innermost heart he knows it is not
true and he fearfully awaits the dread hour of testing, feeling
vaguely that he will never face it but meanwhile putting on a
brave show and trying to think of himself as a knight without
fear and without reproach.

I have another memory of the Manchester Congress.

Ernest Jones, one of the most brilliant of the Chartist leaders,
lived and died in Manchester. He was buried there in Ardwick
Cemetery, and admirers of the great tribune, poet and writer had
erected a modest but handsome monument to his memory.
At the beginning of the twentieth century both grave and
monument had fallen into a neglected and ruinous state. The

[1] Ibid., p. 339.

Trades Union Congress took action, and it was during the Manchester meetings that a new monument was put up. There was an impressive ceremony, attended by many of the Congress members. Davis, Bowerman and Henderson made speeches appropriate to the occasion. They spoke of how Ernest Jones had fought for the people's rights in days when it was difficult and dangerous to do so, that his ideas were an inspiration to the present generation of workers and that the Trades Union Congress and the Labour Party were still having to fight to achieve several important demands which had been made by the Chartist leader more than half a century before. So slowly did life move forward.

I was present when the monument was unveiled and the scene made a very strong impression upon me. There was much that was touching, profound and noble about it. It so happened that at that time I was studying the fate of the Chartist movement and Ernest Jones was one of my historic heroes.

Twelve years passed. In December, 1925, eight years after the October Revolution, I was counsellor at the Soviet Embassy in London and, finding myself in Manchester on business, felt an urge to visit Ernest Jones' grave again. A grey-haired cemetery keeper led me to the familiar monument. Memories of the past crowded in on me and for a moment the present was forgotten. I did not notice that the old man had not gone away but was still at my side, thoughtfully examining the inscription on the monument: 'Born 1819. Died 1869.'

'And what a grand funeral it was! The whole town was there. . . .'

I was taken aback and stared at him.

'What funeral are you talking about?'

'This man's,' he replied, nodding in the direction of Jones' grave.

'How do you know?' I asked incredulously.

'I saw it with my own eyes,' he answered quietly. Then, catching a look almost of terror in my face, he added, apologetically:

'I'm not a ghost from the other world. . . . I was a boy grave-digger at the time of Jones' funeral.'

I closely studied his face. He was certainly very old, this strange relic of a bygone age. His hair was silvery and there were deep furrows in his cheeks, but he was strong and held himself straight. I asked:

'Have you been working here ever since?'

A proud, satisfied look spread over his features. He took his pipe out of his mouth and said with great dignity:

'Next week I shall have been working in Ardwick Cemetery for fifty-six years. I have never left it.'

I was touched to the depths. The old man's last words were:

'Every man has his fate. . . . The longer a man works in one place, the better he works.'

That evening I paid a visit to the offices of the *Manchester Guardian*.

I had a long and most interesting conversation with the well-known Liberal, C. P. Scott, who was its owner and editor. He was a handsome, vigorous old man, approaching eighty years of age, and reminded me of an apostle. His silvery hair was like a halo round his large, expressive face, which seemed to be lit up by his clever, sparkling eyes.

I knew that for many years he had been the mainspring of the *Manchester Guardian* and that it was thanks to him that this 'Lancashire provincial paper' had become one of the most influential press organs in the world. I pressed him for details of the history of the paper, its organization and literary and political associations. He willingly answered my questions and often wandered off into reminiscences of the great men who at one time or another had written for his paper.

'Tell me, Mr. Scott,' I wound up, 'did not Marx and Engels at one time write for your paper? I seem to have heard of it somewhere or other, but cannot say exactly where.'

Scott tilted his apostolic head, reflected for a moment and then began thinking aloud:

'I began working on this paper in 1871. . . . I became editor in 1873. . . . Since that time I have never left the paper. . . .'

He screwed up his eyes once more, and concentrated. The effort furrowed his brow. At last he said:

'No, it was not in my time. . . . If Marx and Engels ever wrote for the *Manchester Guardian* it was before me.'

So Scott had been working for the paper for fifty-four years and been its editor for fifty-one!

The picture of the cemetery keeper suddenly came to mind.

Good heavens! How unchanged life in England is!

CHAPTER TWENTY

Black Towns

WHEN the Manchester Congress was over I did not return to London at once. Chance had taken me north to the heart of old industrial England, where its capitalism was born, and I wanted to have a closer look at this grimy, smoke-blackened region.

In 1912 I traversed the Ruhr from end to end, staying in towns and villages, making the rounds of works and factories and studying the workers' movement. I had thus obtained considerable insight into the Germany of those days.

Now I decided to do the same in England, and after the Trades Union Congress closed I went on a tour of Lancashire and Yorkshire. My Labour Party friend, Jim Middleton, had given me a letter of introduction which opened many doors and hearts. In some places I had friends myself. For a whole month I wandered from town to town and village to village, looking attentively at my surroundings, collecting facts and impressions, making observations and notes. I visited Leigh, Rochdale, Bolton, Blackburn, Burnley, Bradford, Leeds, Halifax, Huddersfield, Sheffield and many other places.

Spartan simplicity and austerity were the keynote of my travels. I had little money, so that I had to practise the most severe economy. Only on the rarest occasions did I take a train. I usually walked, carrying my rucksack, occasionally getting a lift for a few pence on a passing van. At night I put up at village inns and I got my food at the cheapest working-class eating-houses. Sometimes I enjoyed the hospitality of English friends only too willing to open their doors to a 'comrade from Russia'.

By degrees I began to distinguish the features of that gloomy, smoky region and the broad mass of the British proletariat. At that time much seemed strange and surprising, and it was only later, when I knew much more about English history, politics and economics, that I found the explanation (explanation, not justification) of a great deal which I had observed. Yet everything I saw and learned tramping round the industrial north was arresting, interesting and instructive.

During my wanderings in Lancashire and Yorkshire I kept a diary. Most of it was lost during the First World War but part has survived. Perhaps it will be best if I quote two extracts from notes I made at the time.

Burnley
Middle September, 1913

'What a town!

'At one time, 100 to 150 years ago, Lancashire must have been a delightful part of the world, as even now you can see here and there remains of its great natural beauties. There are soft green hills, swathed, as ever in England, in a thin mist, and small woods and coppices nestling in dark patches on the slopes and between the hills. Quiet streams amble down the bottoms of peaceful little valleys. In some places you see toy-like, narrow white bridges thrown across the rivulets, among them perhaps an old "Roman bridge" of somewhat unusual style. This visitor from days of long ago will be grey and weather-beaten, but standing at its post like some sentry from the times of the Caesars. And over hills, woods and streams there is always the wide vault of the low, pale, tranquil sky, which never beckons or draws the eye upwards. It must always have been like that, whether a hundred years ago or in the days of the Romans. . . .

'Yes, Lancashire was lovely then. But now . . .

'Imagine a long, level street with a row of low, two-storey houses on each side. They are not really houses but stocky brick barracks. Each barrack forms a whole row. The interior is divided by partitions into "separate homes", to suit English individualism. Two windows and a door, two windows and a door. I counted more than twenty such "houses" in one row. The smooth walls were of uniform, drab brick without any attempt at ornament. The windows were all alike, small and admitting little light. Each door had a number and an iron knocker instead of a bell. All the numbers and knockers were exactly alike. Porches, shrubs and grass are conspicuous by their absence.

'A wilderness of stone. Stone walls, slippery stone pavements, stone setts in the uneven roads. And soot everywhere! The houses are covered with a thick layer of soot, even exuding from the pores of the brick. Under one's feet grimy flagstones; above one's head thick, black clouds of smoke slowly rising from tall chimneys and hanging suspended in the raw, murky air. The sun seems to be a dim red globe and the people hurrying along the streets look like pale shadows with smoke-begrimed faces. When you blow your nose you leave a black mark on your handkerchief. You look down these grim, drab streets and a feeling of terror creeps into your heart.

'Next you must realize that there are hundreds of other streets exactly like this, all crossing and interlacing, a most fantastic maze. Amongst this chaotic tangle of brick barracks you see the huge factories with their giant chimneys. They are even blacker and more gloomy than the barracks, which are at least lived in. Somewhere in the middle there is a little square with a melancholy town hall, thickly coated with coal dust. At various points the steeples of a few churches, themselves not altogether unlike giant chimneys, rise from the surface of this frozen ocean of masonry. Imagine all this and you get some idea of this town which I am visiting. With its smoke, fumes and the ceaseless roar of machinery, it is just like a stone dragon lurking in a hollow and belching forth smoke and flames at the peaceful, green-clad hills around.

'Such is Burnley, one of the principal textile centres of Great Britain. It is a town of a hundred thousand people. What are they like?

'Yesterday and today I have been wandering about freely, studying the crowds in the streets. Grimy faces, calloused hands, awkward figures. Dark colours almost universal. A gay dress or a fancy tie is a rarity. Few silk hats. Old shirts of the type worn by labourers, scarves knotted round the neck instead of ties, flat caps. Another curious detail: at every step you hear a strange tapping on the pavement. Wooden clogs are very common in the industrial north.

'From outward appearances you can conclude with certainty that this is the kingdom of the proletariat, and this is not surprising. The rich bourgeoisie, the owners of the works and factories, do not live in black, smoke-begrimed Burnley. From the blood and sweat of these tens of thousands of workers comes their hard cash. The "normal" course of this cruel process is greedily supervised by a whole crowd of directors, managers and executives of various kinds. The flow of gold never ceases, but it is spent not in the industrial towns of Lancashire but in London, the south-coast watering-places, on the Riviera or in Egypt, under hot suns and far from the blackened barracks of the Lancashire workers. Yes, Burnley is a workers' town. That can be seen at every step. Hundreds of little shops, pubs, cinemas, fun palaces are all adapted to the needs of working people.

'When the evening sirens sound the factory gates open and a noisy human flood suddenly pours into the long, gloomy streets; the workers are going home. There is a buzz of conversation and they cheerfully jostle along, whistle popular tunes and fire jokes at one another. I always like watching the English proletarian crowd. There is an idea in Russia, and all over the continent, that the English are a prim, dry, stiff-shirt race. This is because the English who go abroad are usually members of the ruling class who look down with contempt on all the "poor foreigners". From them continentals get their notions of English people and the English character. But the ordinary Englishman, especially the workman, is a very different person on his own ground.

'The English workman is very courteous and obliging and has a kindly sense of humour. If he accidentally knocks into you in passing he will stop and apologize. If you do not know the way he will willingly direct you and even make sure that you have understood him properly. If you have run into some slight unpleasantness he will certainly try to brush it off with a joke of some sort; the English are very fond of jokes. They prize a joke above everything else. A man's ranking as a speaker here is determined very largely by his ability to introduce flashes of sceptical humour into his speeches. The English workman is extremely fond of children and they can get anything they want from him. No, there is nothing rude, stiff or standoffish about him, at any rate when you meet him in his own country. You can see that for yourselves in Burnley.

'I am very comfortably situated here, staying with Willie Jameson whom I met at the "Socialist Camp". He and his sister are warm-hearted folk and quite touching in their attentions to their "Russian comrade". Jack Bailby, another friend from the same camp, is also very helpful. They know everyone and everything in their town, and all their connections and acquaintances are at my service. They have given me a great deal of interesting information about local customs and practices and the workers' movement here. It is true that their socialism is very "pink" (even judged by English standards) and of course we often disagree, but I am extremely grateful for their friendly help.

'I am very interested in the spiritual outlook of the English workman. In Manchester I met what I might call the general staff of the British proletariat, its leaders and upper crust. Here in Burnley I meet the working masses. What are they like? What do they think about? Do they realize, and to what extent, the great mission of liberation which history has entrusted to the working class?

'When you get to close quarters with the English working man the first thing that strikes you is his indifference to books and politics. I have been in dozens of workmen's homes, here in Burnley, and elsewhere. I have hardly seen a book, apart from books of a devotional character and books about football.

'Newspapers? Yes, the workman reads newspapers, both the local and the London papers, but they are all bourgeois and only poison his mind. Even the bourgeois papers he reads in his own way; he starts with the last page, which gives the sporting news, and then goes on to the "sensations"—murders, court cases, scandalous divorces, etc., leaving the rest to the end. Usually there is no time or energy left for the "rest".

'Labour organizations? Yes, they do something to rouse the political conscience of the proletariat. Both the Independent Labour Party and the Labour Party produce their own papers, but even apart from their contents one can see that their circulation is small and they do not have much influence on the masses. What about the trade unions? But here perhaps it is better that I should refer to my talk with Ashton yesterday.

'He is the general secretary of the powerful Miners' Federation. He had come to Burnley on business. I happened to meet him at the local branch of the Federation and took advantage of the opportunity to make his acquaintance and discuss the English workers' movement. A picturesque figure is Ashton.

He has a fine head of grey hair and in every word and gesture there is boundless self-confidence and a sort of special trade-union dignity. I put a number of questions to him: among others:

' "How do you account for the fact that the Miners' Federation, with more than seven hundred thousand members, does not have its own paper?"

'Ashton gave me a look of condescending surprise.

' "What use would our own paper be to us? We are a purely industrial organization and pursue no political aims whatever. Why on earth should a limited company or insurance company need its own paper?"

'I admit that I was dumbfounded, so unexpected did I find his argument, especially coming from one of the most distinguished leaders of English trade unionism. . . . Well, if that is their attitude towards the political education of the masses it is no good expecting much.

'But if books and politics play no real part in the life of the average workman, what are his interests?

'To some extent this question is answered by the amount of spare time available to a workman (based on an average nine-hour working day and a forty-two-hour break, from one o'clock on Saturday to 7 a.m. on Monday). How does he spend his leisure?

'Basing my conclusions on what I have myself observed and what I have been told locally, it would seem that it is devoted mainly to three things—the "public bar", the club and sport.

'Let me begin with the "public bar". Some time ago I read in a statistical reference book that on an average every Englishman drinks every year two gallons of pure spirits—a very eloquent figure. Here in Burnley at every step I see striking illustrations to the abstract figures in the statistics. At every street corner there is a public house, sometimes two in a quite small block. At the bar you see whiskey, beer, ale, gin, brandy. You merely have to ask for what you want. You can always find someone in a public house, but it is particularly crowded and noisy in the evenings, when the grim factories are silent after the hard day's work, and before and during holidays. But what happens then! The glass doors of the "public bar" never stop slamming and the place is packed so tight that there would not be room for a pin.

Din of every kind, shouting, loud laughter, grey-blue clouds of smoke, the fat face (it might be a compound of blood and beer) of a barman juggling with amazing skill with a whole battery of taps, tankards and bottles. Amidst such surroundings the working man spends long hours, pushing his way through the crowd, drinking, smoking, talking to his friends, arguing over the last football match or guessing the results of forthcoming races.

'It is a melancholy picture, and becomes even more melancholy when you look closer and suddenly see that one of the most conspicuous figures is a woman. Yes, a woman! A prostitute? Certainly not. All these women are workers or the wives of workers. With a slight stagger and uncertain steps they force their way through to the door. Just outside there are perambulators with tiny infants in them, while older children are running about and shouting. They are waiting for their mothers, who have disappeared into the depths of the hospitable establishment.

'Now for the club. In Russia what we mean by "club", especially a workers' club, is associated with the idea of a wide range of cultural and educational activities, popular lectures on science, political gatherings, a well-assorted library, various kinds of mental recreation.

'In England it is quite different. The whole country is covered with a network of institutions called the Working Men's Club and Institute, usually established and maintained by philanthropic societies, municipalities or employers. Their official ambitions are high-sounding—the social education of working-class youth, the raising of its intellectual level, the promotion of the principles of citizenship, etc., etc.

'But in fact? A few days ago Jack Bailby took me to see the "Burnley Youth Club" in which he had grown up. He was most enthusiastic about it. The club was housed in a large stone building, had several hundred members and, as its manager proudly explained, engaged in all kinds of vigorous activities. What kind of activities? The following dialogue will show:

'Myself: "Is there a library?"

'Manager: "No. We have no library. Why should we? Our members come to the club not to learn but for amusement and recreation. There are some local and London papers in the hall. That's all we need."

'Myself: "Do you arrange lectures, excursions, conferences?"

'Manager: "No, not as a rule. But every Saturday we have dances for the members and they can bring friends."

'Myself: "Do you do anything else?"

'Manager: "We have billiard tables, special rooms for card games, dominoes, chess. A few play games—football, cricket and so on."

'Myself: "Do you sell spirituous liquors in the club?"

'Manager: "Of course. How can you run a club without drinks? No one would come. Have a look."

'He led me to a big room with a bar and an array of bottles, taps and glasses, and even a fat barman—just as in an ordinary public house.

'When we came out Bailby asked me what I thought of the club of his young days. I told him quite frankly. He was obviously offended. But what else could I do? I could not call black white.

'Lastly—sport. Of course sport in itself is a good thing, but here in England it plays a big political role, and a negative one at that. Awakening overwhelming passions in the worker's mind (and the passions are really fierce) it distracts his will and attention from the business of the class struggle. This became particularly clear to me here in Burnley.

'On the day of my arrival Bailby took me to a football match somewhere on the outskirts of the town. I had never seen a football field before and everything about it aroused my curiosity. I deluged him with questions which were probably very naïve from his point of view, though he answered them willingly and in great detail.

'It was the crowd which struck me most of all. It was huge— running into ten thousand, positively colossal in a town of about a hundred thousand inhabitants. The spectators were all working-class people, genuine workers. The most remarkable thing of all was their behaviour. What had become of the legendary English phlegm and self-control? The place was like a boiling cauldron. At every turn of fortune on the football field a wave seemed to sweep over the serried ranks, engulfing them in the same delirium. They shouted, booed, clapped, laughed, roared, frequently rising from their seats and frantically waving their hats and caps. They all seemed like men possessed and I could not help thinking:

' "If the English working man put into the political battle

half the passion he puts into football, what a wonderful country Great Britain would become!" '[1]

Sheffield
Beginning of October, 1913

'Sheffield is a great industrial centre, but very different from Burnley.

'In the first place it is much bigger: the population of Burnley is 110,000 while that of Sheffield is nearly half a million. Secondly —and this is more important—Burnley is the kingdom of textiles while Sheffield is the kingdom of metals. Hence the many differences and distinctions.

'Outwardly Sheffield is very imposing. It spreads over some fine hills, and through it flows a little river with a whole series of picturesque tributaries. It is called the Don. The town has several "sights"—the old church of St. Peter, built six centuries ago, the Theatre Royal, opened at the end of the eighteenth century, the library which has existed for one hundred and fifty years, the Town Hall in the renaissance style, the Corn Exchange, the Ruskin Museum and the famous Cutlery Hall in which all the threads of Sheffield's main industry meet. Everything here would seem beautiful and almost idyllic were it not for dozens of lofty smoking chimneys and the eternal pall of smoke over the city, poisoning the atmosphere.

'I am not as comfortable at Sheffield as I was at Burnley, as I knew no one here when I arrived. I am staying at a cheap little hotel and taking my meals at modest workmen's eating-houses. But I find a great deal that is interesting and instructive, especially the famous Sheffield industries.

'Legend has it that ores were smelted here even in Roman times, i.e. almost two thousand years ago. But it is a historical fact that in the fourteenth century Sheffield was famous for its manufacture of cutlery, and it is quite certain that 1624 saw the birth of the powerful Cutlers' Company which greatly developed this specific branch of industry and gave the city its present world-wide reputation. Of course, Sheffield's industrial activities have extended far beyond the traditional framework. At the present time it makes not only cutlery but saws, sickles, spades,

[1] See Appendix 9.
O

surgical and mathematical instruments and, of course, machinery
of all kinds. At the beginning of the twentieth century Sheffield
had become one of the biggest centres of the metal-working
industry in England with dozens of factories and a vast army of
metal workers.

'I visited several firms engaged in the manufacture of cutlery
and also some engineering shops and have talked with engineers,
charge hands and workmen. I have also made the acquaintance
of the local trade-union leaders (Middleton's letter proved useful)
and attended three trade-union meetings. I have found it all most
interesting and instructive. But the most interesting and instructive experience of all came my way yesterday and, as so
often happens, not in the bright raiment of the unexpected but
as the most ordinary, everyday, almost casual occurrence.

'Yesterday evening I attended a regular meeting of the local
branch of the engineering union. A few days before I had been
introduced to its secretary, Turner, a worker in a machine-tool
works in the city. He is an interesting man, about thirty, intelligent, shrewd, talks well and even reads books on economics
and socialism—an achievement not altogether widespread among
English trade unionists. Before the meeting he said to me:

' "Come to the branch meeting tomorrow and see how we do
our current business."

'I accepted the invitation, expecting nothing more than
routine proceedings, but got something else. . . . But I had better
let the tale speak for itself.

'At the start everything went off as usual. The meeting took
place in a back room of one of the Sheffield public houses. Some
twenty-five to thirty members were present. There was nothing
sensational in the agenda. Turner read out the minutes of the
previous meeting, which were passed without debate or amend-
ment. Then he reported on the subscriptions received during the
past month, complained of the slackness of some members in
paying and proposed measures to remedy this state of affairs.
After a short discussion the meeting approved his proposals.
Then a few minor matters were discussed—financial assistance
for a brother who was ill, the absence of guards on two frames in
a little engineering works, the non-payment of overtime to a
large number of workers and other matters of that kind.

'After forty minutes the business of the meeting had been got through and the members started to go home, leaving seven or eight who obviously wanted to stay on for a chat with their comrades. They gave their orders for more beer, gathered round Turner and then something most interesting happened, something which suddenly enlightened me on another and important side of the English workman.

'After a silent pause in which they all half-emptied their glasses a young man with red hair asked Turner:

' "When does the strike start?"

' "It's not time yet, Jim," Turner quietly replied.

' "What do you mean, it's not time yet?" retorted the red-head, suddenly warming up. "You committee chaps are always prepared to wait and see. You haven't got guts. . . . But in my opinion you'll get nothing by delay. . . . Let's tell the boss to-morrow that we won't work unless he gives us a ten per cent rise, and it's final!"

'All were on the alert at once. One felt that the young man's words had got home. Some of the men sitting at the table said, rather vaguely:

' "Of course. . . . We ought . . . It's time for a rise. . . ."

'I had the impression that the men certainly wanted to agree with Jim but could not bring themselves to say so openly. They all stared expectantly at the secretary, waiting for a lead. Turner took a few puffs at his pipe and then repeated in an authoritative tone:

' "And I tell you that it's not time yet."

' "Why not?" Jim retorted heatedly. "I think it's high time!"

' "No, it's not time yet," Turner replied, even more authoritatively. "We must wait another month or so!"

'After pledging his comrades to secrecy he went on to explain. It appeared that the owner of the works where Turner, the red-head and most of the other men were employed was in the throes of negotiating a big order for machinery for India. Thanks to a girl clerk he knew in the main office, Turner could follow the course of the negotiations. They were going well for the firm but not yet concluded. It would be a month before any contract could be signed.

' "Can't you see?" he said, his eyes now lit up. "If we strike now the boss may lose the Indian order; he'll be furious and, besides, his profits will suffer. . . . We shan't get a rise. But if

we wait for two or three months he will have signed the contract
and it will certainly have a delivery date and there will be
a penalty if he exceeds it. . . . Well, his profit will be at
stake. *Then*'s the time to strike. . . . Meanwhile we must be
patient."

'Turner's words made a great impression on his hearers and
there was a considerable change in the atmosphere. On all sides
you could hear:

' "That's quite a different story. . . . Of course we must
wait. . . . Haste won't do us any good. . . ."

'Even the red-haired Jim quieted down and ceased accusing
the committee of cowardice.

'The conversation immediately turned to India. Two of the
men had previously worked in Bombay and Calcutta and they
started exchanging reminiscences and discussing the country, the
people and the living and working conditions in that vast British
colony. It was very interesting. But what struck me forcibly and
also shocked me was their attitude towards the Indians. One felt
that they looked down on them almost with scorn, as if they
were beings of an inferior race. Even when one of them was
talking about the Indian workers in the textile factory where he
had been employed as a fitter for several years I could not detect
in what he said the slightest sign of any sense of class solidarity
one would expect. And yet he was an ordinary English workman
with calloused hands and factory grime on his face. His last
words were:

' "These Indians only keep wages down."

'The other speaker, who had worked on the railways at
Calcutta for four years, expatiated at great length on the "colour
feeling", i.e. that fundamental antipathy to people with black or
brown skins which, he said, was common to all Europeans in
India. With an intense air of conviction he proclaimed:

' "You can't help it. . . . It's from God!"

'I was most indignant and began to protest, but felt that my
words were falling on stony ground.

'Then the conversation veered to another topic. Jim the red-
head, who had been clamouring for an immediate strike, banged
his tankard down on the table and suddenly burst out:

' "I'm going to Australia! My eldest brother has already been
working in Sydney for four years and has sent for me. He writes

that wages in Australia are good and there's an eight-hour day. When spring comes, I'm off."

' "It's all very well for you," replied an elderly workman whose hair was streaked with grey. "You're young, and not married. . . . It's easy for you to move. I myself wouldn't mind clearing off somewhere—perhaps to Canada. I've relations there. But when you have a family—wife and three children—it wants a lot of thinking about. The fares alone cost a fortune."

'The topic of emigrating overseas at once livened up the party round the table. Not all of them were prepared to emigrate, but all spoke favourably of the idea. They exchanged opinions about the comparative advantages of this or that colony. They argued about where the climate was good or otherwise, where wages were high or otherwise and where work was easy or otherwise to get. In the course of this discussion it emerged that at least three-quarters of those present had relatives overseas—South Africa, Malaya, New Zealand, the Gold Coast, the Bahamas. Wherever they worked or served, they enjoyed a privileged position relative to the local inhabitants and were a cog in the vast administrative and economic machinery of the Empire.

'I could not help thinking of what Engels said about the skilled upper ranks of the English proletariat also benefiting from the exploitation of the colonies. True that all they get are crumbs from the table of the bourgeoisie, but even that has its effect; crumbs too can poison.[1]

'I experienced a feeling that here was a strange case of dual personality. Sitting round a simple wooden table were a number of live, English workmen, drinking beer, smoking pipes and engaged in ordinary human talk. But when I penetrated to what they were talking about they seemed somehow to lose their physical reality and become mere illustrations of Engels' theory. What I had just heard—Turner reckoning on forcing a rise in wages if his firm got the Indian order, and some of his comrades thinking of emigrating to the colonies—what was this but the exploitation of imperial possibilities by a group of English workmen? The objective sense of all this amounted to the "extra feeding" of the upper strata of the proletariat by the British bourgeoisie.

'One final impression.

[1] See Appendix 10.

'Today I was at the house of the cashier of the local printers'
union. He is a very cultured man, reads a lot and likes philo-
sophizing on various lofty themes. A few days ago he put me in a
very difficult position by asking me what I thought about the
relative merits of the Baptists and the Wesleyans.

'He has a nice young wife and a daughter of eight years of
age on whom he dotes. We were having tea and Jessie (as the
little girl was called) was playing close by me. I glanced at her
blonde curly head from time to time and said, intending a
compliment:

' "You're just like a little Russian girl."

'My goodness! You should have seen what happened to my
Jessie! Her little face turned a bright red, tears came into her
eyes, she drew herself up, turned up her nose, stamped her little
foot and burst out:

' "I am proud to be British!"

'At first I was simply dumbfounded. Then I remembered the
meeting yesterday and all became clear. Imperialism again; and
not the religion of the English bourgeoisie only. Its poison gets
into working-class heads too.'

CHAPTER TWENTY-ONE

The Giant in Chains

IN JULY, 1914, on the very eve of the First World War, I
was writing to one of my comrades residing in Switzerland
a long letter about my impressions of the English working-
class movement. Owing to the war this letter was never sent, but
I have kept it and it may be useful to reproduce it here because it
bears witness to my views in the years of exile.

'It is almost two years,' I wrote, 'since I began to take a
close interest in the various aspects of the Labour movement
here and I have finally come to the conclusion that the British
proletariat is a giant in chains.

'Of course it enjoys a degree of political liberty such as no
other working class in Europe can claim. It has the right to
form trade unions and strike, freedom of speech, public meeting
and demonstration, a substantial representation in Parliament
and trade unions with two and a half million members. So you
may wonder what chains I am talking about. Yet I venture to
assert that the British proletariat is a giant in chains, but the chains
are within, not without. It often seems to me that the chains
within are more dangerous than those without, the sort of chains
from which the Russian proletariat, for instance, is now suffering.

'According to the 1911 census, in England seventy-eight per
cent of the population lives in towns, only twenty-two per
cent in the country. This means that at least three-quarters of
the inhabitants belong to the working class and closely related
elements. Here there is no solid mass of the conservative peasantry
which in other countries props up the governing classes. Agri-
culture in England is the affair of the farmers, whose financial
position is precarious. In short, social and economic conditions
exist which should effectively guarantee the working class a
decisive voice in the government, especially under a comparatively democratic constitution. Yet in Great Britain the bourgeoisie is firmly in the saddle, as witness the fact that out of 707

members of the House of Commons only forty-three represent the Labour Party. How can this be explained?

'The explanation is precisely that the British proletariat is a giant in chains. Potentially it has enormous power but in fact it is extraordinarily weak because it is completely entangled in strong internal fetters which keep the conscience and will of the workers' movement—and particularly its leaders—in bourgeois captivity.

'What are these chains? They are many, but three predominate.

'The first is the legalism in anything and everything. The Labour Party members and trade unionists are firmly convinced that everything can be done in accordance with law and within the existing legal framework, i.e. through Parliament and the institutions established by Parliament. The supreme arbiter in the struggle is the ballot-box. No revolutionary action! Legalism, second nature with the Labour leaders, if not inborn, is certainly the fruit of tradition. They are quite unable to think or act outside it.

'This legalism is very closely associated with the philosophy of "gradualness" which is part and parcel of their views and actions in the political and economic sphere. There must be no sudden leaps or sharp turns. Everything must proceed gradually, step by step, by way of slow and almost unnoticeable evolution. "Fabianism" is the acknowledged creed not only of the Webbs, Bernard Shaw, H. G. Wells and other English intellectuals but also of the working-class movement, by which I mean the workers organized in trade unions, most of which are now the skilled upper crust of the proletariat, and especially their leaders.[1]

'The second chain by which the English working-class movement is fettered is semi-conscious imperialism; I say "semi-conscious" because if the average trade-union member or Labour sympathizer is asked point-blank whether he considers that cruel exploitation of colonial peoples is right, the answer is generally

---

[1] In his article, 'British Pacifism and British Dislike of Theory', written in the spring of 1915, Lenin, explaining how successful the British Government had been in arousing 'popular' enthusiasm for the war among the workers, writes that this would have been absolutely impossible 'were not the proletarian masses entirely disorganized and demoralized by the desertion of a minority of the best placed, skilled and organized workers to liberal, i.e. bourgeois, policy. The British trade unions comprise about one-fifth of the wage-workers. The leaders of these trade unions are mostly Liberals, and Marx long ago called them agents of the bourgeoisie.' (Lenin: *On Britain*, p. 233.)

in the negative. Many of them go on to abuse their own capitalists for making millions out of the exploitation of rubber and
gold while paying the native workers a starvation wage. Are they
sincere in saying this? In most cases, and subjectively, yes. But
unfortunately the average English workman does not think
these words out to their logical conclusion or, what is more
important, act on them. So only very few become convinced
opponents of imperialism and come round to the Marxist point
of view.

'An even more important element is the fact that the English
worker, especially the skilled worker, is to a considerable extent
a "partner" of the English capitalist in exploiting colonial peoples.
It is precisely the super-profits of colonial exploitation which
enable the British bourgeoisie to make economic concessions to
the higher ranks of the proletariat from time to time, and it is
only the vast extent of the colonial possessions which enables the
English worker dissatisfied with his position at home to "seek
his fortune" overseas somewhere in the giant British empire.
When such men emigrate it also means that England gets rid of
the more "restless", i.e. the more energetic and revolutionary
of the proletariat. Half instinctively, half consciously, that
particular section of the working class feel its dependence on
the relative benefits derived from the exploitation of the Empire
and such a feeling cannot fail to find expression in its thoughts and
actions. What I have said applies even more to the higher ranks
in the Labour Party and the trade unions.

'The third chain is religion. Wreathed in sweet-smelling
spiritual garlands it may be, but none the less it is a very powerful
and reliable ally of the governing classes.

'At home in Russia the position of religion is extremely
simple. The Orthodox Church in tsarist Russia, particularly
during the eighteenth and nineteenth centuries, was a mono-
polistic, strongly centralized organization, wholly subordinate
to the secular power. In effect it was a government department for
religious affairs, so it followed quite naturally that every Russian
becoming conscious of political life, and whether landowner,
bourgeois, intellectual, worker or peasant, became an enemy not
only of absolutism but also of the Church.

'In England the position is very different.

'In the first place the English Revolution in the seventeenth century was carried through under the banner of religion. The class struggle between the bourgeoisie and the landowners for political power wore the clothing of a war of creeds. With Cromwell Puritanism played the same part as Rousseau's teaching did with the men who carried through the great French Revolution; and such was the influence of this revolutionary-religious ideology of the seventeenth century that the traditions it created have been preserved among the workers right up to the twentieth century.

'Secondly, for many centuries in England the Church was not a single and strictly centralized organization, closely linked with the lay State and supporting it at all times and under all conditions. Here religious life flowed through a number of streams, and not one of them was able to dominate the others unconditionally, and much less suppress them. It is true that one of them, the "Anglican" Church, became the State Church, but even at the present time its adherents are not more than twenty-five per cent of the population of the whole country.

'What about the remaining seventy-five per cent? They are divided into "sects" or "Free" Churches as they call them here. Among them you will find every colour in the political spectrum, from extreme right to extreme left; but—it need hardly be said— the overwhelming majority of the currents of religious thought in Great Britain (whether in the "Established" or "Free" Churches) are opposed to revolution and at best favourable to the Fabian point of view.

'All the Churches have equal rights and there is no discrimination. The worker, even the progressive worker, dutifully respecting ancient traditions and prejudices, seeks and finds the Church best suited to his taste and temperament. The Wesleyan sect, for instance, is very popular in Labour circles and has hundreds of thousands of adherents amongst the proletariat. Very many Labour leaders belong to it and have been lay preachers in their younger days.

'The influence of religion in England is greatly increased by the "independence" (often more apparent than real) of many of the sects or "Free" Churches, some of which frequently indulge in strong criticism of the civil authorities and even the existing social order. There have been times when prominent nonconformists (another name for members of the "Free" Churches) have sided openly with the masses and even become leaders of revolutionary movements. I need mention only the case of Stephens, the Wesleyan minister who was one of the Chartist leaders. It was by no means unique. The "independence" of the nonconformists had a great effect on the masses, who began to reason that the State and religion were not the same thing and should not be mixed up.

'Nor were the Churches alike; there were bad ones, which were only for the rich, and good ones, which sympathized with the workers and should therefore be supported. The result was that there grew up in the minds of millions of simple people the conviction that it was possible to oppose a reactionary government with all their might while remaining a good Christian.

'Such being the case, even the Church of England found itself compelled somehow to veil its close connection with the Government and sometimes play at opposition (of course it was a toothless pretence). More usually, at moments of crisis it assumed the role of conciliator between the Government and the masses. It was fond of making a show of tolerance towards the "radical priests" who were occasionally found in its ranks. At the present moment, for instance, there is much talk in London about the "very left-wing" sermons of a clergyman named Temple. No one is trying to shut him up. Why should they? One Temple amongst the thousands of "loyal" servants of the Church cannot do any harm—on the contrary, the Church can make political capital among the masses out of its "liberalism".

'And the final result? Let me illustrate what I think by a picturesque scene which I recently witnessed.

'I learned that Keir Hardie, the founder and leader of the Independent Labour Party, was to preach at a church in the provinces, and went there to hear him. After the ordinary service, with its prayers and hymns, came the sermon. Keir Hardie went into the pulpit. With his striking, open face and his halo of snowy-white hair, he was like one of those prophets who look down on us from the walls of ancient churches. He took for his text the words from the New Testament: "It is easier for a camel to go through the eye of a needle than for a rich man to enter into the Kingdom of God." He pushed off from this text, and then really let himself go! He wrathfully stormed at all the evils of capitalist society, cursed the bourgeoisie and called

on the proletariat to fight for socialism. And how did he finish up?
With a summons to vote for the Labour Party, the only party
to defend the interests of the workers, at the next election. Once
more—the ballot-box as the final arbiter in all political questions!

'The church was filled to the doors and the big congregation
swept off its feet and moved to the depths by his burning eloquence. Sympathetic murmurs could be heard on all sides,
eyes flashed and clenched fists were raised towards the pulpit.
When he had finished there was a roar of approval, like a wave
breaking on the shore. The people rose in their seats and as they
went out made a narrow path for him to pass to the door, like
Christ leaving the temple. At the porch he was mobbed by a
group of children of various ages. They laughed, shouted, sang
and waved and he smilingly patted their heads and defended
himself as best he could. The scene was almost biblical.

'I could hardly believe my eyes. Where was all this happening? And when? It was happening in the twentieth century in
England, the greatest capitalist country of our time!

'Those are the three main "internal" chains which fetter
the British proletariat at the present time. In such circumstances
can we be surprised that Fabianism and gradualness are the basic
political ideology of the workers' movement here?

'Such being the facts, how can we account for them? I have
spent a great deal of thought on this subject, and can only put
forward one theory which I think may well be the right one.

'England is an island. A strip of water, thirty-five kilometres
wide, separates her from the continent and for the past nine
hundred years has been a barrier against invasion. The result is
that here there has been no big land army such as France, Germany
and Russia have had to keep up because they always had to be
ready to defend their frontiers. England's advantage has had
great political consequences. The governing classes of the continental States, which disposed of powerful armies, used them
not only to fight external enemies but also to buttress their own
position in the country. With guns and bayonets behind them,
they felt far more independent of the masses and therefore feared
them less and treated them with less consideration. In case of
necessity they could resort to open force in defence of their
privileges.

'In England the position is quite different. There was no

large land army at the disposal of the governing classes. There was, of course, a powerful navy, but the number of men in even a very powerful navy was comparatively small, especially up to the twentieth century, and the navy itself is usually at sea, dispersed, and cannot be concentrated quickly in one place. For these reasons the navy is unsuitable for use in the internal political struggle. As a result the ruling classes in England have lacked that sharp weapon with which their counterparts on the continent established and maintained their dictatorship. They have had to resort to more subtle and discreet methods of keeping themselves in power. They did not fail to find them and over the centuries they really did work out such methods. Figuratively speaking, on the continent the masters of life imprisoned the bodies of the workers; the English masters mainly have imprisoned their souls. In the process two influences have been particularly important— the cult of tradition and the cult of compromise.

'Let me take tradition, a real Scheherazade, first. I will give only two characteristic examples.

'In 1605 the Scottish Catholics, dissatisfied with King James I, conspired to blow up the King and all the Members on the day of the solemn opening of Parliament. Barrels of gunpowder were concealed in the vaults of Westminster, and an officer, Guy Fawkes, was to fire the train. The plot was discovered in time and Guy Fawkes and his companions paid with their lives. Three centuries have passed since that time, and now not even a lunatic would think of blowing up Parliament. Yet up to the present day, before every session of Parliament the officials of the House of Commons visit the cellars with lanterns and search them from top to bottom, to satisfy themselves that no gunpowder barrels are concealed anywhere. Why? Only because of tradition. And if you voice your doubts to an Englishman he will answer with a smile: "What's wrong with it? It's a picturesque old custom."

'Another example. At the beginning of the nineteenth century the House of Commons Chamber had room for 450 members. That was because the number of members had been fixed at 450 in the seventeenth century. By the beginning of the last century the number of members had increased to 600, so that on really big days many of them had to sit in the galleries or crowd into the gangways. You would think that they would have enlarged the building. But no! Tradition dictated that the building must not be altered. They put up with the inconvenience and patiently waited. In 1837 there was a great fire and the old House of Commons was burnt down. They built a new one, the one you see on the bank of the River Thames at the present time. Again you would think that the new Chamber would be large enough to accommodate the actual number of members. Not a bit of it! In the name of tradition the new chamber was an exact copy of the old one. As before, it had only 450 seats and so it has remained, although the number of members has risen to 707. Ask an Englishman whether this is a good idea, and he will reply quite seriously: "It's very pleasant to be following in the footsteps of one's ancestors."

'I could give plenty of other instances, but it is hardly necessary. The cult of tradition is deep-rooted in English life, and so widespread that in addition to various political and social curiosities it sustains certain institutions and ideas which are hopelessly out of date, but still of some use to the ruling classes. The House of Lords and the religious prejudices of the masses spring readily to mind. Is not everyone aware that in England tradition still gives legal validity to hundreds of ancient laws which were passed centuries ago but have long outlived their purpose? Of course, in normal times they lie quietly on their shelves. But at certain times, and particularly when the ruling classes want to put pressure on the proletariat, the rusty legal arsenal of days gone by can always produce some mediaeval arquebus or battle-axe which can be used against the working class.

'In the interests of truth I should say that this cult of tradition is not solely the product of deliberate calculations by the ruling classes. Undoubtedly it also owes its existence in great measure to the fact that for nine hundred years England has never known a foreign invasion, so continuity prevailed here far more than in other European countries. Such is the objective factor. Yet none the less the ruling classes long since realized the political advantages they have derived from this situation and began deliberately to canonize the cult of tradition. They surrounded it with an aura of worship and affection, burned incense to it, swore by it as one of the most important pillars of English life. From their point of view they were right: the cult of tradition was—and still is—of inestimable value to them.

'What about the cult of compromise? It also has developed
in the course of centuries, becoming particularly potent after
the revolution in the seventeenth century and the loss of the
American colonies at the end of the eighteeneth century. Of
course it would be wrong to think that the ruling classes always
willingly made concessions to the demands of the masses. Nothing
of the kind! They always rigidly and very stubbornly insisted
—not sticking at bloodshed—on their privileges, occasionally
driving the masses to the brink of open revolt. . . . The brink—
that is the point! After Cromwell they never went further, and
never put the masses in a position where revolt was the only way
out. At the last moment, five minutes before the explosion, they
made concessions, the minimum, of course, but in time to avert
the threatened conflict, at least for the time being.

' "In time" and "by appropriate measures" are indeed the
tactical principles which have guided the ruling classes when they
have bowed to the inevitable and changed course in any dangerous
historical crisis. This has been the essence of their political shrewd-
ness, and it must frankly be admitted that in the last two and a
half centuries they have shown great skill in this respect and
made considerable political capital out of it. Let me give you
two examples to show what I mean.

'The first is the struggle for the parliamentary vote. At the
beginning of the nineteenth century a fierce campaign was
raging for the reform of the old electoral system which ensured
the domination of the House of Commons by the landed gentry.
Many sections of the bourgeoisie, including the most influential,
and a vast number of workers who were just becoming politically
conscious, demanded the right to vote at parliamentary elections.
The struggle for electoral reform became more intense and
violent every year. After the July Revolution in France in 1830
it assumed such forms and dimensions that open revolt was in
the air. The tension was so great that there could have been an
explosion at any moment. The feudal landowners realized the
danger and in 1832 the well-known Reform Bill was passed,
which at once changed the position and averted the danger of
revolution.

'Changed in what way? The English way, of course. The new
electoral law in no way satisfied the demands of the masses. The
old law gave voting rights to three per cent of the population,

the new to four and a half per cent. The big bourgeoisie was satisfied, but the proletariat continued to be shut out of Parliament. By their tactics the landowners destroyed the unity which had previously prevailed in the other camp; they attracted the more moderate elements among the reformers to their own side, and postponed the grant of the parliamentary franchise to the workers for many a long year. Only the reforms of 1867 and 1885, introduced at a time when thunderclouds were beginning to gather on the political horizon, enfranchised the upper crust of the proletariat and the farmers. The mass of the working class got nothing. The final result was that, thanks to the tactical compromise, reached "in time" and "by appropriate measures", the ruling classes have succeeded in preventing the introduction of a truly democratic franchise right up to the present time.[1]

'My second example is the Chartist movement. The disillusionment of the workers over the 1832 reform drew them to the left, and together with some other factors of a political and social order contributed to the creation of that great revolutionary movement among the proletariat which became known as "Chartism". The programme of the Chartists, the so-called "Charter", was on the face of it purely political and had six points: universal suffrage, the secret ballot, equal representation, annual parliaments, abolition of property qualifications for parliamentary candidates and payment of Members. Formally, therefore, the idea was to complete that democratization of the franchise which had been carried halfway by the reforms of 1832.

'But in essence the Chartist movement was more social than political. It was nourished on the terrible poverty of the labouring masses which was the result of their merciless exploitation by capital and the very high cost of living due to the taxes on corn. When they talked of parliamentary reform the Chartists were really thinking of the social and economic transformation of society, and some of their leaders, Stephens the minister, for instance, openly admitted that fundamentally Chartism was not a political question but a "knife-and-fork question".

'The Chartist movement attained really formidable proportions. Millions flocked to its banner. Towards the end of the thirties and the beginning of the forties the situation became

[1] Universal suffrage, in the bourgeois-democratic sense, was attained in England only in two stages, in 1918 and 1928.

particularly ominous for the ruling classes. The Chartists presented petitions to Parliament, bearing millions of signatures, demanding that effect be given to the Charter—but Parliament remained deaf to the appeal. This strengthened the hands of that section among the Chartists which was known as the "Physical Force Party", because it favoured revolutionary methods. In some places riots and revolts began. Everything suggested and everyone said that England would soon see a mighty conflagration which would burn the bourgeois State to the ground.

'But what did the ruling classes do at this critical moment? They decided to make concessions. But how? As ever, on purely English lines. The high duties on corn in Great Britain at that time were profitable to the large landowners but disadvantageous to the industrial bourgeoisie because they increased labour costs. So in the forties Cobden and Bright, then the prophets of English Liberalism, started a great campaign in favour of the abolition of the corn laws. A large section of the bourgeoisie supported them for the reason I have given. The abolition of the duties on corn also promised to do something to reduce the mounting tension in the working classes, which was also to the interests of the bourgeoisie. So in 1846 the English Liberals won a great victory; the duties on corn were repealed. The bourgeoisie killed two birds with one stone; on the one hand labour costs were reduced and the masses were to a certain extent appeased, as the lower cost of living temporarily (very temporarily) improved their material position and weakened their revolutionary zeal. Moreover, in the economic state of the world at the time, when England was the only industrial country among all the agrarian countries in and outside Europe, free trade guaranteed the British bourgeoisie forty years of exceptional prosperity. As a result, Chartism, despite the European revolutions in 1848, began to lose ground more and more and the Labour movement, taking advantage of the favourable economic conditions, increasingly took the line of moderate trade unionism which it still follows.

'In short, thanks to those same tactics of well-timed and adequate measures of compromise, the ruling classes in England emerged scatheless from the most serious crisis without making any political concession whatever to the working class.

'So much for the past. What about the present? The present

P

is no different. Is not Lloyd George in fact playing the same part
—making the inevitable allowance for time and circumstance—
as Cobden and Bright played seventy years ago?

'Yes. The cult of tradition and the cult of compromise over
the centuries have done good service to the ruling classes in
England. But there was an essential condition precedent to all
this—*wealth*. If they had not been exceptionally rich there would
have been nothing with which to make concessions and if there
had been nothing to concede there would have been no cult of
compromise. Then the whole political history of England would
have been very different.

'But the ruling classes were lucky in their history. From the
sixteenth to the eighteenth centuries robbery, force and cunning
enabled them to build up a huge colonial empire on which they
have lived and continue to live, and to build it up in such a way
that a big standing army has not been necessary (the world had
not been divided up then!) on land. The increase of wealth did
not involve the growth of militarism, with all the consequences
it entails. In the nineteenth century there were added the con-
version of England into the world's industrial workshop and a
colossal increase in her foreign trade. In short, a sound and stable
economic basis was created for that political system which, in the
long run, has made the British proletariat a giant in chains.'[1]

[1] See Appendix II.

CHAPTER TWENTY-TWO

The Kidnapping of Sun Yat-Sen

WHAT I am going to relate took place on the 11th October, 1916. I well remember the date, and my story will show why.

I had just come from an international meeting on the war and with me was a friend by the name of Davis. He was Welsh by birth and over sixty years of age. Tall, thin, gauche and with dark hair already turning grey, he resembled one of those rag dolls which can be folded in two. The most remarkable thing about him was his eyes, big, bright eyes with a mad touch in them. Looking at him, you felt at once that he was an unusual phenomenon—genius or lunatic? Such extremes are not often met with; but Davis was a typical English crank. He lived on nothing but milk and nuts, only wore clothes woven by hand and never used any form of transport except horses. There was a great deal of William Morris in his opinions, but he was a member of the Independent Labour Party and an ardent pacifist. He had known very hard times. Something had gone wrong in his life, and in his old age he was earning his bread by petty journalism. His speciality was famous dates. He remembered vast numbers of them and whenever he entered some editorial office he would come out with:

'It's just two hundred years today since . . .', and go on to mention some outstanding event in English political, military, economic or cultural history. Thereupon he was either chased out of the offices or invited to sit down and write a short article on the event in question for the next issue of the paper. He would then scribble his article on scraps of paper without any help from reference books or encyclopaedias. His memory was extraordinary and in the course of a long life he had accumulated a vast store of facts and data.

On this memorable evening I was walking home with him. It was a cold, damp and windy evening. Through narrow streets

we arrived at Portland Place and walked briskly in the direction
of Regent's Park. He suddenly gave a start and stopped in his
tracks. I automatically did the same and looked enquiringly at
him. He did not move but stood gazing raptly at a tall, gloomy
building at the corner of Portland Place and Weymouth Street.
In the half-light from the dim street-lamps (there was a blackout
at the time) I read the number on the house—it was 49. Not
knowing what Davis was up to I murmured:

'What's the matter, Mr. Davis?'

He quickly gave me his half-mad look and asked in turn:

'Have you ever heard of Sun Yat-Sen?'

'Yes,' I replied. 'He is a well-known Chinese revolutionary.'

'Quite right,' he said. 'And do you know what this house—
No. 49—is?'

'No, I don't.'

Davis suddenly became very excited, glared wildly at me
and erupted:

'It's the Chinese Embassy! . . . Today is the 11th October. . . .
It's exactly twenty years today since it happened!'

'What happened?' I asked.

He clutched my hand and dragged me after him.

'Let's go into Regent's Park,' he blurted out as we hurried
along. 'We'll find a seat somewhere and I'll tell you the story. . . .
It's rather a long one.'

When eventually we settled down on a bench in the gloom
of that nasty October evening I heard from his lips a story which
seemed more like some product of fiery Eastern fantasy than a
sober record of something that had actually happened in London.

Towards the end of the eighties young Sun Yat-Sen was
studying medicine at the English university in Hong Kong. Here
he became very friendly with the family of one of his teachers,
Professor James Cantlie. After his university days were over he
took an active part in the national-revolutionary movement in
China and soon became its most prominent leader. The Celestial
Government was soon hot on his heels and its agents searched for
him all over the world. At that time Cantlie, having finished his
work at Hong Kong University, had returned to London and
was living at 46, Devonshire Street, a stone's throw from the

Chinese Legation. This was a pure coincidence, of course, but it played an important part in the drama of which Davis was speaking.

On the 1st October, 1896, Sun Yat-Sen secretly arrived in London for a short stay. No one except Cantlie was to know of his presence here, and he was sure that no one would know. But of course the Chinese revolutionary frequently visited his old friend.

'On the morning of the 11th October, just twenty years ago,' said Davis, 'Sun Yat-Sen was on his way to Cantlie's house when he was suddenly accosted by two Chinese. They began to talk to him in his own Canton dialect. Despite his usual caution, and relying on his incognito, he not only engaged in conversation with them but actually agreed to go with them to where they were staying—just round the corner, they said. But he had hardly crossed the threshold before the door banged to behind him and the great revolutionary was trapped. Only then did he realize that the house his fellow-countrymen lived in was part of the Chinese Legation, but by that time it was too late to escape.

'So the Celestial Government had caught its mortal enemy! It did not dare to kill him in London, however, and ordered its minister in England to smuggle him out on a Chinese ship to China, where he would be beheaded. While all the preparations were being made he found himself a prisoner in the Legation and completely isolated from the outside world. But Sun Yat-Sen was not the sort of man to take reversals of fortune lying down.

'At first,' continued Davis, 'he thought of throwing notes, requesting the finder to inform Cantlie of his arrest, from the window of the room in which he was confined. But this was no good; the only window in his prison looked on to a roof which in turn was overlooked by other high roofs. Then he thought of bribing one of the Legation servants and in that way getting in touch with Cantlie. But all the staff were terrified, and even if some of them sympathized with him they were much too frightened to show it. But the great revolutionary was not going to give in. He considered all the possibilities of rescue and eventually solved his problem.

'The Legation staff included English as well as Chinese. One of them, a certain Mr. Cole, showed obvious sympathy with the

prisoner and the latter soon turned that sympathy to good
account. He explained to Cole that he was himself a Christian
and convinced him that his sole aim was to give China the
same political system which England enjoyed, and that if he
was sent back to China death at the hands of the executioner
awaited him. He fortified his arguments with the promise of a
substantial sum of money. All this made a great impression on
Cole, who was much perturbed and shared his secret with a
compatriot, Mrs. Howe, who was employed as a housekeeper
at the Legation. Mrs. Howe was a kind-hearted woman, and
the fate of the unfortunate captive became a matter of the greatest
concern to her. She agreed to take a note from Sun Yat-Sen to
Cantlie, but only without giving herself away. Accordingly, in
the evening of Saturday, the 17th October, six days after his
arrest, a note in the following terms was slipped under Cantlie's
front door:

' "There is a friend of yours imprisoned in the Chinese
Legation here since last Sunday. They intend sending him out
to China, where it is certain they will hang him. It is very sad for
the poor man, and unless something is done at once he will be
taken away and no one will know it. I dare not sign my name,
but this is the truth, so believe what I say. Whatever you do must
be done at once or it will be too late. His name, I believe, is Lin
Yen Sin."

'Cantlie had been racking his brains, but now had at last
learned what had happened to Sun Yat-Sen. He went into
frenzied action to rescue his friend. But it proved far from easy.

'First he went to the local police [Marylebone District] and
Scotland Yard [Criminal Investigation Department]. They politely
heard him out but did not believe his story and merely shrugged
their shoulders. None of them would admit the possibility of
such a fantastic occurrence in the very heart of the British capital.

'Getting no sense out of the police, he went to the house of
Sir Halliday McCartney, the British representative at the Chinese
Legation. He was not at home. It was Saturday; the sacred
English weekend had begun, official activities had ceased until
Monday and anyone with any self-respect had gone off to the
country.

'That night Cantlie did not sleep, and his head was a fiery
furnace as he grappled with the problem of helping Sun Yat-Sen.

On the morning of Sunday, the 18th, he resorted to various British officials who had previously held high positions in China, and tried to interest them in the fate of the Chinese revolutionary. In vain. They declined to interfere in a matter which they regarded as a tale out of the *Arabian Nights*.

'Meanwhile, another note was received from Sun Yat-Sen, this time delivered by Cole, in which he said that he would be taken to the docks and put on board a Chinese ship during the next two days. Immediate action was called for, and Cantlie visited Scotland Yard again. Notwithstanding his urgent entreaties, Scotland Yard once more declined to do anything in the matter.

'Cantlie was now desperate,' Davis continued, 'and decided to turn to the Foreign Office. Of course the weekend system was in force here too, and the place was empty. All the same, he dug out the official on duty and urgently repeated all he had said previously to the others. At first the young diplomat listened to him as if he were recounting some strange happenings on the moon, but after some time he began to take an interest and even to show considerable sympathy for the Chinese captive. Eventually he promised that when his superior returned to London next day he would make a suitable report. Cantlie was somewhat relieved, but far from satisfied. From the Foreign Office he went straight to the offices of *The Times* newspaper and told the journalist in charge of the kidnapping of Sun Yat-Sen. The journalist decided that he was dealing with a lunatic and, preferring not to irritate him, wrote down what he said and promised to give it to his editor.

'By now it was evening and Cantlie was terribly worried. Suppose the Chinese Legation carried its prisoner off during the night! He decided to hire a detective to keep No. 49 under constant observation. Alas! The weekend made this impossible; even detectives like to have their Sundays free. So he turned himself into a detective and spent the whole night on the corner near the Chinese Legation, never closing his eyes. Simultaneously he made a "psychic" attack on the enemy. During the evening of the 18th he sent to the Legation one of his friends, who told the interpreter who received him that the Foreign Office knew of the kidnapping of Sun Yat-Sen and was taking appropriate measures.'

A strong gust of wind blew through the park, bringing with it cold and damp, but I did not turn a hair and only asked: 'What happened next?'

'What happened next was that the Foreign Office official kept his promise. On Monday the 19th he told his superior of his conversation with Cantlie. The superior was interested. The whole affair was reported to the Foreign Secretary, Lord Salisbury. Now Lord Salisbury was a most respectable Conservative who had no sort of sympathy with revolutionaries—Chinese or any other. But he had his own ideas about standards of civilization, and on these he was very firm. Kidnapping people in the streets and hauling them off to private gaols might be all right in Canton or Peking, but in London . . . In London it was outrageous! It was a gross violation of English standards of civilization. It would lower the world-wide reputation of Great Britain as a cultured and well-ordered country.

'Lord Salisbury decided to intervene. Scotland Yard was given the necessary orders and six detectives suddenly appeared at the Chinese Legation to keep it under observation day and night. Encouraged by this action, the friends of the great revolutionary redoubled their efforts to secure his release. They tried to invoke the Habeas Corpus Act but the court refused the application.

'Then Cole, who by now was wholly on Sun Yat-Sen's side, suggested that he should get on to the roof of the Legation at night and help him to escape that way. But Scotland Yard considered that idea too risky.'

'How did it all end?' I interrupted excitedly.

'Cantlie got his own way in the end,' replied Davis. 'On the 23rd October a three-man delegation—Cantlie, Inspector Jarvis from Scotland Yard and a Foreign Office official—appeared at the Chinese Legation. It was received by Sir Halliday McCartney, whom I have already mentioned. The part he played in this business was very odd, to say the least. The delegation categorically demanded the release of Sun Yat-Sen. At first McCartney tried to dodge a straight answer. Then the Foreign Office man made it clear that if Sun Yat-Sen were not immediately released the Chinese Legation would be searched. Of course a search at the Legation was a most exceptional measure, a violation of long-established diplomatic usage. . . .

But the kidnapping of people in the streets of London, and their forcible detention in a foreign legation, was also an exceptional measure, a violation of long-established diplomatic usage. . . . Anyhow, the official's words had a magic effect; within a few minutes the deeply moved Sun Yat-Sen was being embraced by Cantlie and handed over to the delegation in the basement of the Legation. All four were let out into the street by a back door. The leader of the Chinese Revolution was saved.'[1]

A few minutes' silence followed. I was moved to the depths by what I had heard, turning the kidnapping, arrest and release over and over in my mind. Davis lit a pipe and, puffing it, stared motionless into the night. Finally I asked:

'Where did you get all these details from?'

'It's my speciality,' he replied with a laugh. 'The kidnapping of the leader of the Chinese Revolution in the London streets doesn't happen every day. This was a remarkable date, and I at once found out everything I could about it.'

He puffed at his pipe again, and then added, in a quite familiar tone:

'It wasn't all that difficult. The whole story was in the papers. It was a tremendous sensation. For weeks no one could talk about anything else.'

He reflected for a moment and then continued:

'What an odd trick of fate! Of course, Sun Yat-Sen had twelve unpleasant days to endure, but that was nothing but gain to the Chinese Revolution. I can assure you that years and years of patient, tireless propaganda would not have done as much to popularize his ideas in Europe and America as the kidnapping which fortunately ended so well. . . .'

He lapsed into silence, and then ended on a philosophic note:

'There's a reverse to every medal.'[2]

---

[1] The account of my conversation with Davis is borne out from many other sources, in particular a book, *Sir James Cantlie*, by N. Cantlie and G. Seaver, which was published in London in 1939. The text of Mrs. Howe's note is taken from that book.

[2] See Appendix 12.

PART FOUR

*

The Fall of Tsarism
and the
Return to Russia

CHAPTER TWENTY-THREE

The February Revolution

BELSIZE PARK—a very ordinary Underground station in the north-western part of London. There is nothing in the least bit remarkable about it, but to me it means a great deal. And in 1932, when I came across it in my walks, slightly dimmed memories came back to me.

On that March day all sorts of vague, confused rumours were flying round London from first thing in the morning. For a week previously unusual news had begun to come in from Petrograd—that the queues at the food stores had been getting bigger, the streets of the city were thronged with excited crowds, there were demonstrations in the squares and the Cossacks, brought in to suppress the 'disorders', were behaving with a restraint and irresolution quite out of character. The English papers printed this news day by day, carefully refraining from assessment or comment. Then telegrams and news from Russia suddenly vanished from their pages. It was as if a wind had blown them all away.

Five days passed. Not a word came from Petrograd—no *communiqués* from the front, nothing from political circles, no sensational rumours of new court appointments. What could this strange silence mean?

Something very significant had happened, the London émigrés thought and said, awaiting news from the homeland with beating hearts.

From early that morning confused rumours were flying round the giant city. No one could say where they came from, but all Englishmen were telling their friends that they knew 'from absolutely reliable sources' that great events were taking place in Russia, and the State Duma was in control and that it had set up a responsible government, drawn from all parties.

I did not have a moment's peace all that day. I called at the
offices of several newspapers, made the round of the best-in-
formed London correspondents of the Russian press, dropped
in at the national offices of the Independent Labour Party
(I was on very good terms with some of its members at the
time) and in the evening saw two Members of Parliament whom
I knew. But nowhere could I get any definite news. Rumours,
rumours, nothing but rumours.

The editor of an important Liberal paper remarked por-
tentously:

'Things must be pretty hot in Russia at the moment! . . .
Excellent. . . . We'll soon finish off the Germans!'

A socialist M.P., in reply to my question, adopted a somewhat
patronizing tone:

'Apparently there's a revolution in Russia. . . . I congratulate
you!'

He was silent for a moment and then added:

'Revolutionary armies always fight well, and that means that
before long we shall wipe Prussian militarism from the face of
the earth. Fine! Fine!'

Of course all this speculation was not what I wanted, burning
with anxiety as I was to know what was happening in that distant
land behind the misty horizon and not at all concerned with the
military and political calculations with which the British were
viewing events in Russia. A terrible struggle was going on in my
mind: I very much wanted to believe the enormously exciting
news—at the mere idea of revolution in Russia the blood rushed
to my head and my thoughts took wing—but I was also afraid
to believe it lest my glad hopes should be betrayed and I should
suffer the bitterness of disillusionment. Tired and discontented,
I returned home late at night, had a quick supper and decided
to go straight to bed.

My intentions were frustrated, however. I had hardly risen
from the table when there was a long and insistent ring at the
door. Highly surprised, I ran down and opened the door. In the
darkness I distinguished a tall, spare figure, which burst in, threw
its arms round my neck, kissed my head, nose and moustache
and yelled out:

'Look here! Look here! Read this! There's no tsar in Russia!
Revolution!'

Thereupon the figure brandished a bundle of what looked like ribbons and scraps of paper, smelling strongly of printer's ink.

'What's all this about?' I interjected.

The figure turned out to be Vasiliev, the London correspondent of one of the most important Moscow papers. But what a state he was in! Reserved and phlegmatic in the ordinary way, he shouted, stamped his feet, gesticulated wildly and stopped every few seconds to embrace me. His crumpled hat was over one eye, his overcoat hung from one shoulder and his smart tie, with its diamond pin, was all askew. I had never seen him looking like that before.

'Come up!' I eventually said to my unexpected visitor.

We took the stairs three at a time, and Vasiliev got rid of his coat and threw the bundle of proofs on to the table.

'Read them! I've come straight from the *Daily Telegraph* offices.'

They really were proofs from the London Conservative newspaper. I grabbed the long, narrow strips and my eyes were dazzled with the bold headlines: 'Victory for the People', 'Duma Governs the Country', 'Tsar in the Train between Pskov and Petrograd', 'The Tsar Abdicates', 'Monarchy now Impossible', 'Universal Rejoicing in Russia. . . .'

It was revolution all right, the revolution for which we had been calling so long, for which we had fought so passionately, for which we had sworn to die if need be! And now it had happened! It was a fact! Here it was—the marvellous reality, and achieved under the red flag!

I greedily swallowed every fragment of news, and when I had finished there was only one idea in my head.

'Let's go to the Berzins,' I proposed.

'Fine idea!' my companion enthusiastically agreed, and crammed his smart hat on his head.

A few minutes later we were running through the quiet streets to the home of the Berzins, a kindly, hospitable family of Bolshevik émigrés. When, quite out of breath, we reached the familiar door they were just going to bed.

'There's a revolution in Russia! The Tsar has abdicated! The army is in revolt!' was our joint broadside at the stupefied Berzins.

There was a cross-fire of questions, we all talked at the top of our voices, the proofs passed from hand to hand and then we all agreed on one thing—no bed for us tonight!

Tea was made, we telephoned friends and acquaintances to give them the good news and sent messengers to those who were not on the telephone.

I found it impossible to stay indoors and also sallied forth to call on various comrades. It was already midnight and a quiet, dark, rather misty night. A soft rain was falling. But my heart was jumping with joy. I wanted to wake up sleeping London and shout in her ear: 'Look up! The red flag's flying over the Neva! Long live the revolution!'

A sort of wave of boyish exhilaration seized me. I entered the Underground. It was Belsize Park station. An elegant lady and her no less elegant cavalier were standing by the ticket window. I went up to them, raised my hat and gleefully proclaimed: 'Revolution in Russia! The Tsar's gone! Hurrah!'

The beautiful Englishwoman looked at me as if I were a lunatic, and shrank back against her companion.

While the lift was descending I gave the attendant a friendly tap on the shoulder.

'There's a revolution in Russia! The war will soon be over!'

'The war over?' he laughed. 'Splendid. . . . And the Tsar gone?'

'Yes, the Tsar gone!' I laughed too, suddenly overcome by an unusual feeling of affection for this modest representative of the British proletariat.

In the train I felt like a conqueror. Proudly conscious of my eminence, I looked at the rows of silent English people buried in their papers and commiserated with them: 'My poor friends! You sit there reading, breathing and existing, but you haven't heard of the biggest and most important thing that has ever happened! You don't know that there has been a revolution in Russia!'

I am afraid that I regarded my fellow-travellers with silent contempt.

From the Underground I almost ran to the house where P. V. Karpovich, whom I have mentioned previously, was living. I knocked loudly and imperiously on the door. A sleepy maid reluctantly opened it.

'Is Mr. Karpovich at home?' I bawled.

'Good gracious! It's one o'clock! He's asleep!'

'That doesn't matter, I'll wake him!' And to the no small
terror of the girl I bounded upstairs to Karpovich's room on the
first floor.

'Piotr Vladimirovich, get up!' I yelled, banging on his door.

'Hallo! Hallo! Who's there?' replied a sleepy voice.

I said who I was and banged the door even more furiously.
Eventually it was unlocked and I burst into his room.

'Get up! Get up!' I repeated in my ecstasy. 'There's a revolution
in Russia! They've kicked out the Tsar! The army's in revolt!'

He jumped out of bed, half dressed, almost suffocated me with
a steely hug (he was very strong) and then cried out hoarsely,
part joyful, part threatening:

'You're not lying? Not pulling my leg? Is it really true?'

'Of course it's true! Just read this!'

I thrust the proofs I had brought with me into his hands. He
took a hasty look at them and clutched his head.

'So it's really true!' he murmured, overcome with emotion
and hardly believing his eyes. 'So it's really true! We've lived to
see it! All these years of waiting. . . . Now lettest thou . . . !'

'Come along to the Berzins,' I said. 'I've come to fetch you.
Everybody's meeting there.'

'Immediately! Immediately!'

A few minutes later we were in a taxi driving through the
deserted streets of sleeping London.

There was quite a crowd at the Berzins—twenty already—
and more and more arriving every minute. The bell rang and
the door banged incessantly and the crowded rooms of the
emigrant flat were a scene of noisy rejoicing.

What did we talk about on that dark and foggy March night?
What plans did we make? What sort of a future did we look
forward to? What were our hopes and wishes? What vows did
we make? I cannot say now. All I know is that on that memorable
March night we were living in a world of our own, a world such
as is granted to man only once in a lifetime. It was a world of the
revolutionary inspiration which makes nothing seem impossible.

We separated at the first light, greeting the rising sun with
loud shouts of 'Long live the revolution!'

We all shook hands warmly on leaving and there was a
universal cry:

'To Russia!'

CHAPTER TWENTY-FOUR

The Reactions in England

THE news of the revolution in Petrograd did more than rouse the Russian émigrés who had been swept by the tides of history to the shores of foggy Albion. It fell like a glittering meteor among the British people too, and it was soon clear that there was a dual reaction in the British Isles to this momentous event in history.

The ruling class greeted the Russian Revolution with very mixed feelings. On the one hand they were very pleased at the disappearance of the Romanov clique, which they considered totally unfitted to carry on the war and suspected of being anxious to make a separate peace with Germany. On the other, they regarded the future with much misgiving. A revolution was anathema to the easygoing English bourgeoisie. A revolution in the midst of a terrible war with a powerful enemy was doubly anathema. Two feelings struggled for mastery in the breasts of the British ruling classes and it is probable that the feeling of apprehension was greater than the feeling of relief. After March the men in power concentrated on the question of what the new Government was going to be like. How would it fight— better or worse than the old one? For at the outset no one gave a thought to such possibilities as the October Revolution and what happened afterwards.

Left-wing circles in England, and especially the workers, regarded the Russian Revolution in quite a different light. Imagine a man walking in a terrible storm on a long road leading to an unknown destination. The sky is dark with sinister leaden clouds. The wind is blowing fiercely and the trees are bending to the ground. The heavens ring with thunder, the rain streams down. The unfortunate traveller, shivering and wet to the skin, summons up his last energies and, with despair in his heart and aching limbs, staggers along on his interminable journey.

Suddenly there is a marvellous transformation. The gloomy

banks of clouds disperse and through the gaps the sun shines
down triumphantly on the dark earth. All nature at once comes
to life, a million diamonds sparkle on the rain-soaked fields, the
sombre woods are seen in their green glory, the heavenly vault
turns blue, a rainbow breaks through the clouds. How raptur-
ously the wanderer greets the sun! How hopefully he gazes into
the distances now!

The advanced sections of British democracy felt much like
that when the news of the Russian Revolution arrived. For two
and a half years the nation had been squeezed ever harder and
more grievously in the vice of the world war. Ever greater were
the sacrifices demanded, and the impasse to which humanity
had come looked even more hopeless than before.

And now the thunder of revolution was heard! The English
left wing was startled, as by an electric shock, and hope came to
thousands and thousands of hearts:

'This is the end! The beginning of the end of this inhuman
slaughter!'

English left-wing circles also associated the Russian Revolution with the war, but, unlike the ruling class, they concentrated
on the question whether the revolution would mean the end of
the war. Many, very many, of them believed that it would.

I remember something said to me by Philip Snowden, one
of the leaders of the Independent Labour Party whom I knew
well, a few days after the fall of tsarism:

'The Russian Revolution will mean a speedy end to the war!'

When I asked Massingham, a left-wing democrat and the
editor of the famous weekly, *The Nation*, what he thought of the
revolution he emphatically replied:

'The Russian Revolution means the end of the war!'

The only objection of an old radical, brought up on the
principles of British parliamentarism, was that in Petrograd
there was too much talk about the dictatorship of the proletariat
and too little respect for the ideas of 'pure', i.e. bourgeois,
democracy.

Such was not only the mood of the leaders. The thoughts
and feelings of the masses were even more sympathetic.

On the 31st March, two weeks after the first news of the
events in Petrograd, London democracy staged a triumphal
greeting to the Russian Revolution. The Labour Party, the

JOURNEY INTO THE PAST

socialist parties, the trade unions, various groups of radicals from the bourgeois camp and individual representatives of politics, literature and the arts, came together on that day to send warm greetings to Russia on freeing herself from her chains.

I can remember that meeting as if it were today. The vast Albert Hall, which can hold ten thousand, was packed to the doors. The floor, the circles, the gallery, the gangways and even the platform were a sea of heads and a tumult of exaltation. The great organ at the back of the platform, the platform itself, the boxes and gangways, the roof and walls, were gay with red flags, red ribbons and wreaths of red flowers.

On the platform was the cream of English democracy, picked orators among M.P.s, writers and trade-union leaders, and below and around them thronged a vast and excited mass of workers.

MacDonald spoke.[1] A tense silence descended as his voice rang out like a brass trumpet. He called on the working masses of Great Britain to rouse themselves, open their eyes and turn them to the east where events of world significance were in progress.

Smillie, the miners' leader, spoke. He adjured the English proletariat to abandon their bad old habit of looking down on their continental brothers, and to follow the example of the Russian workers.

There was a speech by Israel Zangwill, one of the brilliant figures in English literature of those days. He caustically attacked the hypocrisy of the reactionary leaders of British imperialism. There could be no peace with them: you could and must talk to them 'only in Russian'.

Then came Nevinson, one of the best British publicists, a tall, lean figure with white hair. He spoke of his meetings with Kropotkin, Stepnyak-Kravchinsky, Vera Figner and many other well-known Russian revolutionaries. He read out a long, long list of victims—Russian workers, peasants and intellectuals—on the altar of the struggle for freedom from the tsarist yoke, victims known and unknown, single names, groups of names. He ended his simple but extremely moving speech with these words:

'The Russians have a splendid custom. When at their meetings they recall the memory of those who have fallen in the struggle

[1] During the First World War MacDonald was a pacifist (see the next chapter).

they all rise, bare their heads and stand in silence for a few moments. Let us follow their example tonight. Friends, let us rise in honour of the countless sacrifices which the Russian people have made to win their freedom!'

The whole vast audience rose as one man. For a short time there was such a hush under the giant dome that you could have heard a pin drop. Then the organ pealed, and the walls resounded to the solemn notes of the Funeral March in memory of the countless martyrs of revolutionary Russia.

The tension reached its peak. The exhilaration was quite out of the ordinary. Many eyes were filled with tears. An English socialist, a sentimental and religious man, who was sitting next to me, turned to me and said:

'It's just like a church in this great hall! And isn't this fervent crowd like a host of worshippers raising their hands to the east, to the sun of the Russian Revolution?'

My neighbour's comparison did not impress me; but I felt that something quite extraordinary was happening in the Albert Hall that evening. In my time I have attended many meetings, large and small, open and secret, stormy and lethargic, peaceful and revolutionary, Russian, German, French, English, Scandinavian. But that meeting in the Albert Hall on the 31st March, 1917, remains in my memory as one of the most vivid moments of my life. At that meeting I passed through a few hours of exaltation such as I had never known before and would never forget, and for the first time I realized that the revolution which had just begun had gigantic potentialities which could make the year 1917 a new and vital landmark in the age-old evolution of humanity.

CHAPTER TWENTY-FIVE

The Socialist Leader

NUMBER 10, Downing Street.

It was not fortuitous that one grey November evening I found myself in this little street which is so well known all the world over. Here, in a three-storey house three hundred years old and sombre with age and grime, is the official residence of the British Prime Minister, and here in the autumn of 1932 lived a man whose name is closely associated in my memory with the first weeks after the fall of tsarism.

I first met Ramsay MacDonald in the spring of 1913. I made his acquaintance through Bruce Glasier, a leading socialist of that day, who heard that I was living in London with a view to studying the British Labour movement, took me under his wing and introduced me into socialist and trade-unionist circles.

I well remember that first meeting with MacDonald. He was then living in Howitt Road, Hampstead, in one of those modest little villas favoured by middle-class English intelligentzia.

It was with some trepidation that I, a young and unknown Russian Social-Democrat, entered that house; after all, I was about to come face to face with one of the most popular leaders of British, and indeed of European, socialism.

MacDonald was then about fifty, but looked very young and vigorous, like most Englishmen of that age. Tall, upstanding and powerful, his dark hair beginning to be tinged with silver, he seemed the incarnation of health and energy. He spoke in a low, deep voice which seemed to have some secret sources of power. Outwardly he had something of the preacher about him, but that was by no means unusual with English political figures.

He gave me a friendly reception, though there was a certain air of condescension about it. This slightly irritated me but I did not show it. Our talk lasted nearly an hour. We discussed

Russia and the revolutionary movement there, England and the English Labour movement, Parliament, the trade unions and many other interesting subjects. Among other things he told me of the history of the Labour Party and the part he had played in its birth and development.

Before we separated we turned to topics of a more intimate nature. I asked him about his past, his origin and education. He was only too willing to tell me and spoke of it very warmly. He had affectionate memories of his native place, Lossiemouth, in northern Scotland, where he was born and spent his youth. He spoke of the poverty in which he had passed his early years, a grandmother who had had great influence on his upbringing and his early life as a schoolmaster.

Then a shadow seemed to pass over his face, he rumpled his hair and suddenly began to talk of his wife. She had recently died. With deep emotion he told me what an enormous part she had played in his life, what a wonderful friend and comrade she had always been and how terribly he felt her loss. He got more and more agitated, constantly getting up and walking about the room. Then, with a penetrating glance at some faraway vision, he murmured:

'In this great sorrow I am sustained by one thought alone—the thought that sooner or later we shall meet again up there. . . .'

He expressively pointed upwards!

I was utterly dumbfounded, and nearly fell off my chair. It would never have entered my head that the leader of the socialist movement could have such a primitive belief in a future life. It was only afterwards that I realized that English socialism is often nourished on religious survivals, and even likes to draw its concepts from the ethics of primitive Christianity.

This first 'shock' was followed by others. Meeting MacDonald, and getting a closer view of his political activities, soon convinced me that he was a typical reformist and legalist of the English type. He would not admit the validity of revolutionary methods in the proletarian struggle, and viewed the coming of socialism in the Fabian fashion as a gradual process carried out by a long series of social reforms. It was not for nothing that Lenin, in his article 'The Manifesto of the Liberal Labour Party', wrote that MacDonald was conducting a 'Liberal Labour policy'.[1]

[1] Lenin, *Collected Works*, vol. 17, p. 286 (Russian edn.).

Marxism was anathema to MacDonald, a fact which often produced angry protest from me. Yet in matters of practical politics
he sometimes did things which met with approval even from
Vladimir Ilych. At the beginning of 1914, when the English
landowners in Northern Ireland (Ulster) revolted against the
Asquith-Lloyd George Liberal Government because it wanted
to introduce Home Rule for Ireland, and officers in the forces
sent against them refused to fight against 'protestant Ulster',
Lenin, in his article, 'Constitutional Crisis in England', quoted
with approval a speech in Parliament in which MacDonald had
pointed out that the officers thought only of fighting against the
workers but when it came to compelling the rich and the pro-
pertied classes to respect the law they refused to do their duty.[1]

Then came the First World War and in England the 'chauvinist bacchanalia' began. Few had the courage to swim against
the tide. Among them were Bernard Shaw and MacDonald,
who, starting from bourgeois pacifism, took the unpopular line
and were exposed to virulent abuse in the press, Parliament and
pulpit.

In November, 1914, Lenin wrote in an article, 'The Position
and Aims of the Socialist International':

'MacDonald and Keir Hardie of the opportunist "Independent
Labour Party" continue to resist chauvinism.'[2]

MacDonald maintained this attitude later, and thus played a
positive role. At the second congress of the Comintern Lenin
said:

'Comrade Gallacher has told us here how he and his comrades
effectively organized the revolutionary movement in Glasgow
in Scotland, how skilful their tactics were during the war and
how they supported the petty-bourgeois pacifists Ramsay
MacDonald and Snowden during their visits to Glasgow, in
such a way as to organize a powerful mass movement against
the war.'[3]

All this had its effect on my relations with MacDonald before
and during the first years of the war. There were many things on
which I disagreed with him, but I kept up the acquaintance
because he helped me greatly with my study of the British

[1] Lenin, op. cit., vol. 20, p. 206 (Russian edn.).
[2] Op. cit., vol. 21, p. 20 (Russian edn.).
[3] Op. cit., vol. 31, p. 233 (Russian edn.).

Labour movement. When the 1914–18 war broke out we had a very important common interest—the struggle against the war. Of course our motives were different but in practice we were often able to work together, just as Gallacher and the other left-wing English socialists managed to do.

The news of the February Revolution in Russia made an enormous impression on him. For several days his favourite remark was 'Ex Oriente lux!'

He often expressed the hope that the Russian Revolution would free humanity from the terrors and sufferings of war. On the 31st March there was, as I have already said, a monster meeting at the Albert Hall to greet the Russian Revolution. He was one of the chief speakers.

Shortly afterwards, the Russian émigrés organized another great meeting in the Kingsway Hall to celebrate the events of February. I presided at this meeting, but MacDonald, Snowden and other socialist leaders were the principal speakers. Mac-Donald made another vivid and powerful speech in which he admitted the enormous significance of the revolution and openly confessed his faith in its mission of salvation.

One fine May morning in 1917 two quite unusual visitors unexpectedly knocked at my door. They were delegates from the Russian cruiser *Askold*, which had arrived at Devonport from Toulon. One of them was a marine and the other a stoker. They told me an exciting story. For nearly a year the *Askold* (6,000 tons) had been refitting in Toulon and during that time the crew had established close relations with the Russian political émigrés living in France. As a result the revolutionary spirit had spread among the sailors. *Agents provocateurs* from the tsarist *Okhrana* had staged a sabotage explosion on board which did the ship no serious harm, but gave the commander an excuse to arrest 150 members of the crew and shoot four. This aroused furious anger among the crew against the commander and senior officers and the atmosphere on the *Askold* became extremely explosive. At the beginning of February, 1917, the cruiser, without completing its refit at Toulon, moved to Devonport, where the work was to be continued. The news of the February Revolution arrived. The officers took fright and started to appease the crew.

In April a ship's committee was formed, which decided to send a
deputation to London to invite political émigrés to visit the
cruiser. Chance led the delegates to me and they urgently asked
me to go with them to Devonport.

Need I say what my feelings were?

I had been reading and thinking so much of the Russian
Revolution and was so passionately yearning to take my part in
the distant, splendid events unrolling in Petrograd, in Moscow
... so far away.... And now the revolution had suddenly come
to me on my own doorstep, here in London, and calling me
to service under the red flag! It was something out of a fairy-
story.

It was immediately decided by the three of us that we should
leave for a visit to the *Askold* that evening, but before train time I
promised my visitors that they should have a tour of London
with myself for guide. Then I thought I would first tell Mac-
Donald of my unusual callers. I went to his house. He became
extremely excited, overwhelmed me with questions and finally
said that he would certainly want to see my remarkable visitors.

'Where?' I said.

'At the House of Commons! Bring them to the Outer Lobby
at one o'clock. We'll have lunch in the dining-room.'

I was thrilled.

Punctually at one o'clock I was at the House of Commons
with my two delegates from the *Askold*. MacDonald was waiting
for us at the rendezvous and took us straight to the dining-room
where he had reserved a table for four. There was rather a scanty
lunch of which, as may well be imagined, my companions
disposed in a few mouthfuls. But this was unimportant. What
was important was that they were sitting at table with the leader
of the Independent Labour Party who was directing a hail of
questions at them about the revolution on the cruiser, the hopes
and aspirations of the crew and the relations between the Russian
sailors and the English sailors and soldiers. He continually stressed
how important it was that the Russian Revolution should lead to
a speedy end to the war.

Very soon our table was the cynosure of all eyes. As usual
the dining-room was packed with Members of Parliament and
their guests, and 'red' MacDonald, engaged in lively conversation
with two sailors in Russian naval uniform, could not fail to be an

object of keen, and not altogether friendly, curiosity on the part of his numerous political opponents.

When lunch was over, MacDonald showed us round the House of Commons, pointing out anything noteworthy. In the library we stopped to have a look at the well-known death-sentence on Charles I which bears the signatures of the Members of Parliament who voted to have him beheaded. MacDonald struck an attitude and said in somewhat theatrical tones:

'We have been a revolutionary nation before, and we will be a revolutionary nation again!'

I could not help frowning. By then I knew him too well not to have doubts about the sincerity of what he said. Of course, I too was hoping that as a result of the war England would take a revolutionary course; so I did not argue with him, but merely thought, 'Time will show'. I could not have imagined to what depths this man would one day descend!

I went to Devonport that evening with my two delegates. The three days I spent on the *Askold* I shall never forget; they were a non-stop meeting. There were meetings for the whole crew, for its active members, for various groups, for the ship's committee. I found myself in the position of an oracle; I had to answer every sort of question, and give my decision on every sort of problem. What troubled the crew most was, what was to be done about the officers? At the meetings where this subject was discussed tempers rose so high that the most extreme measures might be anticipated. It was plain to me that, if that point was reached, the crew would be put under arrest by the British authorities and the cruiser might be requisitioned or sunk by British warships or the shore batteries. So I advised the men to show common sense, get the ship away to Murmansk as quickly as possible and so save it for the Russian Revolution. After stormy debates this suggestion was adopted, and subsequently acted on. But certain officers who were particularly odious to the crew remained behind in England.

At the end of the third day I left the *Askold* and returned to London. On leaving, the crew presented me with a large autographed photo of the cruiser, tied with the black naval ribbon. I have it still. The whole crew assembled on the deck, formed up and gave me naval honours. The English people ashore were somewhat surprised by these salutes, and when the barge deposited me on the quay I caught fragments of conversation:

'What's the matter? Why such a fuss?'

'A Russian admiral has visited the cruiser.'

Mentally, I burst out laughing. A wave of joyous pride swept over me. So that's what things had come to. Naval honours were being given, not to admirals but to revolutionaries!

In May, 1917, I returned to Russia and my relations with MacDonald were interrupted for a long time, during which there were great changes in his fortunes. The seeds of ideological cancer which lurked within him even then, during my émigré years, developed a flourishing growth and ultimately ravaged his whole mental organism.

The October Revolution at once threw him over to the right, though in November, 1917, Lenin was still able to describe him as a 'centrist', i.e. one of those men who fall into the category of 'partisans of routine, corrupted by legalism, perverted by parliamentarism'[1] and so forth. In October, 1918, Lenin spoke of the 'semi-Liberal Ramsay MacDonald.'[2] In August, 1919, he called him a 'drawing-room socialist' who was 'stuffed full of the most academic reformist prejudices'[3] and in July, 1920, a 'thoroughly bourgeois pacifist and conciliator, a petty bourgeois dreaming of a classless government.'[4]

But all this was the flower—the fruit came later, after Lenin's death. By the beginning of 1924 MacDonald, now an avowed enemy of the U.S.S.R., was only concealing his real feelings under smooth, polite phrases. As Prime Minister in the first Labour Government he delayed official recognition of the Soviet Government in every possible way and it was only under extreme pressure from the great mass of the British proletariat that on the 1st February, 1924, diplomatic relations with the U.S.S.R. were established. In the subsequent Anglo-Soviet negotiations for the settlement of disputed claims and other matters he revealed himself as a zealous champion of the interests of British capitalism.

In the years 1929 to 1931, in which MacDonald was again Prime Minister in a Labour Government, he took an openly anti-

[1] Op. cit., vol. 24, p. 55 (Russian edn.).
[2] Op. cit., vol. 28, p. 85 (Russian edn.).
[3] Op. cit., vol. 29, pp. 426, 470 (Russian edn.).
[4] Op. cit., vol. 31, p. 203 (Russian edn.).

Soviet line. He held up the restoration of diplomatic relations which had been broken off by the Conservatives in 1927, opposed the conclusion of a normal trade agreement and so forth. If diplomatic relations were in fact restored, and a trade agreement was ultimately concluded, it was again the result of pressure from the great mass of British workers and also certain commercial circles in the City which wanted to do business with the Soviet State.

But the process of degeneration did not stop there. Before long even the particularly moderate Labour Party was too 'left' for his taste. In the autumn of 1931 MacDonald, Snowden and Thomas were expelled from the Party and formed the ephemeral National Labour Party, which soon went over to the Conservatives. As his reward, and also with the idea of more skilfully bamboozling the masses, the Conservatives, after the general election in 1931 in which they won a brilliant victory, made him Prime Minister in a 'Coalition' Government which was really a Conservative Government. Out of 520 coalition M.P.s, 471 were Conservatives.

All this was going through my head when, one foggy November evening, I stood on the pavement of Downing Street and looked up at the curtained windows of No. 10 where MacDonald was then living. My thoughts ran like this:

What a long way from the persecuted leader of a small Socialist Party to the stately Prime Minister in a Conservative cabinet! Yet how swiftly had the terrible, ominous passage been made! It had taken only fifteen years. It was the classical example of the 'degeneration' of a socialist leader in Britain. But was it only in Britain? Were there not similar cases in France, Italy and other countries? What poisonous plants could grow on 'reformist' soil!

CHAPTER TWENTY-SIX

The Struggle with the British Government over the Return of the Émigrés

KING'S CROSS! Of all London's black and smoky stations this seemed the worst. It was here that, in the spring of 1917, I commenced my journey to my native land, the land which by a mighty effort had thrown off the yoke of autocracy. Here ended my exile, the nine years' wanderings in Switzerland, Germany and England. But how many anxieties, difficulties and obstacles had yet to be overcome before the end!

I have already said that after the fall of tsarism all the political exiles, without distinction of party or creed, passionately longed for one thing only—to return home as soon as possible. Unfortunately, there were great physical and political obstacles to overcome.

As the battle-fronts were constituted at that time the shortest route from England to Russia lay through neutral Scandinavia. That involved a voyage across the North Sea and a landing in Norway from which it was possible some way or other to travel overland to Petrograd. But this voyage across the North Sea was a very considerable obstacle. At that time the British coasts were blockaded by German submarines. The North Sea itself was strewn with mines. Merchant ships sailing at their own risk to Bergen or Trondheim were constantly being torpedoed. I have already related how P. V. Karpovich lost his life in one of those disasters. It was essential to find the large number of émigrés some better and more reliable means of reaching Norway.

The émigrés from Switzerland, Italy and France were seized by the same passion to return home as we were, and were investigating every possible means of achieving their desires. Most of them came to the conclusion that, despite its difficulties and dangers, the northern route across England and Scandinavia was the best. The result was that we Londoners were under constant pressure from Paris, Rome, Geneva and Zürich for a speedy solution of the ticklish transport problem.

We energetically got to work. A general meeting of all the London émigrés was held, which long and heatedly discussed the question of the return to Russia. The meeting appointed a committee to make the necessary arrangements. I was chairman, G. V. Chicherin secretary and among the members were M. M. Litvinov and A. I. Zundelevich. We embarked on protracted negotiations with a series of British departments—the Foreign Office, the War Office, the Admiralty and the Home Office. Chicherin and I had endless discussions with innumerable British officials, but at the outset things went at a snail's pace. British red tape, the novelty of our requests and the real hazards of the crossing between England and Norway all played their part. But there was another factor. The real obstacle was political.

In dealing with the question of the return of Russian émigrés the London authorities were primarily guided by politico-military considerations. They divided the émigrés roughly into two groups—pro-war and anti-war. They were prepared to give every sort of help to the pro-war section which they considered might exercise a useful influence in Russian democratic circles, and more especially the army. When G. V. Plekhanov and P. A. Kropotkin, immediately after the outbreak of the February Revolution, expressed a desire to return to Petrograd, the British Government gave them every facility.

The attitude of London officialdom to the anti-war émigrés, and particularly the Bolsheviks, was quite different. It put every possible obstacle in their way, since it was feared that when they returned to Russia they might 'undermine' the army and prevent the Provisional Government from carrying on the war to a 'victorious conclusion'. The British authorities were particularly hostile to Lenin and his adherents and not too sympathetic even to the Menshevik-Internationalists, the Socialist-Revolutionary Internationalists and all other émigrés of the internationalist school. Under these circumstances the northern route was quite out of the question for Lenin. Chicherin explained the position to the Paris and Zürich committees handling the evacuation of the refugees. In this connection Lenin, in his article 'How We Got Out', wrote:

'The Zürich committee for the evacuation of refugees in which twenty-three groups were represented (including the Central Committee, the Organizational Committee, the Socialist Revolutionaries, the Bund, etc.) passed a unanimous resolution embodying a public declaration that the British Government had decided to deprive the émigré internationalists of any chance of returning to their homeland and taking part in the struggle against the imperialist war.'[1]

In the light of all this, everyone can understand why Vladimir Ilyich was compelled to return to Russia through Germany. And not Vladimir Ilyich only. It is well known that representatives of several other parties and trends, in particular the Bundists and supporters of the Paris paper, Nashe Slovo, travelled in the same train with him and his group.

Our London efforts for the repatriation of the émigrés began with a vigorous campaign against the political discrimination shown by the British authorities in the matter; we insisted that convenient and reliable transport should be guaranteed for the return journey of all émigrés, whatever their opinions or associations.

The practical aspect turned on the right of the émigrés to travel on the steamer Jupiter (unless my memory deceives me, that was its name) on the voyage from England to Norway. The Jupiter was a small, fast ship which, approximately every ten days, escorted by two destroyers, completed the double crossing from Aberdeen to Bergen, carrying government mails, diplomatists, military personnel, civil servants and other official passengers. The voyage on the Jupiter was comparatively safe, and we émigrés claimed that a certain number of places should be reserved for us on each crossing. We knew that several 'privileged' persons from the pro-war camp (Plekhanov and Kropotkin, for instance) had returned to Russia that way, and we were all the more insistent on similar treatment for all émigrés.

The struggle between the committee and the British authorities went on for more than a month, and finally we realized that without the intervention of the Russian ambassador

[1] Op. cit., vol. 24, p. 8 (Russian edn.).

in London we should never get the right to travel by the *Jupiter*. This was a hard blow. In those days there was a deep and unbridged gulf between the émigré colonies and the tsarist embassies abroad. The émigrés regarded these embassies with enmity and suspicion because they always expected intrigues and unpleasantness from that quarter. The embassies for their part looked on the émigré colonies as hotbeds of 'sedition' and fomenters of political agitation against tsarism. There was a permanent condition of warfare between them. Even personal relations between individuals in the two camps were impossible. Whole generations of exiles had grown up under the shadow of such traditions, and so it was easy to understand the dismay of the members of the committee when they were told that it was necessary to obtain the co-operation of the tsarist Embassy before a decision could be given. It was true that there had been a revolution in Russia, that there was no tsar any more and the Provisional Government had taken over. But psychological habits do not fade away overnight. We also knew that no changes had been made in the staff of the London Embassy after February. We understood, however, that there could be no question of repatriation without the Embassy and, after all, repatriation was the important thing. So the psychological barriers were surmounted and one fine April morning Chicherin and I called at the Embassy, which was situated at Chesham House, Chesham Place.

We were received by the Embassy Counsellor, K. D. Nabokov. I well remembered his office, which was not in the main building but in an annexe, connected with the main building by a corridor. Eight years later I was to occupy that same room, also as Counsellor, but to a 'Bolshevik' Embassy. As I have recorded previously,[1] in the spring of 1917 Nabokov was the *chargé d'affaires*.

He greeted us in courteous and almost friendly fashion. He was one of those Liberal officials who at first welcomed the revolution, believing that it could be stopped at the 'February' phase, but openly went over to the counter-revolutionary camp when it was seen that that would not happen.

But in April, 1917, he still had glowing hopes of the triumph of 'reasonable principles' in the Russian Revolution and so we had

[1] See Chapter Six, M. M. Litvinov, p. 65.

R

little trouble in reaching agreement with him on the matter in which we were interested, especially as he had already received a general instruction from Petrograd to co-operate in the repatriation of the émigrés. He undertook to settle the question of sailing on the *Jupiter*, and even promised to affix the Embassy seal to the baggage of the more prominent of the émigrés. This would save it from customs inspection and reduce exit formalities in general.

He kept his word and a few days later the committee received permission from the British authorities to arrange repatriation by the *Jupiter*. The committee was informed prior to each voyage how many places were available, and itself drew up the list of the émigrés nominated. Such an arrangement suited us admirably. Of course this started a lot of disputes between the various parties and groups represented on the committee who were competing for places at each sailing, but after all this was our domestic concern.

CHAPTER TWENTY-SEVEN

Home at Last

THE ever-memorable day marking the end of my years of exile came at last.

I spent the last day saying goodbye to my Russian and English friends, doing my negligible packing and taking a last walk in Hyde Park. The month was May and spring was already with us. The sun blazed down, the birds sang in the trees and young couples strolled arm in arm beneath them. To all this, to the whole great city, to the long years of my exile, I was saying in my mind:

'Farewell! New, unknown, enthralling prospects are beckoning to me.'

The departure of the émigrés from London was kept a secret. The train by which we were to travel was not at a main platform but in one of the sidings at King's Cross. We reached it from somewhere behind the station. The carriage windows had the blinds drawn and the porters spoke in whispers as if at the bedside of a dying man. There were about thirty of us émigrés from the continent as well as from London, and of course we were in the highest spirits.

I cannot remember anything about the journey from London to Aberdeen, except that we left very early in the morning and arrived very late that evening. Our hearts were too full of other thoughts and feelings for us to pay any attention to what was going on around us. At Aberdeen we went straight to the quay and embarked on the *Jupiter*. My cabin mate was an émigré from Paris, Anisimov, who was very frightened of submarines. On the journey between London and Aberdeen he gave me no peace, demonstrating that two destroyers were not enough to escort the *Jupiter* and that we ought to demand at least four. Once on board he fell into a profound melancholy and began to prepare for death, giving me the address of his relatives and asking me to inform them of his demise if I myself survived.

Night came, but the ship remained quietly at her berth. The next day passed. Still no move. The émigrés began to worry. What was the matter? Had some fresh difficulty arisen over our voyage by the *Jupiter*? Towards evening I accosted the captain, an old sea-dog with a red face and bluish nose, and asked why we had not sailed. He laughed and replied:

'I'm waiting for a storm.'

'A storm?' I asked in surprise.

'Yes, a storm. It's less dangerous in a storm. The submarines keep submerged.'

So it was as simple as that!

Two more days passed and there was still no storm. The ship continued to hug the quayside. The passengers got bored, began to make one another's acquaintance. Thus it came to light that in addition to the émigrés we also had on board some British officials and a party of officers from the Russian Military Mission in London who were returning to Russia. Some of the officers were decidedly left wing and soon got on friendly terms with the émigrés.

Finally, on the evening of the third day a fresh wind blew. The captain's face lit up and the crew began to bustle about. The *Jupiter* sailed on the stroke of midnight. All lights were extinguished. The ship glided like a shadow out of the harbour and into the open sea. She was at once caught in huge waves and pitched and rolled unmercifully.

The captain had been right about the storm. It was a real one when it came. Our little *Jupiter* was tossed about like a pea in a bottle. The wind whistled through the rigging. Foaming white rollers swept over the decks. Almost all the passengers were prostrate with sea-sickness. My friend Anisimov was among the worst sufferers. I got off fairly lightly, and crawled out on deck again by morning. Sheltering amongst the baggage under the mast, I gradually got my breath back and had soon almost completely recovered, thanks to the fresh air and salty spray. The sea was extremely rough. At times the escorting destroyers all but disappeared in mountains of foam, and we could see nothing but their masts and funnels. The horizon was a blue-black veil, lit up from time to time by flashes of lightning.

Suddenly there was a clatter of sailors' shoes on the deck and the crew started scuttling about. The captain on the bridge snatched up his binoculars. The *Jupiter* and the destroyers began to signal to each other in code. Our ship swung left while the destroyers, making a beautiful right turn, shot ahead at full speed as if chasing something. I looked hard, straining my eyes, but could see nothing at all.

'What's the excitement about?' I asked a boatswain running past me.

'Submarine on the lee side,' he spluttered; 'but the destroyers are already after it.'

The strong wind brought the sound of firing in the distance.

Half an hour passed and everything gradually quietened down again. The *Jupiter* resumed her previous course and the destroyers, belching out long ribbons of black smoke, returned to their usual stations. We continued on our way to Norway.

'Did they sink the submarine?' I asked the first officer as he was going below.

'No, it got away, unfortunately, but at any rate we've got an open run to Bergen.'

I went below and told Anisimov of the recent excitement. I expected that with his fear of submarines he would be in a terrible panic, but I was wrong. He was lying on his bunk with his face to the wall. His only answer was to wave an arm and mutter:

'Devil take the submarine . . . !'

That is what sea-sickness can do to you!

It took the *Jupiter* twenty-eight hours to cross the North Sea and reach the Norwegian coast. At last it appeared, a long line of rugged cliffs eternally battered by great breakers.

I gazed at it as if it had been the promised land. A little later our *Jupiter*, executing several skilful manœuvres and on the crest of a mighty wave, flew rather than sailed into the narrow entrance of Bergen Fjord. The escorting destroyers turned back and disappeared into the open sea; they were not allowed in the territorial waters of neutral Norway, and in any case our ship was no longer in danger.

The change from the open sea to the fjord was like a fairy-story. The storm, the whistle of the wind, the fury of the waves and the dark skies were behind us; here was a quiet morning, the sea like a mirror, light clouds above and everywhere cascades of sunshine. The pitching and tossing ceased like magic. All the passengers—sallow figures with drawn cheeks and shadows under

the eyes—came to life and began to crawl out on deck. Soon
everyone was wanting some food. In the saloon the stewards
were busy laying a long, wide table for breakfast.

We sailed up Bergen Fjord for four hours. We had a wonderful scene before us—deep blue waters, the great cliffs, patches of
green clinging to their vertical sides, little houses nestling on
ledges, a bright spring sun and silence everywhere—not the
deathly silence which depresses, but the silence in which you can
feel the slow, healthy throb of life. It was as if we had arrived in
another world, a world which we had quite forgotten in wartime
London. We were all resting in deep and tranquil enjoyment of
this marvellous landscape and magic atmosphere, safe from
submarines, Zeppelins and other lethal 'toys' of the First World
War. When the *Jupiter* finally tied up at the quay and we stepped
out on to the stone pavements of Old Bergen some of us could
hardly refrain from feeling sorry that the wondrous fairy-story
was coming to an end.

To me, the rest of the journey across Scandinavia, over the
Russian frontier and on to Petrograd, passed like a dream. There
must have been some reaction after the nervous strain of the hold-
up and the North Sea crossing. But we were wholly absorbed
in thoughts of Russia and the revolution. Sitting in the train, I
almost made myself sick speculating on what was happening in
Petrograd, imagining the crowds in the streets of the capital, the
soldiers at their meetings, the heated debates in the Council of
Workers' Deputies. Before my mind's eye was the panorama of
the whole country—its towns and villages, its works and factories,
its army of millions at and behind the front—in revolt. Such was
my concentration on what lay ahead, such my interest in the
future and the fate of the revolution, that the details of my
journey simply ceased to register on the sensitive film of memory.
So it is difficult for me to recall what happened on my passage
through Norway and Sweden.

I remember that we spent less than twenty-four hours in
Bergen, and the following morning continued by train to
Christiania (now Oslo). I also remember that in Bergen I called
at the offices of a local workers' paper and had a long talk with the
editor about British and Russian affairs. On the following day,

to my surprise, this conversation appeared in the columns of the paper in the form of an interview with me. I remember the unprecedented occurrence at Christiania station when our émigré party was met by the former tsarist consul-general, Kristi, and how at the hotel where we put up for the night I met the first diplomatic 'courier of the Russian Revolution', i.e. the 'courier' sent to London by the Petrograd Council of Workmen's and Soldiers' Deputies. Incidentally, his baggage bore the seal of the Russian Ministry for Foreign Affairs. I remember that Sweden, with its spotless railway carriages, well-kept stations, peaked helmets for its police and other attributes of unusual discipline and order, seemed to me a 'little Germany'. I remember that we spent two days in Stockholm, but where and how I have completely forgotten. I remember that from Stockholm we went north, skirting a bare, gloomy coast, round the Gulf of Bothnia to Haparanda and the frontier between Sweden and Finland, i.e. at that time the frontier between Sweden and Russia. That is all I can remember of this first visit to Scandinavia. I took no notice whatever of the country or its people. Later on, when my diplomatic career began, I got to know them quite well.

Throughout the journey Anisimov irritated me a great deal. Now that he was no longer worried by the sea and the submarines he discovered a fresh subject for alarm and despondency—the fate of the revolution. Recalling the history of our revolutions in the past centuries, and arguing from the experience of 1905, he was constantly wailing that previous revolutions had invariably failed, that the forces of reaction had ultimately prevailed and retained the foundations of their power, even if they threw the masses a few well-gnawed bones. Why should we think that anything would be different now in Russia? No sufficient reason occurred to him, and he was therefore prepared to mourn the death of the revolution forthwith.

'What worries me,' he was always saying, 'is whether the revolution can last or not. My honest opinion is that it can't.'

I answered him pretty sharply, arguing from logic, common sense, the historic experience of the masses, their awakening to the facts of political life and the existence of Marxism as one of the most potent elements in the revolutionary process. But as I, like Anisimov, was basing my arguments on 'reason' and not on facts (the future course of the revolution was then in the lap of the gods), all our discussions bore too abstract a character, and left a feeling of dissatisfaction behind them.

On the tenth day after leaving London we reached Haparanda. Here, separated from Finland by the River Torne, Sweden ended. Across the river we could clearly see the little Finnish town of Tornio, and over its quay the red flag was flying. My heart beat fast at the sight of it. Here was revolutionary Russia!

We crossed the river on a small ferry and disembarked at a pier, immediately under the red flag. We were met by a Russian patrol, a party of cheerful young soldiers, strong, red-cheeked and noisy. Their coats were slung freely over their shoulders, they had discarded shoulder-straps and their only weapon was a big Mauser hanging from their belts. Some of them had red armbands. Frontier discipline was obviously weak; they hardly checked our passports, and took no interest whatever in our baggage. But they poured out their hopes and feelings to the new arrivals.

We had two hours to wait for our train to Petrograd. We made for the station restaurant to fortify the inner man. Then we strolled in the vicinity of the pier. We were quickly surrounded by soldiers who formed groups and started meetings. They asked us émigrés in detail about what was going on abroad. We in turn asked them in detail about what was going on in Russia. I went from group to group, looking and listening. What interested the soldiers most was when the war would end and how soon the English, French and German workers would follow the example of their Russian comrades.

One of the émigrés asked the men, somewhat academically, what their programme was. A tall, handsome N.C.O. answered with a smile:

'We haven't got a programme yet. Finish the war quickly, and then go for the landlords and capitalists. . . . That's all our programme!'

A nearby sailor called out:

'The bloodsuckers! We've had enough.'

The soldiers all round applauded loudly.

I talked with the soldiers too. I did not ask about their programme but tried in a friendly way to find out what were their aims and desires. Various exciting topics were discussed, and although what they said was sometimes a jumble and their ideas vague and confused, one thing was perfectly clear—that these soldiers, among whom were peasants, workers and members of the intelligentzia, were filled with an irresistible and passionate desire to destroy the bad old world to its foundations and not leave one stone upon another.

This made a tremendous impression upon me, but even more impressive was a new and quite special light in the eyes of the men I was talking to. It was the light of thought, the light of intelligence—as though their spirits were being illuminated from within by the rays of a rising spiritual dawn. I had known the Russian soldier since childhood, but never before had I seen anything like that in his eyes. Another and different man stood before me, and I instinctively guessed the gigantic potentialities, only now awakening from sleep, which lurked within him.

A little later I was taking my seat in the train which was to bring me into the cauldron of Petrograd in revolution, and again I met Anisimov. I wanted to laugh at him, but could only rejoice. Summing up the impressions I had received at Tornio, I was suddenly and inexorably convinced—not by any process of reasoning, but in my heart, my instincts, my very being!

Yes, such a revolution will last!

CHAPTER TWENTY-EIGHT

End of a Journey into the Past

THE day came for which I had been waiting. The Foreign Office informed me that the King had returned to London and the ceremony of presenting my letters of credence would take place next day at eleven o'clock in the morning.

At half past ten two State coaches, mounted on the long soft springs of olden days, and each drawn by two horses, arrived at the Embassy. On the box of each coach sat a majestic coachman in a long, dark coat and cape. On his head was a shining silk hat with cockade, on his hands white gloves and he held the reins and a whip on a long handle. The box was so high that the coachman projected from it like a statue from a plinth. At the back, on a footrest, also lifted higher than the roof of the coach, stood two grooms, likewise in livery. The whole picture was redolent of bygone days and the memories of knightly tourneys.

From the first coach stepped a high Foreign Office official who graciously bowed and said that he had been instructed to accompany me from the Embassy to the Palace. He was dressed in the ceremonial gold-embroidered uniform of his office. I was in evening dress, complete with patent leather shoes, black overcoat and silk hat. How different I looked in such attire from the émigré who twenty years before had stood on Folkestone quay!

As we began to go down together from the porch, photographers came running up from all sides and the cameras clicked merrily. The neighbours gathered at entrances to the Embassy grounds and gazed curiously at the unusual ceremony. A groom lowered the folding steps and my companion hastened to make me comfortable in the soft leather seat before taking his place at my side. The second coach was occupied by my 'suite'—the Embassy secretaries whom diplomatic etiquette required to accompany me in my attendance on the King. The cortège started off, and everywhere as we passed through the streets and parks we were a centre of public interest. Pedestrians stopped and closely followed us with their eyes.

On the way my companion, like an excellent host, entertained me in conversation. He pointed out the noteworthy sights, occasionally poking a little fun at English taste and customs. Among other things he mentioned the difference in the ritual of presenting letters of credence as between an ambassador and a minister. In the case of the ambassador there was much more ceremonial. In particular, state coaches were sent only for ambassadors. The others had to use their own cars.

'Perhaps that would be more convenient,' I said half in jest.

'With great respect,' he exclaimed in some indignation, 'all the time-honoured glamour would be lost!'

I at once sensed the Englishman.

At last our coach arrived at the gates of Buckingham Palace and my companion, turning gracefully towards me, said in the same easy tone:

'Would Your Excellency be good enough to observe . . .'

He went on to initiate me into the details of the forthcoming ceremony. Once more I perceived the Englishman.

The journey into the past was over. The present was coming firmly into its own.

Appendices

The perplexity and confusion in Russian émigré circles produced by the war was not confined to Switzerland. N. K. Krupskaya, in her *Reminiscences of Lenin*, writes:

'Fretting as they did in the dreary atmosphere of emigrant life abroad, from which they were so eager to escape, and having had no direct experience of the revolutionary upsurge which had taken place in Russia in recent months [before the outbreak of the war—I.M.] our Bolshevik groups abroad lacked the firmness which our Duma deputies and the Bolshevik organizations in Russia evinced. People were not clear on the question, and spoke mostly about which side was the attacking side.

'In Paris, in the long run, the majority of the group expressed themselves against the war and volunteering, but some of the comrades —Sapozhkov (Kuznetsov), Kazakov (Britman, Svyagin), Misha Edisherov (Davydov, Moiseyev), Ilya, Zefir and others—joined the French army as volunteers. The volunteers—Mensheviks, some of the Bolsheviks, Socialist-Revolutionaries (about eighty men in all)— adopted a declaration in the name of the "Russian Republicans" which was printed in the French press. Plekhanov made a farewell speech in honour of the volunteers before they left Paris. The majority of our Paris group condemned volunteering. But in the other groups too there was no definite clarity on the question.' (English edition, 1959, p. 286.)

If such was the state of affairs in the Bolshevik groups it is easy to imagine what chaos reigned among the other émigré groups—the Mensheviks, Socialist-Revolutionaries, Poles, etc.

On his return to Soviet Russia in October, 1918, M. M. Litvinov (1876–1951) was made a member of the Collegium of the People's Commissariat for Foreign Affairs and in December of the same year was sent on Lenin's proposal to Stockholm, whence he addressed a cable proposing peace to all the Entente powers. As this had no practical results he returned to Moscow at the beginning of 1919. At the end of 1919 he was sent by Lenin to Copenhagen to negotiate the exchange of wounded prisoners of war with a Labour M.P., O'Grady, who represented the British Government. He showed great skill in these negotiations, and in addition to securing the return home of all Russian wounded prisoners, developed the talks into negotiations for a trade agreement between the R.S.F.S.R. and England, which was actually signed (by L. B. Krassin) in London on the 16th March, 1921. This agreement was a great diplomatic triumph for the Soviet Government at the time, as it broke the economic and political blockade which the capitalist world had established against Soviet Russia.[1] In 1921 he was sent as Plenipotentiary Representative and Trade Representative to Estonia, the only country then having diplomatic relations with the R.S.F.S.R. Next year he was appointed Deputy People's Commissar for Foreign Affairs (the People's Commissar was Chicherin), a member of the Collegium of the People's Commissariat for State Control and Deputy Chairman of the Chief Concessions Committee. In 1922 he was a member of the Soviet delegation to the Genoa Conference, and leader of the Soviet delegation at the subsequent conference at The Hague. In December of the same year he presided at the Disarmament Conference in Moscow to which, on the initiative of the Soviet Government, Poland, Lithuania, Latvia, Estonia and Finland were invited. From 1927 to 1930 he was the leader of the Soviet delegation at the Preparatory Disarmament Commission of the League of Nations, in which the U.S.S.R. considered it essential to participate, despite the fact that at that time it was not a member of the League. Here in the name of the Soviet Government he produced first proposals for general disarmament and, when these were rejected, a scheme for partial disarmament, which was also rejected by the representative of the capitalist powers. In 1930 he was appointed People's Commissar for Foreign Affairs, a post which he held for nearly ten years. In 1932 he was the leader of the Soviet delegation at the Disarmament Conference at Geneva. Through the fault of the imperialist Powers, this conference also proved a fiasco.

In 1933 he led the Soviet delegation at the World Economic Conference in London and it was during this period that he concluded a Convention for the Definition of Aggression with Rumania, Poland, Yugoslavia, Czechoslovakia, Turkey, Iran, Afghanistan, Lithuania, Latvia and Estonia. At the end of 1933 he accepted an invitation from Roosevelt to visit Washington, and there on behalf of the Soviet Government signed an agreement for the establishment of diplomatic relations between the U.S.S.R. and the U.S.A. which the latter had avoided for sixteen years. In 1934, acting on a decision of the Soviet Government, he

---

[1] For the details see I. M. Maisky, *Anglo-Sovietskoe torgovoe soglashenie*, 1921 ('Voprosy Istorii', No. 5, 1957).

showed great skill in preparing, and thereafter securing, the entry of the U.S.S.R. into the League of Nations, in which he was the Soviet representative for the next five years. In 1936 he handled the negotiations at the Montreux Conference on the status of the Dardanelles and signed the convention on this subject.

In May, 1939, he was relieved of his duties as People's Commissar for Foreign Affairs, but at the outset of the Great Patriotic War returned to the People's Commissariat for Foreign Affairs as Deputy People's Commissar and was appointed ambassador to the U.S.A. There he remained until 1943 when he returned and worked as Deputy People's Commissar for Foreign Affairs up to 1946, playing a great part in preparing the decisions of the anti-Hitler coalition on Germany and other questions. In that year he left the Soviet Department of Foreign Affairs for the second time. In 1951 he died, at the age of seventy-five, after a heart attack.

He was a member of the Central Committee of the Communist Party, a deputy of the All-Russian Central Executive Committee of Soviets and later of the C.E.C. of the U.S.S.R. and also of the Supreme Soviet of the U.S.S.R. He received the Order of Lenin and the Order of the Labour Red Banner and also the medal 'For Heroic Work'.

In the thirties, when he was in charge of foreign affairs, he was very popular, abroad as well as in the U.S.S.R. His name is closely associated with the struggle for disarmament and collective security which the Soviet Government carried on with such energy. In the days when the reactionaries of the West were staking everything on a war between the U.S.S.R. and Hitler Germany, in the hope that they could stand aside and make no little 'capital' out of it, he put forward the famous slogan 'Peace is indivisible'. That slogan became the banner of all real opponents of war everywhere.

APPENDIX 3

G. V. Chicherin (1870–1936), who returned to the R.S.F.S.R. in January, 1918, was immediately appointed Deputy People's Commissar for Foreign Affairs and subsequently, on Lenin's instructions, signed the Brest Peace Treaty. On the 30th May, 1918, he became People's Commissar for Foreign Affairs and occupied that office until 1930 when his poor health (polyneuritis) compelled his retirement.

The period of his greatest activity was during the civil war and intervention wars when his passionate struggle for peace and against capitalist Europe, finding expression in countless Notes, appeals, declarations, statements, memoranda and so forth, contributed in no small degree to the ultimate victory of Soviet Russia. As a staunch supporter of Lenin's foreign policy he concluded with Turkey, Iran and Afghanistan the first treaties in history with eastern countries which were based on strict observance of the principle of equal rights.

In 1922 he led the Soviet delegation at the Genoa Conference and skilfully defended the interests of Soviet Russia against the imperialist Powers which were trying to put a financial-economic noose round its neck. During the Genoa Conference he negotiated with the German Foreign Minister, Walther Rathenau, and signed the so-called 'Treaty of Rapallo', under which diplomatic relations were restored and both countries abandoned all claims against each other. At the time this treaty was of very great political significance. Coupled with the Anglo-Soviet Trade Agreement concluded in the previous year, it effectively broke the capitalist blockade of Soviet Russia and greatly strengthened its international position.

In 1923 he led the Soviet delegation at Lausanne where the question of the Turkish Straits was considered. Thirteen years later the question of the Straits was reviewed at a fresh conference at Lausanne where, as I have said above, the Soviet representative was Litvinov. In 1925 Chicherin signed a treaty of friendship and neutrality with Turkey, which subsequently was the model for a number of treaties between the U.S.S.R. and other Powers. He was a member of the Central Committee, All-Russian Central Executive Committee of Soviets and Central Executive Committee of the U.S.S.R.

A highly educated and cultured man, speaking three European languages perfectly and most skilful in his dealings with his foreign partners, he enjoyed a great reputation in foreign political and diplomatic circles. Under Lenin's guidance he did very valuable work in the twenties in strengthening the international position of the Soviet Republic.

APPENDIX 4

On his return to Russia in 1920, F. A. Rothstein (1871–1953) was at once appointed ambassador to Persia where he remained until the summer of 1922. Back in Moscow, he spent the next eight years as a member of the Collegium of the People's Commissariat for Foreign Affairs, dealing mainly with press questions. On leaving that department, he was made a member of the editorial board of the Great Soviet Encyclopaedia, at the same time working in the historical sphere, particularly the history of foreign policy and international relations. In 1939 he was elected a member of the Academy and thereafter devoted himself almost exclusively to learned pursuits. From his pen came a number of serious works among which I might mention

From Chartism to Labourism (1922), *The Seizure and Servitude of Egypt* (1925—an expanded version of his *Egypt's Ruin*, published in London in 1910), *From the History of the Prusso-German Empire* (1948), etc.

APPENDIX 5

After her return to Petrograd in 1917 A. M. Kollontay (1872–1952) took a very active part in the Bolshevik struggle against the Provisional Government. After October she became a member of the first Soviet Government as People's Commissar for Public Welfare. During the civil war and intervention she did great political work at the front in the Ukraine, the Donbass and the Crimea. When the fighting was over she returned to Moscow, worked in the Central Committee of the Party and was elected to the All-Russian Central Executive Committee of Soviets.

In 1922 she was appointed Counsellor at our Embassy in Norway, thus beginning her diplomatic career. In 1923 she became Soviet Plenipotentiary and Trade Commissioner in Norway, and next year signed the agreement establishing diplomatic relations between Soviet Russia and Norway. As the first woman ambassador in the world she acquired a wide reputation in foreign countries. In 1926, on behalf of the Soviet Government, she concluded the Soviet-Norwegian Trade Agreement. That same year she was appointed Soviet envoy in Mexico, but for reasons of health (she could not stand the altitudes, averaging 2,278 metres) she had to give up this post after a few months and returned to Norway, where she remained until 1930. She was then transferred to Sweden where she was ambassador for fifteen years (1930–45). During this period she was a member of the Soviet delegation to the League of Nations and in 1944, at the height of the Second World War, played an important part in the negotiations for an armistice between Finland and the powers of the anti-Hitler coalition. In 1945 she returned to Russia and was appointed a Counsellor of the Ministry for Foreign Affairs. She was decorated with the Order of Lenin and two Orders of the Labour Red Banner.

In 1942 she became very ill. The left side of her body was paralysed. Yet right up to her death in 1952 (a month before her eightieth birthday) she preserved a clear head and a most unusual passion for work. It was during these years that she wrote her extremely interesting memoirs, which still await publication.

S

APPENDIX 6

When the October Revolution took place F. M. Stepnyak was quite
at a loss at first. Like many other representatives of her revolutionary
generation it was a considerable time before she understood 'Bolshevik
Russia'. But by degrees her attitude changed. Despite her age (she was
already over sixty) she felt somehow akin to the rapidly rising Soviet
State, and began to realize that there was some bond between the new
revolutionary power and the dreams of her youth.

When I arrived in London in 1925 as Counsellor at our Embassy
I looked her up, and once again knocked at the door of her modest
apartment in Finchley Road. She greeted me with a certain reserve, but
very soon the ice was broken and the old friendship restored. I had
many talks with her about all manner of things—the revolution, the
Soviet Power, the Communist Party, our hopes and plans for the
future. She often fired a lot of difficult questions at me, and insisted on
straight and honest answers. Sometimes we violently disagreed and
could not compose our differences. But what I said always made a
certain impression: I was 'one of the boys' to her, one of the old émigrés
and easier to believe than the new men who were strangers to her.
The transformation which had been going on before was now completed. In June, 1927, when British-Soviet relations were broken off
and our Mission left London, Fanny Markovna was a friend of the
Soviet Union. I went to say goodbye to her. She gave me a warm pat on
the shoulder and said with real feeling:

'I don't always agree with you Bolsheviks, but I know one thing
—Russia is in good hands now.'

She died in London in May, 1945, when she was nearly ninety. A
few years earlier she had, through my wife (who, as I have already
said, was London correspondent of the Institute of Marxism–Leninism)
presented her late husband's papers to the Soviet Union. In recognition
of her revolutionary services and those of S. M. Kravchinsky, the
Soviet Government paid her a pension for many years.

APPENDIX 7

Now, many years after Kibalchich's death and Zundelevich's story, I
am in a position to add a postscript. In August, 1917, after the fall of
tsarism, there was found in the archives of the Police Department a
sealed packet of papers which included Kibalchich's project and some
documents relating to it. They disclosed that he completed his design
on the 23rd March, 1881, six days after his arrest. The prison authorities
told him that it was being submitted to technical experts and day by

APPENDICES

day (his days were strictly numbered) he feverishly waited to hear from them. Not getting any reply, on the 31st March, two days before his execution, he wrote the following letter to the Minister for Internal Affairs:

'In accordance with Your Excellency's instructions, the project of my flying machine has been submitted to a technical committee. Could not Your Excellency give instructions either permitting me to see some member of the committee to discuss this design not later than tomorrow morning, or that I should have a written reply from the experts who have examined my design, also not later than tomorrow morning?'

Of course he did not get any answer to his letter. What had happened was that on the 26th March, 1881, General Komarov, the Commander of the Gendarmerie, handed the document to the Police Department. He had added two notes: (1) 'Put this in the file relating to the 1st March affair; (2) it will hardly be appropriate to submit this to the experts, and in any case it might start inconvenient talk.' The result was that Kibalchich's design was sealed up in an envelope, attached to the relative file and remained undiscovered in the archives of the Police Department for over thirty-six years. It was only the revolution which brought it to light and made it public property.

What was his invention?

In the heading it was described as 'Design for a Flying Machine, by Nikolai Ivanovich Kibalchich, former student at the Institute of Railway Engineers and member of the Russian Social Revolutionary Party.'

The text followed, beginning with these words:

'I am writing this specification in prison a few days before my death. I believe in the practicability of my ideal, and it is this conviction which sustains me in my terrible position. If my project, after careful investigation by technical experts, is admitted to be practical I shall be happy to know that I have rendered a very great service to my country and mankind. I shall then meet death calmly. I therefore implore the scientists who examine my design to be extremely careful and scrupulous in their examination, and give me an answer as soon as possible.'

Going on to the specification, he writes: 'First of all I have to deal with the question—what must be the source of power to set such a machine in motion?' Then after considering steam, electricity and muscular power from that angle, he came to the conclusion that none of these is of any use for flight, and his analysis brought him to the following conclusion:

'In my opinion the source of power must be some slow-burning explosive substance. In fact, in the process of combustion of explosive substances a large quantity of gases are liberated more or less rapidly, gases which at the moment of liberation represent a vast source of energy.'

Later on he puts the question:

'How can we apply the energy of the gases produced by the combustion of explosive substances for some continuous work?'

This was his answer:

'This will be possible only on condition that that vast energy created by the combustion of explosive substances is produced, not all at once, but over a more or less lengthy period of time. If we take a small quantity of granular gunpowder, which explodes instantly on ignition, and compress it under high pressure into the form of a cylinder, and then ignite one end, we shall see that the combustion does not at once affect the whole cylinder but will spread rather slowly from one end to the other, and at a definite speed. . . . Now, suppose that we have a sheet-iron cylinder of known dimensions, hermetically sealed on all sides but with an aperture of definite size in the bottom. Along the axis of this cylinder we place a piece of the compressed gunpowder, also cylindrical in form, and ignite it at one end. On ignition, gases will be given off which will press against the whole internal surface of the metal cylinder: but the pressures on the lateral surface of the cylinder will cancel out, and only the pressure of the gases on the closed bottom of the cylinder will not be subject to counter-pressure, as on the opposite side the gases have an outlet—through the aperture in the bottom. If the cylinder is placed with the closed end upwards, then, at a certain pressure of the gases, which depends both on the internal capacity of the cylinder and on the thickness of the piece of compressed gunpowder, the cylinder must rise.'

Kibalchich included a drawing of his projected flying machine, some observations on its possible performance and set out some interesting ideas on the means of controlling its movements. There were no detailed calculations, of course. How could there be? He wrote: 'When I was at liberty I never had the time to work out my scheme,' and, 'at the present time of course I have no means of procuring the materials I require.'[1]

Thus we have before us only the idea of a flying machine, and not its basic technical data. Yet this idea must deeply move all of us in these days, when it is quite familiar as the principle of the rocket with jet propulsion which has become a concrete technical reality and a thing of such fateful import to the future of humanity.

Much had changed in the world in the thirty-six years during which Kibalchich's project was buried in the police archives. Science forged

[1] See 'N. I. Kibalchich's Design for a Flying Machine', in *Byloe*, 1918, No. 4/5, pp. 113–25.

ahead remorselessly, and at the time when the project emerged from its paper tomb it naturally seemed already out of date. At the turn of the century K. E. Tsiolkovsky had given the world his remarkable works on aeronautics, in which the idea of the rocket with jet propulsion was already clothed in the raiment of exact calculations and mathematical data. So we are fully justified in regarding him as the real father of the cosmic rocket. But we must never forget that he wrote his books fifteen to twenty years after Kibalchich, and wrote them in freedom and with all the sources he needed available to him. Giving him his due, it would still be unjust to forget Kibalchich and his great idea which anticipated the basic lines of future developments in the sphere of aeronautics. It would be equally unjust to forget that real greatness of soul which he displayed in the last tragic days of his life when he put aside all thought of his own fate and devoted himself solely to science and the interests of humanity.

APPENDIX 8

George Lansbury (1859–1941) became a socialist in 1890, municipal councillor in 1903 and Member of Parliament in 1910. He was Minister of Public Works in the second Labour Government (1929–31) and Leader of the Labour Party in the House of Commons from 1931 to 1935. He was twice elected Mayor of Poplar (one of the working-class districts of London) and also organized workers' colonies for the unemployed. At one time he edited the *Daily Herald*.

As a pacifist on principle he was against war, but knew of no way of preventing it except by convincing his opponents. His dogmatic rigidity in this connection is well illustrated by his ridiculous pilgrimage to see Hitler and Mussolini in 1937 when he tried to persuade them not to start a war! It is easy to imagine how long and loud those international bandits must have laughed when the aged apostle of non-resistance came to visit them. In the years before the Second World War Lansbury patronized various English pacifist organizations, some of a highly suspect character. Whatever his personal motives, in practice he did a lot of harm. But such is always the fate of opportunists, even if subjectively they are honest men.

APPENDIX 9

In the forty and more years that have passed since my visit to Lancashire in 1913 there have been notable changes in the way of life of the English workers. Today they take more interest in politics and books can be seen in their homes more often. The trade unions are more sympathetic towards educational work among their members than they were at the beginning of the century and Labour papers have a much bigger circulation among the workers than they had before the First World War. Yet all these changes have not been great enough for quality to develop out of quantity. Football is just as important now as it was in 1913 and as regards the consumption of drink everything seems to be as it was before, as is demonstrated by a curious fact which has more than local significance.

At the beginning of 1958, Simmons, the Labour M.P. for Brierley Hill in Staffordshire, introduced a bill into Parliament providing that clubs should not sell intoxicating liquor to persons under eighteen and that children under fourteen should be debarred from entering any part of a club except a special 'children's room' set apart for them. What happened? The management of the Workmen's Club at Brierley Hill called on him to withdraw his bill, threatening that if he did not do so the six hundred members of the club would not support him at the approaching elections. Some other clubs in the same constituency supported the threat. Since his majority at the election was only 949, the threat was highly significant and could have brought about his defeat. But he stood firm. It is difficult to say how the dispute would have ended if the routine of parliamentary procedure had not made the whole matter unreal. The rules of the House of Commons are such that a bill introduced by a private member stands little chance of becoming law. As a result his bill got stuck somewhere in the complicated machinery of Parliament, and its prospects vanished into thin air.

But it is not the bill which matters. The important thing is the attitude of the workmen's clubs to the attempt to protect the rising generation from the baleful influence of drink. The story shows that in the last forty years there has been no real change in the views of their managements on the consumption of intoxicants by their members.

APPENDIX 10

In a letter to Kautsky dated the 12th September, 1882, Engels writes:
'You ask me what the English workers think about colonial policy. Well, exactly the same as they think about politics in general; the same as what the bourgeois think. There is no workers' party here; there are only Conservative and Liberal-Radicals and the workers gaily share the feast of England's monopoly of the world market and the colonies.'[1]

[1] Marx and Engels, *Selected Correspondence* (English edn. 1934), p. 399.

A year later, on the 30th August, 1883, Engels wrote to Bebel:
'Participation in the domination of the world market was and is the basis of the political nullity of the English workers.'[1]

In the preface to the second German edition of his book *The Position of the Working Class in England*, published in 1892, Engels summarizes his years of observation of British proletarian life as follows:

'The truth is this: during the period of England's industrial monopoly, the English working class have to a certain extent shared in the benefits of the monopoly. These benefits were very unequally parcelled out among them; the privileged minority pocketed most, but even the great mass had at least a temporary share now and then.'[2]

Lenin shared Engels' views. In his article 'In England' (April, 1913) he wrote:

'The opportunism of the British Labour Party is to be explained by the specific historical conditions prevailing in the latter half of the nineteenth century in Britain when the "aristocracy of labour" shared to some extent in the particularly high profits of British capital.'[3]

APPENDIX 11

The description of the British workman and the British Labour movement in the chapters 'The Socialist Camp', 'The Trades Union Congress', 'Black Towns' and 'The Giant in Chains' relates to the beginning of the nineteenth century. More than forty years have elapsed since then and there have been great changes in the world. Much has changed in Britain too, and the greatest change, especially in comparison with 1913 and 1914, has been the decline of the political and economic power of the British bourgeoisie, particularly in the international sphere. But this bourgeoisie has displayed in the past and still displays great tenacity and skill in applying the brakes, and so its decline has not been a steep slope but a slow and gradual descent. These objective circumstances have been reflected in the development of the British Labour movement as well. If the present-day trade unions and the present Labour Party are compared to those of the beginning of the century we can of course see considerable changes in details, but in essentials all remains basically as it was. It has not changed for the better.

The cult of tradition prevails as before in British life. Before each session of Parliament the guard still searches the cellars and when the

[1] Ibid., p. 420.
[2] Marx and Engels, *Selected Works* (English edn. 1951), vol. II, p. 378.
[3] Lenin, *On Britain* (English edn.), p. 157.

House of Commons Chamber, which had been destroyed by a German bomb, had to be rebuilt after the war the new one still had seats for only 450 out of the 600 and more members. The cult of compromise still predominates, though the bourgeoisie finds the stakes raised, in view of the enormous change in the international situation. Now it has even had to resort to the extraordinary step of seducing the 'Labour aristocracy' by giving it the shadow of power in the shape of a 'tame' Labour government. The class war still proceeds in a muted form, and Marxism still finds little favour in the British Labour movement. As before, Fabianism still dominates the minds of the trade union and Labour Party leaders. Religion still plays a large (though less than before) part in forming the world outlook of the rank and file as well as the leaders. The late Stafford Cripps (British Ambassador in Moscow from 1940 to 1942) not infrequently mounted the pulpit just as Keir Hardie used to do. The arrogance of the British workers towards their coloured comrades has to a certain extent diminished, but things are still by no means what they should be in that respect.

The great mass of the British proletariat follows the lead of the Labour Party which at the 1959 election secured over twelve million votes (forty-four per cent of the total votes) while the Communists received only thirty thousand. Even at the present time millions of workers must vote for the Conservatives; with the present social structure in Britain it is impossible to account otherwise for the fact that in the 1959 election the Conservatives polled nearly fourteen million votes (fifty per cent of the total).

Notwithstanding what I have just said, there are solid grounds for thinking that precisely at the present time the British Labour movement is entering upon a new and important phase of its development. The very foundation of the reformism pervading that movement was the exceptional profits derived by the British bourgeoisie from its world trade monopoly and the exploitation of its enormous empire. Today it has no world trade monopoly, and colonial exploitation is diminishing every month. This process strikes at the whole basis of reformism. To this must be added another and quite new factor, the rapidly increasing automation of production which, in the conditions of capitalism, involves prolonged mass unemployment. All this foreshadows an intensification of the class struggle in the not distant future, with all the consequences flowing from it.

Of course the astute and experienced British bourgeoisie will stubbornly cling to life and strive to use various brakes—possibly not without temporary success—to delay their downfall. It is quite probable that in the battle for the victory of socialism the British proletariat too will once again display no little weakness and hesitation—which will cost it dear. Yet all the same the pointer of the barometer of history is clearly set at 'Victory of Socialism'. But it should never be forgotten that this victory will be won on British lines, and will assume forms very different from those of other countries.

APPENDIX 12

In November, 1932, two weeks after I had presented my letters of credence to the King, I paid a visit to that gloomy building, 49 Portland Place. Diplomatic etiquette prescribes that every newly appointed ambassador must pay a visit of courtesy to all other foreign ambassadors previously accredited. In obedience to that rule, I called on a large number of my colleagues. Among them was the Chinese ambassador, who at that time represented the Kuomintang Government. The Embassy building was just as I had seen it sixteen years before. A lackey in sumptuous gold-braided livery opened the door. The Chinese ambassador received me in his study and we conversed for about twenty minutes on various current topics. He was very charming and reminded me twice that he was an admirer of Sun Yat-Sen.

When the conversation was over and I was about to take my leave I asked him:

'If I'm not mistaken, wasn't Sun Yat-Sen interned in this house thirty-six years ago?'

'Perfectly true,' he replied. 'Do you know the story?'

'Yes, I do,' I said, and added: 'Could you show me the place where he was confined?'

'Most willingly,' he exclaimed. 'Follow me.'

The six-storey Embassy building had a long winding staircase by which we ascended to the very top floor. Through a tiny door we entered a low, dark attic, hardly big enough to hold two people. I glanced through the minute window. It looked on to a flat roof, itself overlooked by high-pitched roofs all round. Now I could see for myself why it was impossible for Sun Yat-Sen to throw his note out into the street. The little attic was very like a cell.

'Sun Yat-Sen spent twelve days here,' said the ambassador. 'I want to make this room a little museum.'

There was in fact a portrait of the great revolutionary, framed in the Chinese national colours, on the wall, and on a small table lay his works—books on the history of the Chinese National movement and other matters relating to the development of China after the revolution of 1911.

I stood in his austere prison cell, greatly moved. I felt that at that moment I had touched something of the greatness in history.

Index